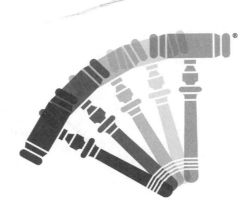

Casenote™ Legal Briefs

CIVIL PROCEDURE

Keyed to Courses Using

**Marcus, Redish, Sherman, and Pfander's
Civil Procedure**

Fifth Edition

Wolters Kluwer
Law & Business

AUSTIN   BOSTON   CHICAGO   NEW YORK   THE NETHERLANDS

© 2010 Aspen Publishers, Inc. All Rights Reserved.
a Wolters Kluwer business
http://lawschool.aspenpublishers.com

To contact Customer Care, e-mail customer.care@aspenpublishers.com, call 1-800-234-1660, fax 1-800-901-9075, or mail correspondence to:

Aspen Publishers
Attn: Order Department
P.O. Box 990
Frederick, MD 21705

Printed in the United States of America.

1 2 3 4 5 6 7 8 9 0

ISBN 978-0-7355-8943-8

About Wolters Kluwer Law & Business

Wolters Kluwer Law & Business is a leading provider of research information and workflow solutions in key specialty areas. The strengths of the individual brands of Aspen Publishers, CCH, Kluwer Law International and Loislaw are aligned within Wolters Kluwer Law & Business to provide comprehensive, in-depth solutions and expert-authored content for the legal, professional and education markets.

CCH was founded in 1913 and has served more than four generations of business professionals and their clients. The CCH products in the Wolters Kluwer Law & Business group are highly regarded electronic and print resources for legal, securities, antitrust and trade regulation, government contracting, banking, pension, payroll, employment and labor, and health-care reimbursement and compliance professionals.

Aspen Publishers is a leading information provider for attorneys, business professionals and law students. Written by preeminent authorities, Aspen products offer analytical and practical information in a range of specialty practice areas from securities law and intellectual property to mergers and acquisitions and pension/benefits. Aspen's trusted legal education resources provide professors and students with high-quality, up-to-date and effective resources for successful instruction and study in all areas of the law.

Kluwer Law International supplies the global business community with comprehensive English-language international legal information. Legal practitioners, corporate counsel and business executives around the world rely on the Kluwer Law International journals, loose-leafs, books and electronic products for authoritative information in many areas of international legal practice.

Loislaw is a premier provider of digitized legal content to small law firm practitioners of various specializations. Loislaw provides attorneys with the ability to quickly and efficiently find the necessary legal information they need, when and where they need it, by facilitating access to primary law as well as state-specific law, records, forms and treatises.

Wolters Kluwer Law & Business, a unit of Wolters Kluwer, is headquartered in New York and Riverwoods, Illinois. Wolters Kluwer is a leading multinational publisher and information services company.

Format for the Casenote Legal Brief

Nature of Case: This section identifies the form of action (e.g., breach of contract, negligence, battery), the type of proceeding (e.g., demurrer, appeal from trial court's jury instructions) or the relief sought (e.g., damages, injunction, criminal sanctions).

Fact Summary: This is included to refresh your memory and can be used as a quick reminder of the facts.

Rule of Law: Summarizes the general principle of law that the case illustrates. It may be used for instant recall of the court's holding and for classroom discussion or home review.

Facts: This section contains all relevant facts of the case, including the contentions of the parties and the lower court holdings. It is written in a logical order to give the student a clear understanding of the case. The plaintiff and defendant are identified by their proper names throughout and are always labeled with a (P) or (D).

Palsgraf v. Long Island R.R. Co.
Injured bystander (P) v. Railroad company (D)

N.Y. Ct. App., 248 N.Y. 339, 162 N.E. 99 (1928).

NATURE OF CASE: Appeal from judgment affirming verdict for plaintiff seeking damages for personal injury.

FACT SUMMARY: Helen Palsgraf (P) was injured on R.R.'s (D) train platform when R.R.'s (D) guard helped a passenger aboard a moving train, causing his package to fall on the tracks. The package contained fireworks which exploded, creating a shock that tipped a scale onto Palsgraf (P).

🏛 RULE OF LAW
The risk reasonably to be perceived defines the duty to be obeyed.

FACTS: Helen Palsgraf (P) purchased a ticket to Rockaway Beach from R.R. (D) and was waiting on the train platform. As she waited, two men ran to catch a train that was pulling out from the platform. The first man jumped aboard, but the second man, who appeared as if he might fall, was helped aboard by the guard on the train who had kept the door open so they could jump aboard. A guard on the platform also helped by pushing him onto the train. The man was carrying a package wrapped in newspaper. In the process, the man dropped his package, which fell on the tracks. The package contained fireworks and exploded. The shock of the explosion was apparently of great enough strength to tip over some scales at the other end of the platform, which fell on Palsgraf (P) and injured her. A jury awarded her damages, and R.R. (D) appealed.

ISSUE: Does the risk reasonably to be perceived define the duty to be obeyed?

HOLDING AND DECISION: (Cardozo, C.J.) Yes. The risk reasonably to be perceived defines the duty to be obeyed. If there is no foreseeable hazard to the injured party as the result of a seemingly innocent act, the act does not become a tort because it happened to be a wrong as to another. If the wrong was not willful, the plaintiff must show that the act as to her had such great and apparent possibilities of danger as to entitle her to protection. Negligence in the abstract is not enough upon which to base liability. Negligence is a relative concept, evolving out of the common law doctrine of trespass on the case. To establish liability, the defendant must owe a legal duty of reasonable care to the injured party. A cause of action in tort will lie where harm,

though unintended, could have been averted or avoided by observance of such a duty. The scope of the duty is limited by the range of danger that a reasonable person could foresee. In this case, there was nothing to suggest from the appearance of the parcel or otherwise that the parcel contained fireworks. The guard could not reasonably have had any warning of a threat to Palsgraf (P), and R.R. (D) therefore cannot be held liable. Judgment is reversed in favor of R.R. (D).

DISSENT: (Andrews, J.) The concept that there is no negligence unless R.R. (D) owes a legal duty to take care as to Palsgraf (P) herself is too narrow. Everyone owes to the world at large the duty of refraining from those acts that may unreasonably threaten the safety of others. If the guard's action was negligent as to those nearby, it was also negligent as to those outside what might be termed the "danger zone." For Palsgraf (P) to recover, R.R.'s (D) negligence must have been the proximate cause of her injury, a question of fact for the jury.

▶ ANALYSIS
The majority defined the limit of the defendant's liability in terms of the danger that a reasonable person in defendant's situation would have perceived. The dissent argued that the limitation should not be placed on liability, but rather on damages. Judge Andrews suggested that only injuries that would not have happened but for R.R.'s (D) negligence should be compensable. Both the majority and dissent recognized the policy-driven need to limit liability for negligent acts, seeking, in the words of Judge Andrews, to define a framework "that will be practical and in keeping with the general understanding of mankind." The Restatement (Second) of Torts has accepted Judge Cardozo's view.

━━

Quicknotes
FORESEEABILITY A reasonable expectation that change is the probable result of certain acts or omissions.

NEGLIGENCE Conduct falling below the standard of care that a reasonable person would demonstrate under similar conditions.

PROXIMATE CAUSE The natural sequence of events without which an injury would not have been sustained.

━━

Party ID: Quick identification of the relationship between the parties.

Concurrence/Dissent: All concurrences and dissents are briefed whenever they are included by the casebook editor.

Analysis: This last paragraph gives you a broad understanding of where the case "fits in" with other cases in the section of the book and with the entire course. It is a hornbook-style discussion indicating whether the case is a majority or minority opinion and comparing the principal case with other cases in the casebook. It may also provide analysis from restatements, uniform codes, and law review articles. The analysis will prove to be invaluable to classroom discussion.

Issue: The issue is a concise question that brings out the essence of the opinion as it relates to the section of the casebook in which the case appears. Both substantive and procedural issues are included if relevant to the decision.

Holding and Decision: This section offers a clear and in-depth discussion of the rule of the case and the court's rationale. It is written in easy-to-understand language and answers the issue presented by applying the law to the facts of the case. When relevant, it includes a thorough discussion of the exceptions to the case as listed by the court, any major cites to the other cases on point, and the names of the judges who wrote the decisions.

Quicknotes: Conveniently defines legal terms found in the case and summarizes the nature of any statutes, codes, or rules referred to in the text.

Aspen Publishers is proud to offer *Casenote Legal Briefs*—continuing thirty years of publishing America's best-selling legal briefs.

Casenote Legal Briefs are designed to help you save time when briefing assigned cases. Organized under convenient headings, they show you how to abstract the basic facts and holdings from the text of the actual opinions handed down by the courts. Used as part of a rigorous study regimen, they can help you spend more time analyzing and critiquing points of law than on copying bits and pieces of judicial opinions into your notebook or outline.

Casenote Legal Briefs should never be used as a substitute for assigned casebook readings. They work best when read as a follow-up to reviewing the underlying opinions themselves. Students who try to avoid reading and digesting the judicial opinions in their casebooks or online sources will end up shortchanging themselves in the long run. The ability to absorb, critique, and restate the dynamic and complex elements of case law decisions is crucial to your success in law school and beyond. It cannot be developed vicariously.

Casenote Legal Briefs represents but one of the many offerings in Aspen's Study Aid Timeline, which includes:

- *Casenote Legal Briefs*
- *Emanuel Law Outlines*
- *Examples & Explanations* Series
- *Introduction to Law* Series
- Emanuel *Law in a Flash* Flashcards
- Emanuel *CrunchTime* Series

Each of these series is designed to provide you with easy-to-understand explanations of complex points of law. Each volume offers guidance on the principles of legal analysis and, consulted regularly, will hone your ability to spot relevant issues. We have titles that will help you prepare for class, prepare for your exams, and enhance your general comprehension of the law along the way.

To find out more about Aspen Study Aid publications, visit us online at *http://lawschool.aspenpublishers.com* or email us at *legaledu@wolterskluwer.com*. We'll be happy to assist you.

Get this Casenote Legal Brief as an AspenLaw Studydesk eBook today!

By returning this form to Aspen Publishers, you will receive a complimentary eBook download of this Casenote Legal Brief in the AspenLaw Studydesk digital format.* Learn more about AspenLaw Studydesk today at *www.AspenLaw.com*.

Name	Phone ( )

Address	Apt. No.

City	State	ZIP Code

Law School	Year (check one) □ 1st □ 2nd □ 3rd

Cut out the UPC found on the lower left corner of the back cover of this book. Staple the UPC inside this box. Only the original UPC from the book cover will be accepted. (No photocopies or store stickers are allowed.)

> **Attach UPC inside this box.**

Email (Print legibly or you may not get access!)

Title of this book (course subject)

ISBN of this book (10- or 13-digit number on the UPC)

Used with which casebook (provide author's name)

Mail the completed form to: Aspen Publishers, Inc.
Legal Education Division
130 Turner Street, Bldg 3, 4th Floor
Waltham, MA 02453-8901

* Upon receipt of this completed form, you will be emailed a code for the digital download of this book in AspenLaw Studydesk format. The AspenLaw Studydesk application is available as a 60-day free trial at *www.AspenLaw.com*.

For a full list of print titles by Aspen Publishers, visit *lawschool.aspenpublishers.com*.
For a full list of digital eBook titles by Aspen Publishers, visit *www.AspenLaw.com*.

Make a photocopy of this form and your UPC for your records.

For detailed information on the use of the information you provide on this form, please see the PRIVACY POLICY at www.aspenpublishers.com.

How to Brief a Case

A. Decide on a Format and Stick to It

Structure is essential to a good brief. It enables you to arrange systematically the related parts that are scattered throughout most cases, thus making manageable and understandable what might otherwise seem to be an endless and unfathomable sea of information. There are, of course, an unlimited number of formats that can be utilized. However, it is best to find one that suits your needs and stick to it. Consistency breeds both efficiency and the security that when called upon you will know where to look in your brief for the information you are asked to give.

Any format, as long as it presents the essential elements of a case in an organized fashion, can be used. Experience, however, has led *Casenotes* to develop and utilize the following format because of its logical flow and universal applicability.

NATURE OF CASE: This is a brief statement of the legal character and procedural status of the case (e.g., "Appeal of a burglary conviction").

There are many different alternatives open to a litigant dissatisfied with a court ruling. The key to determining which one has been used is to discover *who is asking this court for what.*

This first entry in the brief should be kept as *short as possible.* Use the court's terminology if you understand it. But since jurisdictions vary as to the titles of pleadings, the best entry is the one that addresses who wants what in this proceeding, not the one that sounds most like the court's language.

RULE OF LAW: A statement of the general principle of law that the case illustrates (e.g., "An acceptance that varies any term of the offer is considered a rejection and counteroffer").

Determining the rule of law of a case is a procedure similar to determining the issue of the case. Avoid being fooled by red herrings; there may be a few rules of law mentioned in the case excerpt, but usually only one is *the* rule with which the casebook editor is concerned. The techniques used to locate the issue, described below, may also be utilized to find the rule of law. Generally, your best guide is simply the chapter heading. It is a clue to the point the casebook editor seeks to make and should be kept in mind when reading every case in the respective section.

FACTS: A synopsis of only the essential facts of the case, i.e., those bearing upon or leading up to the issue.

The facts entry should be a short statement of the events and transactions that led one party to initiate legal proceedings against another in the first place. While some cases conveniently state the salient facts at the beginning of the decision, in other instances they will have to be culled from hiding places throughout the text, even from concurring and dissenting opinions. Some of the "facts" will often be in dispute and should be so noted. Conflicting evidence may be briefly pointed up. "Hard" facts must be included. Both must be *relevant* in order to be listed in the facts entry. It is impossible to tell what is relevant until the entire case is read, as the ultimate determination of the rights and liabilities of the parties may turn on something buried deep in the opinion.

Generally, the facts entry should not be longer than three to five *short* sentences.

It is often helpful to identify the role played by a party in a given context. For example, in a construction contract case the identification of a party as the "contractor" or "builder" alleviates the need to tell that that party was the one who was supposed to have built the house.

It is always helpful, and a good general practice, to identify the "plaintiff" and the "defendant." This may seem elementary and uncomplicated, but, especially in view of the creative editing practiced by some casebook editors, it is sometimes a difficult or even impossible task. Bear in mind that the *party presently* seeking something from this court may not be the plaintiff, and that sometimes only the cross-claim of a defendant is treated in the excerpt. Confusing or misaligning the parties can ruin your analysis and understanding of the case.

ISSUE: A statement of the general legal question answered by or illustrated in the case. For clarity, the issue is best put in the form of a question capable of a "yes" or "no" answer. In reality, the issue is simply the Rule of Law put in the form of a question (e.g., "May an offer be accepted by performance?").

The major problem presented in discerning what is *the* issue in the case is that an opinion usually purports to raise and answer several questions. However, except for rare cases, only one such question is really the issue in the case. Collateral issues not necessary to the resolution of the matter in controversy are handled by the court by language known as *"obiter dictum"* or merely *"dictum."* While dicta may be included later in the brief, they have no place under the issue heading.

To find the issue, ask *who wants what* and then go on to ask *why did that party succeed or fail in getting it.* Once this is determined, the "why" should be turned into a question.

The complexity of the issues in the cases will vary, but in all cases a single-sentence question should sum up the issue. *In a few cases,* there will be two, or even more rarely, three issues of equal importance to the resolution of the case. Each should be expressed in a single-sentence question.

Since many issues are resolved by a court in coming to a final disposition of a case, the casebook editor will reproduce the portion of the opinion containing the issue or issues most relevant to the area of law under scrutiny. A noted law professor gave this advice: "Close the book; look at the title on the cover." Chances are, if it is Property, you need not concern yourself with whether, for example, the federal government's treatment of the plaintiff's land really raises a federal question sufficient to support jurisdiction on this ground in federal court.

The same rule applies to chapter headings designating sub-areas within the subjects. They tip you off as to what the text is designed to teach. The cases are arranged in a casebook to show a progression or development of the law, so that the preceding cases may also help.

It is also most important to remember to *read the notes and questions* at the end of a case to determine what the editors wanted you to have gleaned from it.

HOLDING AND DECISION: This section should succinctly explain the rationale of the court in arriving at its decision. In capsulizing the "reasoning" of the court, it should always include an application of the general rule or rules of law to the specific facts of the case. Hidden justifications come to light in this entry; the reasons for the state of the law, the public policies, the biases and prejudices, those considerations that influence the justices' thinking and, ultimately, the outcome of the case. At the end, there should be a short indication of the disposition or procedural resolution of the case (e.g., "Decision of the trial court for Mr. Smith (P) reversed").

The foregoing format is designed to help you "digest" the reams of case material with which you will be faced in your law school career. Once mastered by practice, it will place at your fingertips the information the authors of your casebooks have sought to impart to you in case-by-case illustration and analysis.

B. Be as Economical as Possible in Briefing Cases

Once armed with a format that encourages succinctness, it is as important to be economical with regard to the time spent on the actual reading of the case as it is to be economical in the writing of the brief itself. This does not mean "skimming" a case. Rather, it means reading the case with an "eye" trained to recognize into which "section" of your brief a particular passage or line fits and having a system for quickly and precisely marking the case so that the passages fitting any one particular part of

the brief can be easily identified and brought together in a concise and accurate manner when the brief is actually written.

It is of no use to simply repeat everything in the opinion of the court; record only enough information to trigger your recollection of what the court said. Nevertheless, an accurate statement of the "law of the case," i.e., the legal principle applied to the facts, is absolutely essential to class preparation and to learning the law under the case method.

To that end, it is important to develop a "shorthand" that you can use to make margin notations. These notations will tell you at a glance in which section of the brief you will be placing that particular passage or portion of the opinion.

Some students prefer to underline all the salient portions of the opinion (with a pencil or colored underliner marker), making marginal notations as they go along. Others prefer the color-coded method of underlining, utilizing different colors of markers to underline the salient portions of the case, each separate color being used to represent a different section of the brief. For example, blue underlining could be used for passages relating to the rule of law, yellow for those relating to the issue, and green for those relating to the holding and decision, etc. While it has its advocates, the color-coded method can be confusing and time-consuming (all that time spent on changing colored markers). Furthermore, it can interfere with the continuity and concentration many students deem essential to the reading of a case for maximum comprehension. In the end, however, it is a matter of personal preference and style. Just remember, whatever method you use, underlining must be used sparingly or its value is lost.

If you take the marginal notation route, an efficient and easy method is to go along underlining the key portions of the case and placing in the margin alongside them the following "markers" to indicate where a particular passage or line "belongs" in the brief you will write:

N   (NATURE OF CASE)
RL   (RULE OF LAW)
I   (ISSUE)
HL   (HOLDING AND DECISION, relates to
     the RULE OF LAW behind the decision)
HR   (HOLDING AND DECISION, gives the
     RATIONALE or reasoning behind the
     decision)
HA   (HOLDING AND DECISION, APPLIES
     the general principle(s) of law to the facts
     of the case to arrive at the decision)

Remember that a particular passage may well contain information necessary to more than one part of your brief, in which case you simply note that in the margin. If you are using the color-coded underlining method instead of margin notation, simply make asterisks or checks in the margin next to the passage in question in the colors that indicate the additional sections of the brief where it might be utilized.

The economy of utilizing "shorthand" in marking cases for briefing can be maintained in the actual brief writing process itself by utilizing "law student shorthand" within the brief. There are many commonly used words and phrases for which abbreviations can be substituted in your briefs (and in your class notes also). You can develop abbreviations that are personal to you and which will save you a lot of time. A reference list of briefing abbreviations can be found on page xii of this book.

C. Use Both the Briefing Process and the Brief as a Learning Tool

Now that you have a format and the tools for briefing cases efficiently, the most important thing is to make the time spent in briefing profitable to you and to make the most advantageous use of the briefs you create. Of course, the briefs are invaluable for classroom reference when you are called upon to explain or analyze a particular case. However, they are also useful in reviewing for exams. A quick glance at the fact summary should bring the case to mind, and a rereading of the rule of law should enable you to go over the underlying legal concept in your mind, how it was applied in that particular case, and how it might apply in other factual settings.

As to the value to be derived from engaging in the briefing process itself, there is an immediate benefit that arises from being forced to sift through the essential facts and reasoning from the court's opinion and to succinctly express them in your own words in your brief. The process ensures that you understand the case and the point that it illustrates, and that means you will be ready to absorb further analysis and information brought forth in class. It also ensures you will have something to say when called upon in class. The briefing process helps develop a mental agility for getting to the *gist* of a case and for identifying, expounding on, and applying the legal concepts and issues found there. The briefing process is the mental process on which you must rely in taking law school examinations; it is also the mental process upon which a lawyer relies in serving his clients and in making his living.

Abbreviations for Briefs

Table of Cases

Choosing a System of Procedure

Quick Reference Rules of Law

Band's Refuse Removal, Inc. v. Borough of Fair Lawn

Disposal company (P) v. City contractor (D)

N.J. Super. Ct., App. Div., 62 N.J. Super. 522, 163 A.2d 465 (1960).

NATURE OF CASE: Appeal of order declaring municipal contract void.

FACT SUMMARY: In an action challenging a municipal contract, the judge used the trial as a vehicle for conducting an investigation into the underlying transaction.

🏛 RULE OF LAW
A judge may not assume the role of advocate in a trial over which he presides.

FACTS: The Borough of Fair Lawn, N.J. (D), awarded a refuse collection contract to Capasso (D). Band's Refuse Removal, Inc. (P) challenged the legality of the contract. At trial the judge largely took over the prosecution of the case, calling his own witnesses, creating his own issues, and doing his own cross-examination and direct examination, citing the public importance of the case as justification for this. At the close of the trial, he voided the contract and awarded over $300,000 in damages.

ISSUE: May a judge assume the role of advocate in a trial over which he presides?

HOLDING AND DECISION: (Goldmann, J.) No. A judge may not assume the role of advocate in a trial over which he presides. The power of a judge to take an active role in the trial of a case must be exercised with the greatest restraint. While the judge may do this to move a trial along, he may not assume the role of advocate. Courts must both be impartial and give the appearance of impartiality. The conduct of the judge in this instance fell far short of that. He called witnesses not wanted by Band's Refuse Removal, Inc. (P) and essentially took on the plaintiff's case. This was inappropriate and seriously prejudiced the defense of the case. Reversed and remanded.

▶ ANALYSIS

The rules in this area are quite nebulous. There is no question that a court can actively participate in trials, especially at the federal level. The point at which a judge goes too far will essentially be a matter of degree.

■■■■

Quicknotes

AMICI CURIAE A third party not implicated in the suit, which seeks to file a brief, containing information for the court's consideration, in conformity with its position.

CONFLICT OF INTEREST Refers to ethical problems that arise, or may be anticipated to arise, between an attorney and his client if the interests of the attorney, another client or a third party conflict with those of the present client.

CROSS-EXAMINATION The interrogation of a witness by an adverse party either to further inquire as to the subject matter of the direct examination or to call into question the witness's credibility.

DIRECT EXAMINATION The initial interrogation of a witness, conducted by the party who called the witness.

■■■■

Kothe v. Smith

Patient (P) v. Doctor (D)

771 F.2d 667 (2d Cir. 1985).

NATURE OF CASE: Appeal of sanctions levied in medical malpractice action.

FACT SUMMARY: A court sanctioned Smith (D) for not settling in what the court believed to be a timely fashion.

🏛 RULE OF LAW
A court may not sanction a party for refusing to settle.

FACTS: Kothe (P) sued Smith (D) for medical malpractice. At a pretrial conference, the judge expressed a view that the value of the case was $20,000 to $30,000 and urged settlement. Smith (D) offered no more than $5,000. After one day of trial, the case settled for $20,000. The trial judge then sanctioned Smith (D) $2,480 for refusing to settle in a timely fashion. Smith (D) appealed.

ISSUE: May a court sanction a party for refusing to settle?

HOLDING AND DECISION: (Van Graafeiland, J.) No. A court may not sanction a party for refusing to settle. Although the law favors the voluntary settlement of civil suits, judges may not effect settlements through coercion. While judges have the power to bring the parties together to discuss settlement, judges may not use such powers as a vehicle for clubbing a litigant into settlement. The ultimate decision as to whether a case shall be settled or tried rests in the parties, not the courts. Reversed and remanded.

▶ ANALYSIS

The extent to which judges involve themselves in settlements varies greatly, not only among the jurisdictions but among individual courts as well. Generally speaking, judges would rather see a case settled than be tried. The extent to which a judge will attempt to bring this about often depends on the judge himself.

■══■

Quicknotes

SETTLEMENT An agreement entered into by the parties to a civil lawsuit agreeing upon the determination of rights and issues between them, thus disposing of the need for judicial determination.

■══■

The Rewards and Costs of Litigation

Quick Reference Rules of Law

Fuentes v. Shevin

Chattel owner (P) v. Municipality (D)

407 U.S. 67 (1972).

NATURE OF CASE: Constitutional challenge to Florida and Pennsylvania's prejudgment replevin procedures on due process grounds.

FACT SUMMARY: Fuentes (P) had her stove and stereo picked up by the sheriff prior to the adjudication of a suit filed by Firestone for nonpayment of the installment sales contract.

🏛 **RULE OF LAW**
Procedural due process requires that parties whose rights are to be affected are entitled to be heard at a meaningful time, and in order that they may enjoy that right, they must be notified.

FACTS: Two prejudgment replevin statutes were attacked on due process grounds. Florida's statute permitted "[a]ny person whose goods or chattel are wrongfully detained by any other person . . . a writ of replevin to recover them." Florida did not require a convincing showing that the goods were wrongfully detained before seizure. A person merely filed a complaint and requested a writ of replevin alleging that the goods had been wrongfully detained. A bond equal to twice the value of the property was filed, and the officer assigned picked up the chattels at the same time as he served the other party with the summons and complaint. After the property has been seized, the party eventually has a right to a hearing as the defendant in the suit that was filed, which plaintiff is required to pursue. While the Pennsylvania law was similar to Florida's in most respects, the party whose goods have been seized may never be granted a hearing. The writ of replevin was an independent action, and a lawsuit was not required. Therefore, to obtain a hearing, the party must himself initiate suit. Both statutes allowed the party whose property was seized to post a counterbond equal to twice the value of the property within three days of the replevin in order to retain possession of the property. If they did not, the property was transferred to the party who sought the writ. Fuentes (P), a Florida resident, had her stove and stereo picked up by the sheriff after she had fallen behind on her payments to Firestone Tire and Rubber Co. because of a dispute over repairs under her service policy. Firestone filed a complaint and requested that the property be seized. The complaint and summons were served simultaneously with the writ of replevin. Appellants attacking the Pennsylvania statute also fell behind in their payments and had their property repossessed. Finally, another Pennsylvania resident, Washington (P), had been divorced from a local deputy sheriff and was involved in a custody battle with him. He used the replevin process to have their child's

clothing, furnishings, and toys picked up. Both statutes were upheld by their respective state courts. The U.S. Supreme Court combined the actions since they dealt with the same constitutional issues. The various plaintiffs in this action challenged the constitutionality of the prejudgment replevin statutes, claiming that they procedurally violated the Due Process Clause of the Fourteenth Amendment.

ISSUE: Does procedural due process require that parties, whose rights are to be affected, are entitled to be heard at a meaningful time, and in order that they may enjoy that right, they must be notified?

HOLDING AND DECISION: (Stewart, J.) Yes. Procedural due process requires that a party whose rights are being affected be given a meaningful opportunity to be heard, and in order that he may enjoy that right, he must be notified. The constitutional right to be heard is a basic aspect of the duty of government to follow a fair process of decision-making when it acts to deprive a person of his possessions. This right to be heard minimizes substantively unfair or mistaken deprivations of property, a danger that is especially great when the state seizes goods simply upon the application of and for the benefit of a private party. Without due process of law, there would be no safeguards to protect a person's property from governmental interference. The right to speak out in one's own defense before an impartial arbitrator is a fundamental right which must be protected. If the right to notice and a hearing is to serve its full purpose, then it is clear that it must be granted at a time when the deprivation can still be prevented. While return of possessions and damages can be granted at a later hearing, nothing can undo the fact that a person's property was arbitrarily taken from him without procedural due process of law. That the hearing required by due process is subject to waiver, and is not fixed in form, does not affect its root requirement that an individual be given an opportunity for a hearing before he is deprived of any significant property interest, except for extraordinary situations where some valid governmental interest is at stake that justifies postponing the hearing until after the event. The statute's requirements of requesting a writ, posting bond, and stating in a conclusory fashion that the property is wrongfully held, merely tests the applicant's own belief in his rights. Since his private gain is at stake, the danger is all too great that his confidence in his cause will be misplaced. While possession may be reinstated by the posting of a counterbond, it is well settled that a temporary, nonfinal

Continued on next page.

deprivation of property is nonetheless violative of the Due Process Clause of the Fourteenth Amendment. Moreover, the Due Process Clause encompasses both the possessory rights to property and situations where the title is in dispute. The Court distinguished *Sniadach v. Family Financial Corporation*, 395 U.S. 337 (1969), and *Goldberg v. Kelly*, 397 U.S. 254 (1970), which dealt with prejudgment garnishment statutes on the basis that the reasoning was similar and had nothing to do with the absolute necessities of life. These cases also required a hearing prior to a deprivation of rights, and, while emphasizing the special importance of wages and welfare benefits, they did not create a limited constitutional doctrine. Situations requiring a postponement of notice and hearing are truly unusual. They require an important governmental purpose, a special need for prompt action, and they must be initiated by and for the benefit of the government as opposed to a private individual (e.g., war effort, economic disaster, etc.). The contention that the parties waived their constitutional rights is also without merit since waiver requires clear and explicit language indicating exactly the rights to be waived. For the above-mentioned reasons, both Florida's and Pennsylvania's prejudgment replevin statutes violate the Due Process Clause of the Fourteenth Amendment. Vacated and remanded.

DISSENT: (White, J.) The dissenters noted that state proceedings were in progress on this issue when the action was commenced, so jurisdiction should have been refused since there was an adequate remedy at law. There were conflicting interests here. There was the debtor who is in default and the creditor who desired either his money or the return of his property, the question being which party has a better right to possession prior to the hearing. The creditor wanted to prevent the further use and deterioration of his property, but the majority ignored his property rights totally. The creditor was in business to make money. His posting of the bond was a reasonable guarantee that frivolous claims would not be pursued. The current procedure protected the rights of both parties, and there appeared to be no compelling reason why possession should be retained by the debtor in default rather than by the creditor. Moreover, a counterbond was available to the debtor who honestly believed that the creditor was wrongfully attempting to repossess the property. Finally, it was very doubtful that the proposed hearing would in fact result in protections for the debtor substantially different from those the present law provided. An additional difficulty in the majority's reasoning was that all a creditor has to do in order to avoid the hearing requirement was to place an express waiver clause in the credit contract.

▶ ANALYSIS

In California, Michigan, and a large number of other states, the writ of replevin is now referred to as claim and delivery. In California, this action is contained in §§ 511.010 *et seq.* of the Code of Civil Procedure. A hearing is required for the granting of a writ of possession (comparable to the prior writ of replevin) under the guidelines set out in § 512.010. Exceptions are made for property feloniously taken, credit cards, and property acquired in the normal course of trade or business for commercial use. It must be alleged that the property is not necessary for the support of the defendant or his family and that there is a danger that the property will become unavailable to levy, its value will be substantially impaired, and it is necessary to protect the property (§ 512.020). At the hearing, the court will make its determination based on affidavits, pleadings, and other evidence on record. Upon showing a good cause, the court may admit additional evidence or continue the hearing until the new evidence can be obtained (§ 512.050). Finally, with regard to waiver of a hearing requirement, it appears that it is permissible if the parties are acting at arm's length and have equal bargaining power, *D. H. Overmeyer Co. v. Frick Co.*, 405 U.S. 174 (1972); however, if the consumer has no option but to buy on credit, the parties are not equal in bargaining power and the clause is unconscionable, *Kosches v. Nichols*, 327 N.Y.S.2d 968 (1971). This is but another example of consumer protection. The businessman can waive his constitutional rights, but the consumer cannot.

■==■

Quicknotes

PROCEDURAL DUE PROCESS The constitutional mandate that if the state or federal government acts so as to deny a citizen of a life, liberty or property interest the individual is first entitled to notice and the right to be heard.

REPLEVIN An action to recover personal property wrongfully taken.

■==■

Connecticut v. Doehr

State (D) v. Property-owning defendant (P)

501 U.S. 1 (1991).

NATURE OF CASE: Appeal from reversal of a grant of summary judgment in favor of the plaintiff who had secured a prejudgment attachment under state law.

FACT SUMMARY: When DiGiovanni (D) had Doehr's (P) home attached in conjunction with a suit against Doehr (P) for assault and battery, Doehr (P) brought this action, claiming the Connecticut statute that allowed prejudgment attachment without prior notice or hearing was unconstitutional.

> ## RULE OF LAW
> Prejudgment attachment of real estate without affording prior notice or the opportunity for a prior hearing to the individual whose property is subject to attachment does not satisfy due process requirements.

FACTS: In conjunction with a suit for assault and battery against Doehr (P), DiGiovanni (D) submitted an application for an attachment on Doehr's (P) home. The underlying suit did not involve Doehr's (P) real estate nor did DiGiovanni (D) have any preexisting interest in Doehr's (P) home. Doehr (P) received notice of the attachment only after the property had been attached. Rather than pursue any of his state remedies, Doehr (P) brought this action against DiGiovanni (D) in federal district court, claiming that the Connecticut (D) statute that allowed such prejudgment attachment without prior notice or hearing was unconstitutional under the Due Process Clause of the Fourteenth Amendment. The district court upheld the statute, granting summary judgment in favor of DiGiovanni (D). A divided panel of the court of appeals reversed. DiGiovanni (D) appealed.

ISSUE: Does prejudgment attachment of real estate without affording prior notice or the opportunity for a prior hearing to the individual whose property is subject to attachment satisfy due process requirements?

HOLDING AND DECISION: (White, J.) No. Prejudgment attachment of real estate without affording prior notice or the opportunity for a prior hearing to the individual whose property is subject to attachment does not satisfy due process requirements. For a property owner like Doehr (P), attachment ordinarily clouds title, impairs the ability to sell or otherwise alienate the property, taints any credit rating, reduces the chance of obtaining a home equity loan or additional mortgage, and can even place an existing mortgage in technical default where there is an insecurity clause. Furthermore, the risk of erroneous deprivation that Connecticut (D) permits here is substantial. Finally, absent allegations that Doehr (P) was about to transfer or encumber his real estate, DiGiovanni's (D)

interest in attaching the property does not justify burdening Doehr's (P) ownership rights in the absence of a hearing to determine the likelihood of recovery. By failing to provide for a preattachment hearing without at least requiring a bond or a showing of some exigent circumstance, the provision clearly falls short of the demands of due process. The judgment of the court of appeals is affirmed and remanded.

CONCURRENCE: (Rehnquist, C.J.) The Connecticut attachment statute, as applied in this case, fails to satisfy the Due Process Clause of the Fourteenth Amendment. However, the Court should await concrete cases that present questions involving bonds and exigent circumstances before attempting to decide when and if the Due Process Clause of the Fourteenth Amendment requires them as prerequisites for a lawful attachment.

▶ ANALYSIS

A survey of state attachment provisions reveals that nearly every state requires either a preattachment hearing, a showing of some exigent circumstance, or both, before permitting an attachment to take place. As noted by the Court, disputes between debtors and creditors more readily lend themselves to accurate ex parte assessments of the merits. Tort actions, like the assault and battery claim at issue here, do not. Although a majority of the Court did not reach the issue, Justices Marshall, Stevens, O'Connor, and White deemed it appropriate to consider whether due process also required a plaintiff to post a bond or other security in addition to requiring a hearing or showing of some exigency. They concluded that it did. It was this part of the opinion that the concurrers refrained from joining.

■━■

Quicknotes

ATTACHMENT The seizing of the property of one party in anticipation of, or in order to satisfy, a favorable judgment obtained by another party.

PROCEDURAL DUE PROCESS The constitutional mandate that if the state or federal government acts so as to deny a citizen of a life, liberty or property interest the individual is first entitled to notice and the right to be heard.

■━■

Carey v. Piphus

Court (D) v. Suspended student (P)

435 U.S. 247 (1978).

NATURE OF CASE: Appeal of award of damages for civil violations.

FACT SUMMARY: Damages in excess of a nominal amount were awarded in absence of proof of injury.

🏛 RULE OF LAW
In an action based on denial of procedural due process, only nominal damages may be awarded in the absence of actual injury.

FACTS: Piphus (P) was suspended from school for several days. He was reinstated but brought an action under 28 U.S.C. § 1983 anyway, contending he was denied procedural due process. The district court found no actual injury and dismissed. The court of appeals reversed, holding that Piphus (P) was entitled to injunctive relief and also that denial of procedural due process was compensable even in the absence of actual injury. The Supreme Court accepted review of the latter portion of the appellate court's holding.

ISSUE: In an action based on denial of procedural due process, may damages in excess of a nominal amount be awarded in the absence of proof of injury?

HOLDING AND DECISION: (Powell, J.) No. In an action based on denial of procedural due process, only nominal damages may be awarded. The basic purpose of § 1983 is to compensate individuals for injuries caused by the deprivation of constitutional rights. The structure under which this is done borrows from tort law. Just as tort law requires injury for compensation to be merited, so does § 1983. It cannot be assumed that denial of procedural due process, in itself, is an injury. Many will suffer no distress when such denial leads to no injury, and in such cases compensation would be inappropriate. It is injury caused by deprivation not the deprivation itself that is compensable. Here, no evidence on the issue of injury was put forth, so actual damages would be inappropriate. Reversed and remanded.

▶ *ANALYSIS*

The decision was apparently rather purposefully limited in scope. The Court always limited its terms to procedural due process. Substantive due process was not mentioned. Also, the Court said in a footnote that punitive damages might be awarded in the absence of actual injury.

Quicknotes

INJUNCTIVE RELIEF A court order issued as a remedy, requiring a person to do, or prohibiting that person from doing, a specific act.

NOMINAL DAMAGES A small sum awarded to a plaintiff in order to recognize that he sustained an injury that is either slight or incapable of being established.

PROCEDURAL DUE PROCESS The constitutional mandate that if the state or federal government acts so as to deny a citizen of a life, liberty or property interest the individual is first entitled to notice and the right to be heard.

PUNITIVE DAMAGES Damages exceeding the actual injury suffered for the purposes of punishment, deterrence and comfort to plaintiff.

■━■

Smith v. Western Electric Co.

Smoke-injured employee (P) v. Utility company (D)

Mo. Ct. App., 643 S.W.2d 10 (1982).

NATURE OF CASE: Appeal of dismissal of action seeking injunctive relief against alleged workplace safety violations.

FACT SUMMARY: Smith (P), claiming that his employer's tobacco policy threatened his health, sought an injunction mandating adoption of safer practices.

🏛 RULE OF LAW
An employee may seek an injunction mandating that he be provided with a safer workplace.

FACTS: Smith (P) was employed by Western Electric Company (Western) (D). Western (D) had minimal restrictions on smoking by employees. Smith (P), who had a history of respiratory problems, began to experience serious health problems as a result of exposure to the smoke. Attempts to move Smith (P) around the premises proved unsuccessful. Smith (P) then brought an action against Western (D), seeking an injunction mandating that he be given a smoke-free working environment. The trial court dismissed, holding that no basis for injunctive relief existed. Smith (P) appealed.

ISSUE: May an employee seek an injunction mandating that he be provided with a safe workplace?

HOLDING AND DECISION: (Dowd, J.) Yes. An employee may seek an injunction mandating that he be provided with a safe workplace. It is well established that, where monetary damages would prove inadequate, an individual may seek an injunction enforcing some right he claims has been violated. Here, Missouri law requires that an employer take reasonable steps to ensure workplace safety. An employee contending that his workplace is unsafe has, as a legal remedy, the option to wait until an injury occurs and then sue for damages. This is an unreasonable expectation, and therefore the legal remedy in such a situation is inadequate. This being so, an action to compel a safe environment through injunction is appropriate. Here, Smith (P) is entitled to a hearing on the merits. Reversed.

▶ ANALYSIS

Although the matter discussed by the court here is the main criterion in assessing the suitability of injunctive relief, other criteria may apply. One is whether the action has merit. Others are based on policy considerations, such as whether the injunction is amenable to judicial administration.

■=■

Quicknotes

INJUNCTION A court order requiring a person to do or prohibiting that person from doing a specific act.

LEGAL REMEDY Compensation for violation of a right or injuries sustained that is available in a court of law, as opposed to in equity.

■=■

Venegas v. Mitchell

Client (D) v. Attorney (P)

495 U.S. 82 (1990).

NATURE OF CASE: Appeal from a judgment allowing a contingency-fee agreement in a civil rights case to stand.

FACT SUMMARY: After Mitchell (P) won Venegas's (D) underlying civil rights suit, a dispute arose between the two as to whether Mitchell (P) was entitled to the 40 percent contingency fee negotiated in their contract.

🏛 RULE OF LAW
The plaintiff in a civil rights action may enter into a contingency-fee agreement with his attorney, even where such a fee exceeds subsequent court-awarded attorney fees.

FACTS: In the underlying 42 U.S.C. § 1983 action that Venegas (D) filed against the city of Long Beach, California, he signed a contingency-fee agreement with Mitchell (P), his attorney, for a fee of 40 percent of the gross amount of any recovery. Venegas (D) subsequently consented to the association of co-counsel who would share any contingent fee equally with Mitchell (P). After Venegas (D) obtained a judgment for $2.08 million, the court awarded him $117,000 in attorney's fees, with $75,000 attributable to the work done by Mitchell (P). After Mitchell (P) withdrew as counsel of record and Venegas (D) obtained different counsel for his appeal, Mitchell (P) asserted a $406,000 attorney's lien against the judgment proceeds representing his half of the 40 percent fee. The district court refused to disallow or reduce the fee, finding it reasonable. The court of appeals affirmed. Venegas (D) appealed.

ISSUE: May the plaintiff in a civil rights action enter into a contingency-fee agreement with his attorney even when such a fee exceeds subsequent court-awarded attorney fees?

HOLDING AND DECISION: (White, J.) Yes. The plaintiff in a civil rights action may enter into a contingency-fee agreement with his attorney, even when such a fee exceeds subsequent court-awarded attorney fees. The aim of the rule is to enable civil rights plaintiffs to employ reasonably competent lawyers without cost to themselves if they prevail but there is nothing in § 1988 to regulate what plaintiffs may or may not promise to pay their attorneys if they lose or if they win. Depriving plaintiffs of the option of promising to pay more than the statutory fee if that is necessary to secure counsel of their choice would not further § 1988's general purpose of enabling plaintiffs in civil rights cases to secure competent counsel. The Court has no occasion to address the extent of the federal courts' authority to supervise contingent fees.

▶ ANALYSIS

A cause of action under § 1983 belongs to the injured individual, and, in at least some circumstances, that individual's voluntary waiver of a § 1983 cause of action may be valid. If § 1983 plaintiffs may waive their causes of action entirely, there is little reason to believe that they may not assign part of their recovery to an attorney if they believe that the contingency arrangement will increase their likelihood of recovery. A contrary decision would place § 1983 plaintiffs in the peculiar position of being freer to negotiate with their adversaries than with their own attorneys.

■■■

Quicknotes

CONTINGENCY FEE AGREEMENT A fee agreement between an attorney and client that is contingent upon the ultimate disposition of the case and comprises a percentage of the party's recovery.

■■■

Describing and Defining the Dispute

Quick Reference Rules of Law

13. Relation Back of Amendments.   (1) An amended complaint may not be dismissed under *30* Fed. R. Civ. P. Rule 12(b)(6) where it does not on its face show that it is barred by the statute of limitations. (2) Under Fed. R. Civ. P. Rule 15(c), an amended complaint that adds a party as a defendant relates back to the original complaint where the added party is a subsidiary of the originally named defendant, and where, even though the plaintiff was aware of the subsidiary's identity and name, the plaintiff was mistaken as to its status as a successor-in-interest. (Goodman v. Praxair, Inc.)

Gillispie v. Goodyear Service Stores

Assault victim (P) v. Store employees (D)

N.C. Sup. Ct., 258 N.C. 487, 128 S.E.2d 762 (1963).

NATURE OF CASE: Appeal of a decision granting a demurrer in action to collect damages in a personal injury case.

FACT SUMMARY: Employees of Goodyear Service Stores (D) trespassed on Gillispie's (P) property, assaulted her, and caused her to be put in a public jail.

🏛 RULE OF LAW
Facts must be alleged in the complaint upon which plaintiff's cause of action is based.

FACTS: Gillispie (P) alleged that she and each of the employees of the Goodyear Service Stores (D), as well as the store, were citizens and residents of North Carolina. The remaining allegations of the complaint and the prayer for relief were as follows: "4. On or about May 5, 1959, and May 6, 1959, the defendants, without cause or just excuse and maliciously, came upon and trespassed upon the premises occupied by the plaintiff as a residence, and by the use of harsh and threatening language and physical force directed against the plaintiff assaulted the plaintiff and placed her in great fear, and humiliated and embarrassed her by subjecting her to public scorn and ridicule, and caused her to be seized and exhibited to the public as a prisoner, and to be confined in a public jail, all to her great humiliation, embarrassment and harm. 5. By reason of the defendants' malicious and intentional assault against and humiliation of plaintiff, the plaintiff was and has been damaged and injured in the amount of $25,000. 6. The acts of the defendants as aforesaid were deliberate, malicious, and with the deliberate intention of harming the plaintiff, and the plaintiff is entitled to recover her actual damages as well as punitive damages from the defendants and each of them. Therefore, the plaintiff prays that she have and recover of the defendants the sum of $25,000 as damages and $10,000 in addition thereto as punitive damages, and that she have such other and further relief as may be just and proper." Goodyear Service Stores (D) demurred to the complaint on the grounds that the complaint did not state facts sufficient to constitute a cause of action and that there was a misjoinder of parties and causes of action. The court sustained the demurrer, and Gillispie (P) appealed the decision.

ISSUE: Can pleadings which contain only conclusions of law state a proper cause of action?

HOLDING AND DECISION: (Bobbitt, J.) No. A complaint must contain a plain and concise statement of the facts constituting a cause of action. Facts must be set out in the complaint that constitute a cause of action and not merely state the conclusions of the pleader. The re-quirement is that a complaint must allege the material, essential, and ultimate facts upon which plaintiff's right of action is based. When the complaint is challenged by a demurrer, only the facts alleged and not the pleader's conclusions are deemed admitted in determining if the complaint states a cause of action. Gillispie (P) alleged in a single sentence that Goodyear Service Stores (D), "without cause or just excuse and maliciously," trespassed upon premises occupied by her as a residence, assaulted her, and caused her to be seized and confined as a prisoner. The complaint stated no facts upon which these legal conclusions could be predicated. Gillispie's (P) allegations do not disclose what occurred, where it occurred, who did what, the relationships between defendants and plaintiff, or of defendants inter se, or any other factual data that might identify the occasion or describe the circumstances of the alleged wrongful conduct of Goodyear Service Stores (D). There was no factual basis to which the court could apply the law. When considered in the light most favorable to Gillispie (P), the complaint fails to state a cause of action. Demurrer affirmed.

▶ *ANALYSIS*

It is often difficult to distinguish between evidentiary facts, ultimate facts, and conclusions of law. Only ultimate facts can properly be included in pleadings. One test used to determine which is which is when no other facts or conclusions can be drawn from a fact then it is a legal conclusion. If the next logical deduction that can be drawn from a fact is a legal conclusion, then it is an ultimate fact. If the next logical deduction from the pleaded fact is another fact, then it is an evidentiary fact. Because it is so difficult to determine the fine line between the ultimate facts, conclusions of law, and evidentiary material, some states are using notice pleading as the federal courts do. Notice pleading only requires that enough facts be pleaded to put the opposing party on notice of the charges against him. In states that still require that only ultimate facts are pleaded, complaints must be carefully drawn. If it appears that there is a basis for a valid cause of action but the pleadings are not properly drawn, courts are quite liberal in allowing the complaint to be amended.

■■■

Quicknotes

COMPLAINT The initial pleading commencing litigation which sets forth a claim for relief.

Continued on next page.

DEMURRER The assertion that the opposing party's pleadings are insufficient and that the demurring party should not be made to answer.

JOINDER The joining of claims or parties in one lawsuit.

MATERIAL FACT A fact without the existence of which a contract would not have been entered.

■═■

United States v. Board of Harbor Commissioners

Federal government (P) v. Environmental polluters (D)

73 F.R.D. 460 (D. Del. 1977).

NATURE OF CASE: Motion for more definite statement in action based on allegedly illegal discharge into navigable waters.

FACT SUMMARY: The Government (P) filed an action alleging the discharge of oil into navigable water, without alleging specifics as to what occurred.

RULE OF LAW
A complaint need not allege the specifics of the transaction of which complaint is made.

FACTS: The Government (P) filed an action against various entities based on the alleged discharge of oil into navigable waters, in violation of 33 U.S.C. § 1321(b)(3). Defendants, SICO Company (D) and NASCO (D), moved for a more definite statement, contending that the complaint did not allege the amounts discharged or the actions which caused the discharge.

ISSUE: Must a complaint allege the specifics of the transaction of which complaint is made?

HOLDING AND DECISION: (Latchum, C.J.) No. A complaint need not allege the specifics of the transaction of which complaint is made. Fed. R. Civ. P. 8 requires only that a complaint reasonably notify the defendant of the nature of the claim being made against him. Specifics are to be uncovered via discovery as permitted in Rules 26 through 36. Here, the complaint stated the nature of the claim and met the requirements of Rule 8. Motion denied.

▌ *ANALYSIS*

Motions for a more definite statement are authorized under Fed. R. Civ. P. 12(e). The motion is analogous to the common law bill of particulars. Both are remnants of the era when formal discovery did not exist, and the pleadings were the only source of information litigants had on each other. Formal discovery has made the motion largely obsolete.

■═■

Quicknotes

COMPLAINT The initial pleading commencing litigation which sets forth a claim for relief.

DISCOVERY Pretrial procedure during which one party makes certain information available to the other.

■═■

McCormick v. Kopmann

Wife of decedent (P) v. Truck driver (D)

Ill. App. 3d Dist., 23 Ill. App. 2d 189, 161 N.E.2d 720 (1959).

NATURE OF CASE: Appeal of denial of motion for directed verdict.

FACT SUMMARY: McCormick (P) brought this action against Kopmann (D) for causing an accident in which her husband was killed. She also sued Huls (D) for violating a state law by serving the decedent alcohol. Kopmann (D) moved for a directed verdict.

🏛 RULE OF LAW
A complaint may contain inconsistent allegations, even though the proof of one negates any fault on the basis of the other.

FACTS: McCormick's (P) husband was killed when his automobile collided with Kopmann's (D) truck. McCormick (P) brought this wrongful death action against Kopmann (D), alleging that he drove over the center line of the road and thereby caused the accident. In a separate allegation in the same complaint, McCormick (P) alleged that another defendant, Huls (D), violated the Dram Shop Act by serving the decedent alcohol after he was intoxicated and that this caused the accident. Kopmann (D) moved for a directed verdict on the ground that the decedent's intoxication constituted contributory negligence and precluded relief as against Kopmann (D). The motion was denied, and the jury returned a verdict against Kopmann (D). Kopmann (D) appealed.

ISSUE: May a complaint contain inconsistent allegations even though the proof of one negates any fault on the basis of another?

HOLDING AND DECISION: (Reynolds, J.) Yes. Sound policy weighs in favor of alternative pleading so that controversies may be sealed and complete justice may be accomplished in a single action. While in Count I, McCormick (P) alleged that the decedent was free from any contributory negligence and in Count IV alleged that he was intoxicated while driving, nothing indicates that McCormick (P) knew in advance of trial which of the averments were true. Thus, McCormick (P) had the right to adduce all proof she had under both counts. Furthermore, the allegations which are inconsistent with those against Kopmann (D) are not binding admissions on the part of McCormick (P). This would force a plaintiff into an election of theories for recovery, and that is not the aim of the pleading laws. A complaint, therefore, may contain inconsistent allegations even though the proof of one negates any fault on the basis of the other. Affirmed.

▶ ANALYSIS

Inconsistent pleading is nearly a universally permitted procedure in pleading a case. Since the trial is supposed to be a fact-determining event, it would not be logical to require a plaintiff to choose which set of facts is "true" before trial when different possibilities exist.

■■■

Quicknotes

COMPLAINT The initial pleading commencing litigation which sets forth a claim for relief.

CONTRIBUTORY NEGLIGENCE Behavior on the part of an injured plaintiff falling below the standard of ordinary care that contributes to the defendant's negligence, resulting in the plaintiff's injury.

PLEADING A statement setting forth the plaintiff's cause of action or the defendant's defenses to the plaintiff's claims.

■■■

Zuk v. Eastern Pennsylvania Psychiatric Institute of the Medical College of Pennsylvania

Doctor (P) v. Institute (D)

103 F.3d 294 (3d Cir. 1996).

NATURE OF CASE: Motions for attorney's fees and sanctions.

FACT SUMMARY: Lipman (D) appealed from an order of sanctions imposed upon him under 28 U.S.C.A. § 1927 and Fed. R. Civ. P. 11, in a copyright infringement suit.

RULE OF LAW

Sanctions may not be imposed upon an attorney pursuant to 28 U.S.C.A. § 1927 where the attorney fails to make a reasonably adequate inquiry into the facts and law before filing the lawsuit.

FACTS: Zuk (P), a psychologist on Eastern Pennsylvania Psychiatric Institute's (EPPI) (D) faculty, had an EPPI (D) technician film two of his family therapy sessions in the early 1970s. Zuk (P) had duplicates made of the films so that they could be rented from EPPI's (D) library. Zuk (P) later wrote a book that included transcripts from the sessions. The book was registered in 1975 with the U.S. Copyright Office. In 1980 Zuk (P) was furloughed and he asked that the copies of the tape be returned to him. EPPI (D) refused and continued to rent the films. A suit for copyright infringement was later brought on Zuk's (P) behalf. EPPI (D) moved to dismiss under Fed. R. Civ. P. 12(b) and the motion was granted. EPPI (D) then filed a motion for attorney's fees under 17 U.S.C.A. § 505 and a Fed. R. Civ. P. 11 motion for sanctions. The court concluded that Zuk (P) and his counsel, Lipman (D), were liable to EPPI (D) for $15,000 in attorney's fees. Zuk (P) settled leaving Lipman (D) liable for $8,750. Lipman (D) appealed.

ISSUE: May sanctions be imposed upon an attorney pursuant to 28 U.S.C.A. § 1927 where the attorney fails to make a reasonably adequate inquiry into the facts and law before filing the lawsuit?

HOLDING AND DECISION: (Rosenn, J.) No. Sanctions may not be imposed upon an attorney pursuant to 28 U.S.C.A. § 1927 where the attorney fails to make a reasonably adequate inquiry into the facts and law before filing the lawsuit. The court first reviews the district court's decision to impose sanctions under 28 U.S.C.A. § 1927. That section requires attorneys who multiply proceedings in a case unreasonably and vexatiously to satisfy the excess costs incurred as a result. The primary purpose of the section is to deter intentional and unnecessary delay. Here, the court imposed sanctions for failure to make a reasonably adequate inquiry into the facts and law before bringing suit. Thus, the statute is inapplicable. Moreover, the statute imposes sanctions only on counsel and not on the client. Moreover, the court may only impose § 1927 sanction upon a finding of willful bad faith. Here, there was no such finding. Therefore, the sanctions order must be vacated since the district court did not divide the sanctions between the § 1927 violation and Fed. R. Civ. P. 11. Affirmed in part and vacated in part.

ANALYSIS

The court went on to address the issues that would arise on appeal, namely the type and amount of sanctions that should properly be imposed under Fed. R. Civ. P. 11. A 1983 amendment deleted the willfulness requirement and imposed a duty on counsel to reasonably inquire as to both the facts and law. The court concluded that the district court did not err in concluding that Lipman (D) did not reasonably inquire as to the facts and law before filing the present suit.

Quicknotes

BAD FAITH Conduct that is intentionally misleading or deceptive.

COPYRIGHT INFRINGEMENT A violation of one of the exclusive rights granted to an artist pursuant to Article I, section 8, clause 8 of the United States Constitution over the reproduction, display, performance, distribution, and adaptation of his work for a period prescribed by statute.

SANCTIONS A penalty imposed in order to ensure compliance with a statute or regulation.

Mitchell v. Archibald & Kendall, Inc.

Gunshot victim (P) v. Business owner (D)

573 F.2d 429 (7th Cir. 1978).

NATURE OF CASE: Appeal from dismissal of complaint for failure to state a claim.

FACT SUMMARY: Mitchell (P) brought this action for injuries sustained when criminal assailants shot him while he was parked on a street adjacent to Archibald & Kendall, Inc.'s (A & K) (D) business, but the district court dismissed for failure to state a claim upon which relief could be granted.

🏛 RULE OF LAW
A complaint failing to include facts constituting a cause of action may be dismissed under Fed. R. Civ. P. 12(b)(6).

FACTS: Mitchell (P) and his family arrived to deliver certain items to Archibald & Kendall, Inc. (A & K) (D) at its place of business. Mitchell (P) was told to wait for another truck to unload at the loading dock. Mitchell (P) was directed onto an adjacent street, where he sat in his truck waiting, when two assailants approached, demanded his money, and shot him in the face with a 12-gauge shotgun when he refused their demands. Mitchell (P) filed a complaint against A & K (D) for serious injuries sustained therefrom, alleging that A & K (D) had repeated experiences of assaults and had breached a duty to Mitchell (P) by not taking steps to prevent such incidents. The district court dismissed the complaint on the grounds that the public street was not part of A & K's (D) premises. Mitchell (P) appealed, arguing that the adjacent street was part of A&K's (D) "premises," and contending that the district court had improperly made a factual finding in dismissing the case because factual disputes cannot be resolved on motion under Fed. R. Civ. P. 12(b)(6).

ISSUE: May a complaint failing to include facts constituting a cause of action be dismissed under Fed. R. Civ. P. 12(b)(6)?

HOLDING AND DECISION: (Pell, J.) Yes. Upon the facts stated in the complaint, the district court was able to properly determine that the crime occurred on the street as opposed to A & K's (D) premises. The complaint did not present the theory that the street was part of the premises. Mitchell (P) appealed before the dismissal became final, thus destroying any right to file an amended complaint by electing to stand on the original deficient complaint. On the face of the complaint, Mitchell (P) was seeking recovery for an attack on a public street, and the district court properly dismissed on the grounds that no right of action exists under these circumstances for an attack on a public street. A complaint failing to include facts constituting a cause of action may be dismissed under Fed. R. Civ. P. 12(b)(6). Affirmed.

DISSENT: (Fairchild, C.J.) The complaint alleged that A & K (D) ordered Mitchell (P) to wait on a street where it knew or should have known that he would be in danger of attack. The affirmative conduct of A & K (D) gave rise to a duty to warn.

▌ANALYSIS

Under Fed. R. Civ. P., pleadings are to be liberally construed. In this case, Mitchell (P) did allege facts that could be inferred to give rise to a tort cause of action. It is true that the inclusion of the street as part of A & K's (D) premises was not part of the complaint as drafted, but upon the facts as set forth in the complaint a duty to warn of a known danger was arguably created.

■=■

Quicknotes

CAUSE OF ACTION A fact or set of facts the occurrence of which entitles a party to seek judicial relief.

COMPLAINT The initial pleading commencing litigation which sets forth a claim for relief.

DUTY TO WARN An obligation owed by an owner or occupier of land to persons who come onto the premises, to inform them of defects or active operations which may cause injury.

■=■

Tellabs, Inc. v. Makor Issues & Rights, Ltd.

Corporation (D) v. Shareholder (P)

551 U.S. 308 (2007).

NATURE OF CASE: Appeal from reversal of dismissal of action brought under the Private Securities Litigation Reform Act of 1995 for securities fraud.

FACT SUMMARY: Shareholders (P) of Tellabs, Inc. (Tellabs) (D), who brought suit under the Private Securities Litigation Reform Act of 1995 (PSLRA) claiming that Tellabs (D) and its officers (D) had intentionally deceived investors about the true value of the company's stock, contended that they had pled with particularity facts giving rise to a "strong inference" that Tellabs (D) and the officers (D) had acted with the required scienter.

📜 **RULE OF LAW**
Under the Private Securities Litigation Reform Act of 1995 (PSLRA), to qualify as "strong" within the intendment of § 21D(b)(2), an inference of scienter must be found by a reasonable person to be cogent and at least as compelling as any opposing inference of nonfraudulent intent.

FACTS: Shareholders (P) of Tellabs, Inc. (Tellabs) (D) who purchased stock over a seven-month period filed a class action under the Private Securities Litigation Reform Act of 1995 (PSLRA) alleging that Tellabs (D) and Notebaert (D), then Tellabs's (D) CEO and president, had engaged in securities fraud in violation of § 10(b) of the Securities Exchange Act of 1934 and SEC Rule 10b-5. Specifically, the shareholders (P) alleged that during the seven-month period, Notebaert (D) (and by imputation Tellabs (D)) falsely reassured public investors, in a series of statements, that Tellabs (D) was continuing to enjoy strong demand for its products and earning record revenues when, in fact, Notebaert (D) knew the opposite was true. When it was finally revealed, after the seven-month class period, that demand for Tellabs's (D) products had dropped significantly, the price of its stock per share plunged from a high of $67 to a low of around $16. The district court dismissed the action without prejudice, and the shareholders (P) amended their complaint to add 27 confidential sources and other new, more specific allegations, but the district court again dismissed, this time with prejudice. The court of appeals reversed, finding that the requirement in PSLRA that plaintiffs must "state with particularity facts giving rise to a strong inference that the defendant acted with the required state of mind" had been met. The court of appeals held that the "strong inference" standard would be met if the complaint "allege[d] facts from which, if true, a reasonable person could infer that the defendant acted with the required intent." Tellabs (D) appealed, and the United States Supreme Court granted certiorari.

ISSUE: Under the Private Securities Litigation Reform Act of 1995 (PSLRA), to qualify as "strong" within the intendment of § 21D(b)(2), must an inference of scienter be found by a reasonable person to be cogent and at least as compelling as any opposing inference of nonfraudulent intent?

HOLDING AND DECISION: (Ginsburg, J.) Yes. Under the Private Securities Litigation Reform Act of 1995 (PSLRA), to qualify as "strong" within the intendment of § 21D(b)(2), an inference of scienter must be found by a reasonable person to be cogent and at least as compelling as any opposing inference of nonfraudulent intent. As a check against abusive litigation in private securities fraud actions, PSLRA includes exacting pleading requirements that require plaintiffs to state with particularity both the facts constituting the alleged violation, and the facts evidencing scienter, i.e., the defendant's intention "to deceive, manipulate, or defraud." As set out in § 21D(b)(2), plaintiffs must "state with particularity facts giving rise to a strong inference that the defendant acted with the required state of mind." However, Congress left the key term "strong inference" undefined. The key issue in this case is whether the court of appeals' formulation of that term is adequate; it is not, because it does not capture the stricter demand Congress sought to convey by its use of that term. Congress did not shed much light on what facts would create a strong inference or how courts could determine the existence of the requisite inference. With no clear guide from Congress other than its intention to strengthen existing pleading requirements, courts of appeals have diverged in construing the term "strong inference." Among the uncertainties are whether courts should consider competing inferences in determining whether an inference of scienter is "strong." Thus, the Court's task is to prescribe a workable construction of the "strong inference" standard that promotes the PSLRA's twin goals of curbing frivolous, lawyer-driven litigation, while preserving investors' ability to recover on meritorious claims. The Court establishes the following prescriptions: First, faced with a motion to dismiss a § 10(b) action, courts must, as with any motion to dismiss for failure to plead a claim on which relief can be granted, accept all factual allegations in the complaint as true. Second, courts must consider the complaint in its entirety, as well as other sources courts ordinarily examine when ruling on motions to dismiss. The inquiry is whether all of the facts alleged, taken collectively, give rise to a strong inference of scienter, not whether any individual allegation, scrutinized in isolation, meets that standard.

Continued on next page.

Third, in determining whether the pleaded facts give rise to a "strong" inference of scienter, the court must take into account plausible opposing inferences. The court of appeals expressly declined to engage in such a comparative inquiry, but Congress did not merely require plaintiffs to allege facts from which an inference of scienter rationally could be drawn. Instead, Congress required plaintiffs to plead with particularity facts that give rise to a "strong"—i.e., a powerful or cogent—inference. To determine whether the plaintiff has alleged facts giving rise to the requisite "strong inference," a court must consider plausible, nonculpable explanations for the defendant's conduct, as well as inferences favoring the plaintiff. The inference that the defendant acted with scienter need not be irrefutable, but it must be more than merely "reasonable" or "permissible"—it must be cogent and compelling. In this way, the inference is "strong" in light of other explanations. Tellabs (D) contends that when competing inferences are considered, as per this formulation, Notebaert's (D) evident lack of pecuniary motive will be dispositive. While motive can be a relevant consideration, and personal financial gain may weigh heavily in favor of a scienter inference, the absence of such a motive is not fatal. Because allegations must be considered collectively, the significance that can be ascribed to an allegation of motive, or lack thereof, depends on the entirety of all the facts alleged. Finally, the court of appeals was unduly concerned that a court's comparative assessment of plausible inferences would impinge upon the Seventh Amendment right to jury trial. Congress, as creator of federal statutory claims, has power to prescribe what must be pleaded to state the claim, just as it has power to determine what must be proved to prevail on the merits. It is Congress's prerogative, therefore, to allow, disallow, or shape the contours of § 10(b) private actions, including the pleading and proof requirements thereof. Vacated and remanded.

CONCURRENCE: (Scalia, J.) The Court's test fails in one key respect: an inference that is merely "at least as compelling as any opposing inference" cannot be said to be a "strong inference." Instead, the test should be whether the inference of scienter is more plausible than the opposing inference of innocence. It is up to Congress to determine the appropriate pleading standard and the Court's job to give meaning to the standard devised by Congress. Thus, here, "strong inference" must be given its ordinary meaning.

CONCURRENCE: (Alito, J.) The best interpretation of the PSLRA is that only those facts that are alleged "with particularity" may properly be considered in determining whether the allegations of scienter are sufficient. To this extent, the majority is incorrect that the complaint's omissions and ambiguities weigh against an inference of scienter, since such an approach is no different from normal pleading review. Also, Justice Scalia's interpretation properly aligns the pleading test under the PSLRA with the test that is used at the summary-judgment and judgment-as-a-matter-of-law stages, whereas the majority's test would

introduce a test previously unknown in civil litigation. Thus, it seems more likely that Congress meant to adopt a known quantity and thus to adopt Justice Scalia's approach.

DISSENT: (Stevens, J.) Congress's intent in enacting a heightened pleading requirement in the context of securities fraud litigation was to protect defendants from the costs of discovery and trial in unmeritorious cases. This purpose is akin to protecting those suspected of criminal conduct from producing their private effects unless there is probable cause to believe them guilty of misconduct. Thus, the better standard to apply in this case is probable cause, which in common parlance means the same as "strong inference," and with which judges are more familiar. Moreover, it is doubtful that Congress intended to adopt a standard that makes it more difficult to commence a civil case than a criminal case. Applying this standard to the facts, it is clear that there was probable cause that Notebaert (D) acted with the requisite scienter.

▶ ANALYSIS

On remand, the court of appeals ruled that the allegations in the complaint met the PSLRA's pleading requirements. In reaching this conclusion, Judge Posner said that the idea of drawing a "strong inference" from factual allegations is inconsistent with the prevalent practice of notice pleading. Even when a plaintiff is required by Rule 9(b) of the Federal Rules of Civil Procedure to plead facts (such as the when and where of an alleged fraudulent statement), the court must treat the pleaded facts as true and "draw all reasonable inferences in favor of the plaintiff." To draw a "strong inference" in favor of the plaintiff might seem to imply that the defendant had pleaded facts or presented evidence that would, by comparison with the plaintiff's allegations, enable a conclusion that the plaintiff had the stronger case; and therefore that a judge could not draw a *strong* inference in the plaintiff's favor before hearing from the defendant. But comparison is not essential, and obviously is not contemplated by the PLSRA, which requires dismissal in advance of the defendant's answer unless the complaint itself gives rise to a strong inference of scienter. A defendant will usually have evidence to present in his defense, so a complaint that on its face, and without reference to the defendant's case, creates only a weak or bare inference of scienter, suggesting that the plaintiff would prevail only if there were no defense case at all, would be quite likely to fail eventually when the defendant had a chance to put on his case, which would normally be after pretrial discovery. Apparently, Congress does not believe that weak complaints should put a defendant to the expense of discovery in a complex securities-fraud case, such as the one at issue in this decision.

■■■

Continued on next page.

Quicknotes

FRAUD A false representation of facts with the intent that another will rely on the misrepresentation to his detriment.

INFERENCE A deduction from established facts.

SCIENTER Knowledge of certain facts; often refers to "guilty knowledge," which implicates liability.

■═■

Swierkiewicz v. Sorema, N.A.

Terminated employee (P) v. Employer (D)

534 U.S. 506 (2002).

NATURE OF CASE: Appeal from dismissal of a complaint for failure to plead facts sufficient to establish a prima facie case.

FACT SUMMARY: Swierkiewicz (P), a 53-year-old native of Hungary, filed suit against Sorema, N.A. (D), his former employer, for employment discrimination. His complaint was dismissed because the complaint was found not to contain specific facts establishing a prima facie case of discrimination under the framework set forth by *McDonnell Douglas Corp. v. Green*, 411 U.S. 792 (1973).

🏛 **RULE OF LAW**
An employment discrimination complaint need not contain specific facts establishing a prima facie case under the framework of *McDonnell Douglas Corp. v. Green*, 411 U.S. 792 (1973).

FACTS: Swierkiewicz (P), a 53-year-old native of Hungary, filed suit against Sorema, N.A. (D), his former employer, alleging that he had been fired on account of his national origin in violation of Title VII of the Civil Rights Act of 1964 and on account of his age in violation of the Age Discrimination in Employment Act of 1967 (ADEA). In affirming the district court's dismissal of the complaint, the court of appeals relied on its settled precedent requiring an employment discrimination complaint to allege facts constituting a prima facie case of discrimination under the framework set forth in *McDonnell Douglas Corp. v. Green*, 411 U.S. 792 (1973). The court held that Swierkiewicz (P) had failed to meet his burden because his allegations were insufficient as a matter of law to raise an inference of discrimination. The U.S. Supreme Court granted review.

ISSUE: Does an employment discrimination complaint need to contain specific facts establishing a prima facie case under the framework of *McDonnell Douglas Corp. v. Green*, 411 U.S. 792 (1973)?

HOLDING AND DECISION: (Thomas, J.) No. An employment discrimination complaint need not contain specific facts establishing a prima facie case under the framework of *McDonnell Douglas Corp. v. Green*, 411 U.S. 792 (1973). Instead, it must contain only "a short and plain statement of the claim showing that the pleader is entitled to relief" as required by Fed. R. Civ. P. 8(a)(2). The *McDonnell Douglas* framework—which requires the plaintiff to show (1) membership in a protected group, (2) qualification for the job in question, (3) an adverse employment action, and (4) circumstances supporting an inference of discrimination—is an evidentiary standard, not a pleading requirement. The Court has never indicated that the requirements for establishing a prima facie case apply to pleading. Moreover, the precise requirements of the prima facie case can vary with the context and were never intended to be rigid, mechanized, or ritualistic. Also, it may be difficult to define the precise formulation of the required prima facie case in a particular case before discovery has unearthed relevant facts and evidence. Consequently, the prima facie case should not be transposed into a rigid pleading standard for discrimination cases. Imposing the Second Circuit's heightened standard also conflicts with Rule 8(a)(2)'s express language, which requires simply that the complaint "give the defendant fair notice of what the plaintiff's claim is and the grounds upon which it rests." Given the Federal Rules' simplified standard for pleading, a court may dismiss a complaint only if it is clear that no relief could be granted under any set of facts that could be proved consistent with the allegations. Here, Swierkiewicz's (P) complaint easily satisfies Rule 8(a)'s requirements because it gives Sorema (D) fair notice of the basis for his claims and the grounds upon which they rest. In addition, it states claims upon which relief could be granted under Title VII and the ADEA. Thus, the complaint is sufficient to survive Sorema's (D) motion to dismiss. Reversed and remanded.

▌ **ANALYSIS**

This case unequivocally supports the notice pleading of Rule 8(a)(2) in the employment discrimination area by making it clear that detailed fact pleading is not required. The case thus continues the trend of repudiating heightened pleading requirements in all types of federal cases.

■═■

Quicknotes

PRIMA FACIE CASE An action where the plaintiff introduces sufficient evidence to submit the issue to the judge or jury for determination.

■═■

Bell Atlantic v. Twombly

Telephone companies (D) v. Telephone subscribers (P)

550 U.S. 544 (2007).

NATURE OF CASE: Appeal of judgment on the pleadings.

FACT SUMMARY: Telephone and Internet subscribers alleged in a complaint that local telephone companies were violating antitrust laws. The district court dismissed the complaint for failure to state a claim, and the Court of Appeals for the Second Circuit reversed.

🏛 RULE OF LAW
In order for a complaint to survive dismissal on the pleadings, the complaint must include enough facts to state a claim to relief that is plausible on its face.

FACTS: Telephone and internet subscribers alleged in a complaint that local telephone companies were violating antitrust laws by agreeing not to compete with each other and by agreeing to exclude other potential competitors, which allowed monopoly power in the market. The district court dismissed the complaint for failure to state a claim, and the Second Circuit Court of Appeals reversed.

ISSUE: In order for a complaint to survive dismissal on the pleadings, must the complaint include enough facts to state a claim to relief that is plausible on its face?

HOLDING AND DECISION: (Souter, J.) Yes. In order for a complaint to survive dismissal on the pleadings, the complaint must include enough facts to state a claim to relief that is plausible on its face. In this case, in order to state an antitrust claim under the Sherman Act, the complaint must state enough factual matter to suggest that an agreement between the alleged conspirators was made. The complaint fails to show a plausible claim. The holding in *Conley v. Gibson*, 355 U.S. 41 (1957), which stated that a "complaint should not be dismissed for failure to state a claim unless it appears beyond doubt that the plaintiff can prove no set of facts in support of his claim which would entitle him to relief" must have been read by the court of appeals to say that any statement showing the theory of a claim will suffice, unless its factual impossibility may be shown from the face of the pleadings. But the standard interpreted by the *Conley* case should now be set aside, insofar as it has been held up as a minimum standard of adequate pleading for a complaint to survive dismissal. Because antitrust conspiracy was not suggested by the facts in the complaint, the complaint failed to state a claim and must be dismissed. Enough facts to state a claim to relief that is plausible on its face is required for a complaint to survive. That the claim is conceivable is not enough. It must be plausible. Reversed.

DISSENT: (Stevens, J.) This case alleges that the telephone companies acted in concert to cheat customers. Plaintiffs alleged the conspiracy, and because the complaint was dismissed in advance of the answer, the allegation has not even been denied. The case should therefore proceed. The departure from settled procedural law seems to stem from the enormous expense of private antitrust litigation, and the risk that jurors may mistakenly conclude that evidence of parallel conduct proves that the parties acted in accordance with agreement when they in fact merely made similar independent decisions. These concerns do not justify the dismissal of an adequately pleaded complaint. The court seems to have appraised the plausibility of the ultimate factual allegation, rather than its legal sufficiency.

▶ ANALYSIS

The court was careful to say, in the text of the opinion and in footnotes, that it did not apply a heightened pleading standard or broaden the scope of Rule 9. The risk of abusive litigation in certain subjects, like antitrust, requires the plaintiff to state factual allegations with greater particularity than Rule 8 requires, and the Court's concern in this case was not that the allegations in the complaint were insufficiently particularized, but that the complaint failed to show a plausible claim to relief. It is the totality of the claim in the complaint that the Court says must indicate a plausible claim, which is beyond merely conceivable.

Quicknotes

PLEADING A statement setting forth the plaintiff's cause of action or the defendant's defense to the plaintiff's claims.

SHERMAN ACT Prohibits unreasonable restraint of trade.

Shepard Claims Service, Inc. v. William Darrah & Associates

Claims processor (P) v. Service partner (D)

796 F.2d 190 (6th Cir. 1986).

NATURE OF CASE: Appeal of denial of motion to set aside a default.

FACT SUMMARY: Negligence on the part of William Darrah & Associates' (D) counsel resulted in a default being entered.

🏛 RULE OF LAW
Where a plaintiff will not be prejudiced and a meritorious defense is shown, a default should be set aside if it was the result of mere negligence.

FACTS: Shepard Claims Service, Inc. (Shepard) (P) sued William Darrah & Associates (Darrah) (D) for breach of contract. Counsel for Darrah (D) obtained an extension of time in which to answer. Due to secretarial error, the date on which an answer was to be due was misstated in a confirming letter. Darrah's (D) counsel did not review the letter before it was mailed. When the date indicated on the letter passed, Shepard (P) obtained an entry of default. Darrah (D) moved to set it aside. The district court found that setting aside the default would not prejudice Shepard (P) and that Darrah (D) could present a meritorious defense. The court nonetheless denied the motion, citing the negligence of Darrah's (D) counsel. Darrah (D) filed an interlocutory appeal.

ISSUE: Where a plaintiff will not be prejudiced and a meritorious defense is shown, should a default be set aside if it was the result of mere negligence?

HOLDING AND DECISION: (Lively, C.J.) Yes. Where a plaintiff will not be prejudiced and a meritorious defense is shown, a default should be set aside if it was the result of mere negligence. Under Fed. R. Civ. P. 55(c), a default entry may be set aside for "good cause." Cases decided under the rule have formulated three questions to be answered in deciding on such a motion: (1) whether the plaintiff will be prejudiced; (2) whether the defendant has a meritorious defense; and (3) whether culpable conduct of the defendant led to the default. Culpable conduct has been considered to be something worse than mere negligence. A willful disregard for the rules of civil procedure has generally been required for conduct to be considered culpable. Therefore, if the first two questions are answered in favor of the defendant, and the defendant is guilty only of negligence, it is an abuse of discretion not to set aside a default entry. Such was the case here. Reversed and remanded.

▌ *ANALYSIS*

Entries of default are governed by Fed. R. Civ. P. 55(b). Setting aside default judgments is governed by Fed. R. Civ.

P. 60(b). The terms for setting aside default judgments are more stringent than for a mere entry of default. This is due to the judicial policy favoring the finality of judgments.

■=■

Quicknotes

DEFAULT JUDGMENT A judgment entered against a defendant due to his failure to appear in a court or defend himself against the allegations of the opposing party.

INTERLOCUTORY APPEAL The appeal of an issue that does not resolve the disposition of the case, but is essential to a determination of the parties' legal rights.

NEGLIGENCE Conduct falling below the standard of care that a reasonable person would demonstrate under similar conditions.

■=■

David v. Crompton & Knowles Corp.

Machine operator (P) v. Manufacturer (D)

58 F.R.D. 444 (E.D. Pa. 1973).

NATURE OF CASE: Motion to amend answer in an action based on personal injury.

FACT SUMMARY: Crompton & Knowles Corp. (D) denied manufacturing a certain machine on lack of information, although the facts relevant to the issue of its connection to the machine were within its knowledge and control.

🏛 RULE OF LAW
A denial based on lack of information will be deemed an admission if the facts relevant to the issue are within the denying party's knowledge and control.

FACTS: David (P) was injured by a machine manufactured by Hunter, predecessor to Crompton & Knowles Corp. (Crompton) (D). David (P) filed suit in federal court seeking damages. As to the allegation that Crompton (D) manufactured the machine, Crompton (D) denied on lack of information. Crompton (D) later moved to amend its answer to deny the allegation. This was based on the realization that the contract purchasing Hunter's assets disclaimed assumption of liabilities. The court first addressed the issue of whether the denial on lack of information should be considered an admission or denial.

ISSUE: Will a denial based on lack of information be deemed an admission if the facts relevant to the issue are within the denying party's knowledge and control?

HOLDING AND DECISION: (Huyett, J.) Yes. A denial based on lack of information will be deemed an admission if the facts relevant to the issue are within the denying party's knowledge and control. Normally, a denial on lack of information will be deemed the same as a denial. However, such an averment will be deemed an admission when the matter is obviously one of which the defendant has knowledge. When the information relevant to this is within the defendant's control, such a case exists. Here, the relevant information was the denial of successor liability in the contract. This was obviously within the control of Crompton (D), and its denial on the lack of information was therefore invalid.

▶ ANALYSIS

Some states permit defendants to generally deny all allegations on a plaintiff's complaint. This is not the case in federal court, under the Fed. R. Civ. P. There, each paragraph must be separately denied, admitted, or denied on lack of information. A bad-faith denial can lead to subsequent sanctions.

Quicknotes

ADMISSIONS A voluntary acknowledgment by a party as to the existence of specific facts.

BAD FAITH Conduct that is intentionally misleading or deceptive.

SANCTIONS A penalty imposed in order to ensure compliance with a statute or regulation.

Wigglesworth v. Teamsters Local Union No. 592

Whistleblower (P) v. Union (D)

68 F.R.D. 609 (E.D. Va. 1975).

NATURE OF CASE: Motion to dismiss counterclaim in action based on violation of federal labor laws.

FACT SUMMARY: Certain officials of the Teamsters Local Union No. 592 (D), when sued for violation of labor laws by Wigglesworth (P), counterclaimed for defamation.

🏛 RULE OF LAW

A party sued for violation of federal labor laws may not raise defamation as a compulsory counterclaim when it does not arise out of the same transaction or occurrence forming the basis of the complaint.

FACTS: Wigglesworth (P) sued the Teamsters Local Union No. 592 (D) and various officials thereof for violations of federal labor laws. At the same time, he publicly accused the various officials of being associated with organized crime. The various individual defendants counterclaimed for defamation. Wigglesworth (P) moved to dismiss for lack of subject matter jurisdiction.

ISSUE: May a party sued for violation of federal labor laws raise defamation as a compulsory counterclaim when it does not arise out of the same transaction or occurrence forming the basis of the complaint?

HOLDING AND DECISION: (Warriner, J.) No. A party sued for violation of federal labor laws may not raise defamation as a compulsory counterclaim when it does not arise out of the same transaction or occurrence forming the basis of the complaint. Fed. R. Civ. P. 13 makes a counterclaim compulsory if it arises out of the transaction or occurrence forming the basis of the complaint. In this manner, a counterclaim not having a basis for federal subject matter jurisdiction may nonetheless be adjudicated in federal court. Whether a counterclaim arises out of the same transaction depends mainly upon their logical relationship. Here, the two separate events complained of are quite distinct, being separated both by time and distance. One was in reaction to the other. In no sense can they be considered the same transaction, and therefore the counterclaim was not compulsory. As there is no independent basis for federal jurisdiction in the counterclaim, it must be dismissed. Motion granted.

▶ ANALYSIS

Under Fed. R. Civ. P., counterclaims come under two basic types. The first is the compulsory counterclaim, which must be brought at the time of answer or is waived. The second type is the permissive counterclaim. It need not be brought at the time of answer. Unlike the compulsory counterclaim,

it must always have independent federal subject matter jurisdiction.

Quicknotes

COMPULSORY COUNTERCLAIM An independent cause of action brought by a defendant to a lawsuit, in order to oppose or deduct from the plaintiff's claim, that arises out of the same transaction or occurrence that is the subject matter of the plaintiff's claim and does.

DEFAMATION An intentional false publication, communicated publicly in either oral or written form, subjecting a person to scorn, hatred or ridicule, or injuring him or her in relation to his or her occupation or business.

PERMISSIVE COUNTERCLAIM Any claim brought against the plaintiff by the defendant that does not arise out of the subject matter of the original action.

SUBJECT MATTER JURISDICTION The authority of the court to hear and decide actions involving a particular type of issue or subject.

David v. Crompton & Knowles Corp.

Machine operator (P) v. Manufacturer (D)

58 F.R.D. 444 (E.D. Pa. 1973).

NATURE OF CASE: Motion to amend answer in an action based on personal injury.

FACT SUMMARY: Crompton & Knowles Corp. (D) attempted to amend its answer to deny an allegation after substantial time had passed since it obtained the knowledge that the amendment would be proper.

🏛 RULE OF LAW
If a party waits a lengthy period of time between discovery facts making an amendment appropriate and moving to amend, the motion may be denied.

FACTS: David (P) was injured by a machine manufactured by Hunter, predecessor of Crompton & Knowles Corp. (Crompton) (D). David (P) filed suit, seeking damages. Crompton (D) denied, on lack of information, manufacturing the machine. Crompton (D) later moved to amend its answer to deny this allegation, this being based on the realization that the contract purchasing Hunter's assets disclaimed assumption of liabilities. By the time the motion was made, the statute of limitations had run on David's (P) claim.

ISSUE: If a party waits a lengthy period of time between discovering facts, making an amendment appropriate, and moving to amend, may the motion be denied?

HOLDING AND DECISION: (Huyett, J.) Yes. If a party waits a lengthy period of time between discovering facts, making an amendment appropriate, and moving to amend, the motion may be denied. Generally speaking, the law favors liberality of amendment. However, when such amendment will prejudice the opposing party, leave to amend will be denied. Where a lengthy period of time has passed, it is common for prejudice to exist. In this instance, the statute of limitations has passed on David's (P) claim. No new action can be filed. Crompton (D) presumably had access to the contract with Hunter since the execution of the contract. Consequently, Crompton (D) cannot say it is relying on newly discovered information. In light of this, to permit the denial would reward Crompton (D) for its lack of diligence, which would prejudice David (P). Motion denied.

▌ *ANALYSIS*

There are several ways in which the passage of time can prejudice a party moving to amend. One example is that cited in this case. Another common instance is loss of evidence over time.

Quicknotes

DAMAGES Monetary compensation that may be awarded by the court to a party who has sustained injury or loss to his or her person, property or rights due to another party's unlawful act, omission or negligence.

DISCOVERY The pretrial procedure during which one party makes certain information available to the other.

STATUTE OF LIMITATIONS A law prescribing the period in which a legal action may be commenced.

Goodman v. Praxair, Inc.

Contracting party (P) v. Parent of other contracting party's successor (D)

494 F.3d 458 (4th Cir. 2007) (en banc).

NATURE OF CASE: Appeal from dismissal of action asserting breach of contract and wage claims.

FACT SUMMARY: Goodman (P) contended that his action asserting breach of contract and wage claims against Praxair Services, Inc. (D) should not have been dismissed under Fed. R. Civ. P. Rule 12(b)(6) because his amended complaint did not on its face indicate that it was barred by the statute of limitations, and because Fed. R. Civ. P. Rule 15(c) saved the amended complaint from being barred by the statute of limitations by permitting it to relate back to the date of the original complaint, since naming Praxair, Inc. (D) in the original complaint, instead of correctly naming Praxair Services, Inc. (D) (Praxair, Inc.'s (D) subsidiary), was the kind of mistake permitting relation-back under Rule 15(c).

🏛 RULE OF LAW

(1) An amended complaint may not be dismissed under Fed. R. Civ. P. Rule 12(b)(6) where it does not on its face show that it is barred by the statute of limitations.

(2) Under Fed. R. Civ. P. Rule 15(c), an amended complaint that adds a party as a defendant relates back to the original complaint where the added party is a subsidiary of the originally named defendant, and where, even though the plaintiff was aware of the subsidiary's identity and name, the plaintiff was mistaken as to its status as a successor-in-interest.

FACTS: Goodman (P) entered into a contract with Tracer Research Corp. (Tracer) in 1998. On December 19, 2000, Tracer was sent a letter by the Environmental Protection Agency (EPA). Based on the contents of the EPA letter, Goodman (P) contended he was entitled to payment of $650,000 in fees under his contract with Tracer, instead of the $30,000 that Tracer had paid him. In 2002, Praxair Services, Inc. (D), a wholly owned subsidiary of Praxair, Inc. (D), acquired Tracer. Goodman (P) brought suit in state court for breach of contract and wage claims, naming Praxair, Inc. (D) as the defendant, alleging that it was the successor in interest to Tracer—even though he was aware that Tracer had been merged into Praxair Services, Inc. (D). The case was removed to federal court, where Praxair, Inc. (D) moved to dismiss the action on the basis that Praxair Services, Inc. (D), not it, was Tracer's successor in interest. Goodman (P) then amended the complaint on April 5, 2004 by adding Praxair Services, Inc. (D) as a defendant and adding an alter ego claim against Praxair, Inc. (D). Both defendants moved to dismiss under Fed. R. Civ. P. Rule 12(b)(6), on the grounds

that Goodman's (P) claims were barred by the state's statute of limitations. The district court granted the defendants' motion to dismiss, finding that the claims were barred by the statute of limitations and that Rule 15(c), which provides when an amended pleading relates back to the original date of the pleading, did not save Goodman's (P) amended complaint. The court of appeals granted review.

ISSUE:

(1) May an amended complaint be dismissed under Fed. R. Civ. P. Rule 12(b)(6) where it does not on its face show that it is barred by the statute of limitations?

(2) Under Fed. R. Civ. P. Rule 15(c), does an amended complaint that adds a party as a defendant relate back to the original complaint where the added party is a subsidiary of the originally named defendant, and where, even though the plaintiff was aware of the subsidiary's identity and name, the plaintiff was mistaken as to its status as a successor-in-interest?

HOLDING AND DECISION: (Niemeyer, J.)

(1) No. An amended complaint may not be dismissed under Fed. R. Civ. P. Rule 12(b)(6) where it does not on its face show that it is barred by the statute of limitations. Fed. R. Civ. P. 12(b)(6) tests the sufficiency of a complaint. The statute of limitations defense is an affirmative defense on which the defendants carry the burden of proof. Thus, ordinarily, a 12(b)(6) motion cannot reach the merits of a statute of limitations defense. A relatively rare exception occurs where all the facts sufficient to rule on the affirmative defense are alleged in the complaint and appear on its face. Here, however, not all such facts appear on the face of Goodman's (P) complaint. The complaint alleges neither a date when the contract was breached nor a date when Goodman (P) may have discovered the breach. Its allegation that money was owed does not mean that the contract on which it was owed had been breached. The complaint does not allege when Tracer received the letter or when it provided a copy to Goodman (P). Moreover, the complaint contains no allegations of when any demand for payment was made by Goodman (P) or of when Tracer refused to pay. Instead, the complaint merely alleges that Tracer "failed and refused to pay" Goodman (P). Therefore, it cannot be said that the complaint alleges when the cause of action accrued. Also, in some instances, the date a claim accrues is extended until that time at which the plaintiff should have discovered his injury. Here, Goodman's

Continued on next page.

(P) complaint, original or amended, does not provide facts sufficient to apply this discovery rule. For these reasons, the district court erred in dismissing Goodman's (P) complaint under Rule 12(b)(6). Reversed as to this issue.

(2) Yes. Under Fed. R. Civ. P. Rule 15(c), an amended complaint that adds a party as a defendant relates back to the original complaint where the added party is a subsidiary of the originally named defendant, and where, even though the plaintiff was aware of the subsidiary's identity and name, the plaintiff was mistaken as to its status as a successor-in-interest. Under Fed. R. Civ. P. 15(c), an amendment that changes the party against whom a claim is asserted relates back to the date of the original pleading if (1) the claim in the amended complaint arose out of the same transaction that formed the basis of the claim in the original complaint; (2) the party to be brought in by the amendment received notice of the action such that it will not be prejudiced in maintaining a defense to the claim; and (3) it should have known that it would have originally been named a defendant "but for a mistake concerning the identity of the proper party." These requirements balance two competing policies: simplicity in pleadings and their liberal amendment vs. providing defendants with predictable statutes of limitations. Here, by adding Praxair Services, Inc. (D) as a party, Goodman (P) "changed" the party he was suing for purposes of Rule 15(c). He did not, as the defendants assert, have to drop Praxair, Inc. (D) to achieve such a change. Such a restrictive reading of "change," as proposed by the defendants, would not serve any policy. Leaving Praxair, Inc. (D) in as a party would not be unfair to it. The only potential unfairness would be to Praxair Services, Inc. (D), but protections for such potential unfairness are included in Rule 15(c)(1)(B) and (C), not by restrictively reading "change." Thus the liberal amendment policy of the Fed. R. Civ. P. becomes paramount, so that the amended complaint made a "change" as required by Rule 15(c)(1). The next issue, therefore, is whether Goodman's (P) naming of Praxair Services, Inc. (D) in the amended complaint corrected the kind of mistake contemplated by Rule 15(c). Goodman (P) mistakenly thought that Praxair, Inc. (D) had become Tracer's successor-in-interest. The district court ruled that such a mistake is not covered by Rule 15(c), which it found would only cover a mistake of corporate identity or misnomer in this case. Rule 15(c), by promoting the policy of liberal amendment, does not concern itself with an amending party's state of mind except as it relates to mistake. In that regard, the concern is primarily with notice to the new party and the effect the amendment will have on that new party. These concerns preserve for the new party the protections of the statute of limitations: the new party is not prejudiced where it should have known that it was the party that would have been sued but for the plaintiff's

"mistake." For example, such policy concerns would support barring the substitution of "Doe" defendants after the limitations period has run because most new defendants would either be prejudice by the substitution or would not have had proper notice, since naming Doe defendants self-evidently is no "mistake" such that the Doe substitute has received proper notice. Here, Praxair Services, Inc. (D) was not prejudiced by being added as a defendant, and, given the identity of interest between it and its parent corporation and the fact that they share attorneys, there would not have been any surprise to it when the complaint was amended. Praxair Services, Inc. (D) knew that it was Trace's successor and therefore it knew or should have known within the limitations period that it was the proper party to Goodman's (P) suit. For these reasons, the requirements for relation-back under Rule 15(c)(3) have been met. Reversed as to this issue. Reversed and remanded.

CONCURRENCE IN PART: (Gregory, J.) The majority is correct that the statute of limitations defense cannot be determined from the face of the complaint, but it errs in determining that the amended complaint relates back to the original complaint. The majority's approach will decrease the incentives for plaintiffs to thoroughly investigate their cases before filing suit. Instead, the Rule 15(c) should be read only as forgiving mistakes that are clerical and inconsequential—not those that arise from errant lawyering. Otherwise, more lawsuits will be filed against incorrect defendants, who will be forced to bear the costs of defending themselves until the correct defendants are found. Following 20-year precedent, the court should not have permitted Goodman (P) to relate his amendment back, since he intended to sue Tracer's successor-in-interest, but simply failed to determine that the party he wanted to sue was Praxair Services, Inc. because of the corporations' confusing corporate relationships. If Goodman (P) is permitted to relate back his amended complaint, a future plaintiff will be free to file suit against a placeholder defendant while continuing to search for the proper one any time the plaintiff can make a plausible claim that he believed the originally named defendant was the correct one, provided the other requirements of Rule 15(c) are met.

▶ ANALYSIS

The "but for a mistake" language in Rule 15(c)(3)(B) has led to differing interpretations by the courts. Some have divided cases involving amendments to correct typographical errors from cases involving amendments to correct a lack of knowledge of the proper party, and have created another category of amendments resulting from strategic error. Moreover, the majority of courts agree that Rule 15(c)(3) does not permit substitution for "Doe" defendants

Continued on next page.

after the limitations period has run, and do so on the basis of the Rule's "mistake" language. The court in this case obviously did not support such parsing of the "mistake" language, but instead focused on the underlying policy considerations.

■≡■

Quicknotes

CAUSE OF ACTION   A fact or set of facts the occurrence of which entitles a party to seek judicial relief.

RELATION-BACK DOCTRINE   Doctrine which holds that a party may not amend its pleading to set forth a new or different claim or defense unless it involves the subject matter of the original pleading; under Fed. R. Civ. P. 15, if a party amends its pleading as a matter of course before a responsive pleading is served, such amendment is said to relate back to the original pleading if it involves the subject matter of the original pleading.

STATUTE OF LIMITATIONS   A law prescribing the period in which a legal action may be commenced.

■≡■

CHAPTER 4

Establishing the Structure and Size of the Dispute

Quick Reference Rules of Law

Southern Methodist University Association of Women Law Students v. Wynne and Jaffe

Student organization (P) v. Law firm (D)

599 F.2d 707 (5th Cir. 1979).

NATURE OF CASE: Appeal of pretrial order in gender discrimination action.

FACT SUMMARY: Various plaintiffs in a gender discrimination action under Title VII of the Civil Rights Act wished to proceed anonymously.

🏛 RULE OF LAW
Plaintiffs in a gender discrimination action under Title VII of the Civil Rights Act may not proceed anonymously.

FACTS: Various individuals and entities brought an action under Title VII of the 1964 Civil Rights Act against two Dallas-area law firms for alleged gender bias. Several individual plaintiffs sued anonymously. The defendants moved to compel disclosure of the plaintiffs. The trial court ordered disclosure, and an interlocutory appeal was taken.

ISSUE: May plaintiffs in a gender discrimination action under Title VII of the Civil Rights Act proceed anonymously?

HOLDING AND DECISION: (Ainsworth, J.) No. Plaintiffs in a gender-based discrimination action under Title VII of the Civil Rights Act may not proceed anonymously. Fed. R. Civ. P. 10(a) provides that an action shall contain the names of the parties. There is no specific exception to this in Title VII. Courts have carved out an exception to this rule in certain types of cases involving particularly private matters, such as abortion. However, a gender discrimination action does not fall within such a category, particularly one against a private party under Title VII. Since no particularly private matter is involved in such an action, the usual rule of Fed. R. Civ. P. 10(a) must be followed. Affirmed.

▌ *ANALYSIS*

Parties are named anonymously or fictitiously for a variety of reasons. Rarely will plaintiffs be granted anonymity for reasons of privacy, as the court stated herein. Fictitiously named defendants usually are anonymous due to lack of knowledge on the part of a plaintiff as to their true identities.

■■■

Quicknotes

GENDER-BASED DISCRIMINATION Unequal treatment of individuals without justification on the basis of their sex.

INTERLOCUTORY APPEAL The appeal of an issue that does not resolve the disposition of the case, but is essential to a determination of the parties' legal rights.

■■■

Kedra v. City of Philadelphia
Civil rights plaintiff (P) v. Municipality (D)

454 F. Supp. 652 (E.D. Pa. 1978).

NATURE OF CASE: Motion to dismiss for improper joinder in civil rights action.

FACT SUMMARY: Kedra (P), suing for civil rights violations, joined parties and claims spanning a lengthy period of time.

RULE OF LAW
The fact that certain claims and parties relevant thereto span a lengthy period of time will not, in itself, prevent joinder.

FACTS: Kedra (P) and her children filed a civil rights action against the City of Philadelphia (D), stemming from an alleged series of incidents constituting police brutality. The incidents involved various individuals over a 15-month period. Several defendants moved to dismiss, contending that joinder had been improper due to the expansive length of time involved.

ISSUE: Will the fact that certain claims and parties relevant thereto span a lengthy period of time in itself prevent joinder?

HOLDING AND DECISION: (Luongo, J.) No. The fact that certain claims and parties thereto span a lengthy period of time will not in itself prevent joinder. The joinder provisions of the Federal Rules are very liberal. The impulse is toward entertaining the broadest possible scope of action consistent with fairness to the parties. As long as a claim or party is "reasonably related" to the main claim, joinder will be appropriate. Here, even though the various acts of which complaint is made span a considerable period of time, they are part of an alleged pattern. Consequently, sufficient relationship for joinder exists. Motion denied and decision deferred.

ANALYSIS

Joinder rules often interact with jurisdictional mandates. State-law claims are often joined to the claim brought in federal court, even though they could not originally have been brought there. This is known as "pendent jurisdiction."

■=■

Quicknotes

JOINDER The joining of claims or parties in one lawsuit.

PENDENT JURISDICTION A doctrine granting authority to a federal court to hear a claim that does not invoke diversity jurisdiction if it arises from the same transaction or occurrence as the primary action.

■=■

Insolia v. Philip Morris, Inc.

Smokers (P) v. Tobacco companies (D)

186 F.R.D. 547 (E.D. Wis. 1999).

NATURE OF CASE: Suit for money damages alleging claims of fraud.

FACT SUMMARY: Philip Morris, Inc. (D) moved to sever the claims of three plaintiffs under Fed. R. Civ. P. 21 on the basis that the plaintiffs were improperly joined.

RULE OF LAW
Parties may be joined under Fed. R. Civ. P. 20 only if their claims involve the same transaction or series of transactions or a common question of law or fact predominates.

FACTS: Three former smokers and their spouses brought a civil suit for money damages against major tobacco companies and two tobacco trade organizations. The smokers (P) argued their claims arose from an industry-wide conspiracy to deceive consumers as to the addictive and deadly characteristics of cigarettes. The smokers' (P) motion to certify a class of all Wisconsin residents who smoked for over 20 years and had been diagnosed with lung cancer was denied on the basis that common questions of law or fact did not predominate. Philip Morris, Inc. (D) then moved to sever the actions of the three plaintiffs into three separate actions under Fed. R. Civ. P. 21, on the basis that such claims had been joined improperly under Fed. R. Civ. P. 20, since they did not arise from the same transaction or series of transactions and did not share a common question of law or fact.

ISSUE: May parties be joined under Fed. R. Civ. P. 20 only if their claims involve the same transaction or series of transactions or a common question of law or fact predominates?

HOLDING AND DECISION: (Crabb, J.) Yes. Parties may be joined under Fed. R. Civ. P. 20 only if their claims involve the same transaction or series of transactions or a common question of law or fact predominates. Here the plaintiffs' claims do not arise from the same transaction or series of transactions and do not satisfy Fed. R. Civ. P. 20. The facts of the individual claims indicate they are not related to each other. The smokers (P) began smoking at different ages, smoked different brands of cigarettes and quit smoking for different reasons and under different circumstances. The only common thread is an assertion that there existed an industry-wide conspiracy regarding the harmful effects of smoking. Here, joinder would not further the intent of Fed. R. Civ. P. 20. The plaintiffs argue the contrary, relying on *Hohlbein v. Heritage Mutual Ins. Co.*, 106 F.R.D. 73 (E.D. Wis. 1985). There, the court recognized that some factual differences existed between the claims but concluded that it satisfied Fed. R. Civ. P. 20 since they resulted from a consistent pattern or practice of employment conduct on the part of the defendant. Here, the alleged misconduct took place over decades not years. Furthermore, five tobacco companies, rather than one employer, are involved. Subjecting the jury to evidence pertaining to some of the defendants and not to others would have a prejudicial effect on the jury's decision and prejudice the tobacco company's (D) ability to protect its rights.

ANALYSIS

Fed. R. Civ. P. 20 governs permissive joinder of parties. Subsection (a) permits joinder of several parties asserting a right to relief "with respect to or arising out of the same transaction, occurrence, or series of transactions or occurrences." In addition, the claims must assert a common "question of law or fact."

Quicknotes

JOINDER The joining of claims or parties in one lawsuit.

QUESTION OF LAW An issue regarding the legal significance of a particular act or event, which is usually left to the judge to ascertain.

PREJUDICE A preference of the court toward one party prior to litigation.

Janney Montgomery Scott, Inc. v. Shepard Niles, Inc.

Investment bank (P) v. Corporate subsidiary (D)

11 F.3d 399 (3d Cir. 1993).

NATURE OF CASE: Appeal from grant of motion for judgment on the pleadings in a breach of contract action.

FACT SUMMARY: Shepard Niles, Inc. (D) moved to dismiss for failure to join Underwood, its parent and co-obligor to the contract Janney Montgomery Scott, Inc. (P) sued on, on the grounds that Underwood was both necessary and indispensable under Rule 19.

🏛 RULE OF LAW
If a contract imposes joint and several liability on its co-obligors, complete relief can be granted in a suit when only one of the co-obligors has been joined as a defendant.

FACTS: Janney Montgomery Scott, Inc. (Janney) (P), an investment banking corporation, entered into an investment banking agreement with Underwood, a closely held corporation. Janney (P) agreed to serve as an advisor to Underwood and its subsidiaries, including Shepard Niles, Inc. (Niles) (D), and to assist them in obtaining private placement financing to refinance Niles's (D) debt obligations. Later, when Janney's (P) efforts had yet to show results, Underwood negotiated with Unibank to provide private placement financing that Niles (D) needed. Janney (P) did not introduce Unibank to Underwood, but Janney (P) alleged that it provided substantial advice and support to Underwood and Niles (D) throughout the negotiations. Janney (P) contended that under its agreement with Underwood, this advice and support entitled it to a contingent fee which it sought, unsuccessfully, to recover from Niles (D). Janney (P) filed a breach of contract action against Underwood in state court. Janney (P) then filed a breach of contract action against Niles (D) in federal district court. Niles (D) moved for judgment on the pleadings based on Janney's (P) failure to join Underwood as an indispensable party. The district court granted Niles's (D) motion and Janney (P) appealed.

ISSUE: Can complete relief be granted in a suit when only one of two co-obligors to a contract has been joined as a defendant?

HOLDING AND DECISION: (Hutchinson, J.) Yes. If a contract imposes joint and several liability on its co-obligors, complete relief can be granted in a suit when only one of the co-obligors has been joined as a defendant. Fed. R. Civ. P. 19 determines when joinder of a party is compulsory. A court must first determine whether a party should be joined if "feasible" under Rule 19(a). If the party should be joined but joinder is not feasible because it would destroy diversity, the court must then determine whether the absent party is "indispensable" under Rule 19(b). If the party is indispensable, the action cannot go forward. Analysis of whether joinder is "feasible," i.e., which parties are "necessary" under Rule 19(a), is a multi-step process. Under Rule 19(a), the court must inquire whether complete relief can be given to the parties to the action in the absence of the unjoined party. Rule 19(a)(1)(A) inquires whether complete relief can be granted to the persons who are already parties to the action. Here, because there is a strong trend in favor of the principle that co-obligors on a contract are jointly and severally liable for its performance and the agreement between Niles (D) and Underwood as co-obligors can be construed to be joint and several liability, Underwood is not a necessary party under Rule 19(a)(1)(A). Though the district court did not hold Underwood to be a necessary party under Rule 19(a)(1)(A), it did conclude that Underwood's joinder was compulsory under Rule 19(a)(1)(B)(i) and 19(a)(1)(B)(ii). Rule 19(a)(1)(B)(i) requires a court to decide whether determination of the right of present parties would impair an absent party's ability to protect its interest in the subject matter of the litigation. Here, the district court held that Underwood was a necessary party because any decision in the federal action would be a persuasive precedent against Underwood in the ongoing state action. On the contrary, however, Underwood, a co-obligor, is not a party whose joinder Rule 19(a)(1)(B)(i) requires because continuation of the federal litigation in Underwood's absence will not create a precedent that might persuade another court to rule against Underwood on principles of stare decisis or some other unidentified basis not encompassed by the rules of collateral estoppel or issue preclusion. The district court erred in holding that the mere possibility that its decision in the present action would be a "persuasive precedent" in any subsequent state action against Underwood could impair Underwood's interest under Rule 19(a)(1)(B)(i). Therefore, Underwood is not an absent party whose joinder is compulsory, if feasible, under Rule 19(a)(1)(B)(i). Rule 19(a)(1)(B)(ii) asks whether continuation of this action in the absence of Underwood would expose Niles (D) to the substantial risk of incurring double or inconsistent obligations by reason of the claimed interest. The district court answered in the affirmative because Niles (D) could be found liable under the agreement in the federal action while Underwood may be found liable in the state court action that Janney (P) has filed against it. The possibility that Niles (D) may bear the whole loss if it is found liable is not the equivalent of

Continued on next page.

double or inconsistent liability. It is instead the common result of joint and several liability and should not be equated with prejudice. Inherent in the concept of joint and several liability is the right of a plaintiff to satisfy its whole judgment by execution against any one of multiple defendants who are liable to him, thereby forcing the debtor who has paid to protect itself by an action for contribution against the other joint obligors. Niles (D) is free to implead Underwood, using Fed. R. Civ. P. 14, to assert its claim for contribution or indemnity upon principles of restitution, if it is ultimately found liable to Janney (P). The continuation of this case in the absence of Underwood does not subject Niles (D) to double or inconsistent liabilities. Therefore, Underwood is not a necessary party under Rule 19(a)(1)(B)(ii). To summarize, Underwood's joinder is not necessary under Rule 19(a)(1)(A) because the district court can give complete relief to Janney (P) and Niles (D) in this action. It is thus unnecessary to decide whether the district court abused its discretion when it decided that Underwood was an indispensable party under Rule 19(b). Reversed.

▌ ANALYSIS

Note that Niles (D), not Underwood, filed the Rule 12(c) motion for judgment on the pleadings for failure to join Underwood as an indispensable party. This is because Underwood, as an absent party, did not have status to object to its nonjoinder, and therefore must rely on Niles (D), as the defendant, to protect its interests. Alternatively, Underwood might have utilized one of two devices to join the suit and achieve the same result—intervention or interpleader.

■══■

Quicknotes

COLLATERAL CONTRACT A contract made prior to or contemporaneous with another contract.

JOINDER The joining of claims or parties in one lawsuit.

JOINT AND SEVERAL LIABILITY Liability amongst tortfeasors allowing the injured party to bring suit against any of the defendants, individually or collectively, and to recover from each up to the total amount of damages awarded.

■══■

Clark v. Associates Commercial Corp.

Tractor owner (P) v. Commercial lender (D)

149 F.R.D. 629 (D. Kan. 1993).

NATURE OF CASE: Motion to dismiss a third-party complaint in an action in tort and contract for damages to person and property.

FACT SUMMARY: Associates Commercial Corp. (Associates) (D) repossessed Clark's tractor. Clark (P) sued Associates (D) for damages to his person and property. Associates (D) brought a third-party complaint seeking indemnity against the employee and two subcontractors who had effected the repossession.

🏛 RULE OF LAW
Under Fed. R. Civ. P. 14(a), impleader is proper only if the third-party defendant is or may be liable to the third-party plaintiff for all or part of the plaintiff's claims against the third-party plaintiff.

FACTS: Clark (P) brought an action against Associates Commercial Corp. (Associates) (D) for damages to his person and property when agents of Associates (D) repossessed by force a tractor that was collateral for a loan that Associates (D) had made to Clark (P). Clark (P) alleged causes of action in tort and contract (by negative implication in the security agreement prohibiting the secured party from proceeding contrary to a plaintiff's rights under the Uniform Commercial Code (U.C.C.)). Associates (D) then filed a third-party complaint seeking indemnity from its agents who had effected the repossession. Associates (D) alleged that it hired Howard, one of the third-party defendants, and Howard, without the knowledge of Associates (D), hired two other persons to help with the repossession. Howard and the other third-party defendants then moved to dismiss Associates' (D) third-party complaint and Clark (P) moved to strike the third-party complaint, or in the alternative, for a separate trial of the issues it raised.

ISSUE: Under Fed. R. Civ. P. 14(a), is impleader proper only if the third-party defendant is or may be liable to the third-party plaintiff for all or part of the plaintiff's claims against the third-party plaintiff?

HOLDING AND DECISION: (Belot, J.) Yes. Under Fed. R. Civ. P. 14(a), impleader is proper only if the third-party defendant is or may be liable to the third-party plaintiff for all or part of the plaintiff's claims against the third-party plaintiff. Here, the third-party defendants, Howard et al., allege that Associates' (D) claim is based on "implied indemnity," which is no longer recognized in Kansas. They note that under the Kansas comparative fault statute, each defendant is liable only in proportion to his relative fault. Because impleader is proper only if the party has a right to relief under the governing substantive law, the third-party defendants contend that Associates (D) has no valid claim for indemnity against them. However, the basis for Associates' (D) indemnity claim against the third-party defendants is an agency theory, whereby Associates (D) seeks to hold its alleged agents liable for any amounts that Associates (D) is found liable to Clark (P). The State of Kansas continues to recognize the right of an employer to seek indemnity against his employees for liability resulting from the employees' tortious acts. Thus, Associates (D) has properly impleaded the third-party defendants. Clark (P) also opposes Associates' (D) third-party complaint, arguing that his claims against Associates (D) are based upon duties imposed under the U.C.C. and by contract, and thus, third-party defendants have "no duty" under the contract between Clark (P) and Associates (D). But, a proper third-party complaint does not depend upon the existence of a duty on the parts of the third-party defendants toward the plaintiff. Also, a third-party defendant need not be necessarily liable over to the third-party plaintiff in the event the third-party plaintiff is found liable toward plaintiff. Although Rule 14 does not allow a defendant to assert an independent claim for relief from a liability that does not arise out of the plaintiff's claim against the defendant, Rule 14(a) expressly allows impleader of a person who is or may be liable to the third-party plaintiff for all or part of the plaintiff's claim against the third-party plaintiff. The third-party claim need not be based on the same theory as the main claim, and impleader is proper even though Howard's liability is not automatically established once Associates' (D) liability to Clark (P) has been determined. Therefore, Associates (D) has stated a valid claim for indemnity against the third-party defendants. Motion denied.

▶ ANALYSIS

The impleader suit is rooted historically in a common law practice called "vouching to warranty." Under the common law, if a person holding title to land came under attack regarding the validity of the title, he could "vouch in" his grantor because the grantor had warranted the title. The grantor then might or might not take part in the action, but would be bound by the outcome of the action if he was later sued by the grantee. Vouching warranty is rarely used today because two lawsuits must necessarily take place. Like vouching in warranty, impleader is used to resolve like questions of fact and law, but accomplishes it in one lawsuit without delay or inconsistent results.

■━■

Continued on next page.

Quicknotes

IMPLEADER Procedure by which a third party, who may be liable for all or part of liability, is joined to an action so that all issues may be resolved in a single suit.

INDEMNITY The duty of a party to compensate another for damages sustained.

■══■

State Farm Fire & Casualty Co. v. Tashire

Insurance company (P) v. Claimant (D)

386 U.S. 523 (1967).

NATURE OF CASE: Action in the nature of an interpleader in a tort action.

FACT SUMMARY: State Farm Fire & Casualty Co. (P) insured one of three individuals involved in a collision involving a Greyhound bus and attempted to interplead all claimants.

🏛 RULE OF LAW
Insurance companies can invoke the federal interpleader before claims against them have been reduced to judgment. A party to a multiparty litigation can only interplead the claimants seeking the funds of that party.

FACTS: In September 1964, a Greyhound bus collided with a pickup truck in northern California. Two of the passengers aboard the bus were killed; 33 others were injured, as were the bus driver and the driver of the truck and its passenger. Four of the injured passengers filed suit in California state courts seeking damages in excess of $1 million. Greyhound, the bus driver, the driver of the truck, and the owner of the truck, who was the passenger in the truck, were named as defendants. Before these cases could come to trial, State Farm Fire & Casualty Co. (State Farm) (P) brought this action in the nature of interpleader in the U.S. District Court for the District of Oregon. State Farm (P) had in force an insurance policy with respect to the driver of the truck providing for bodily injury liability up to $10,000 per person and $20,000 per occurrence. State Farm (P) asserted that claims already filed against it far exceeded its maximum amount of liability under the policy. It paid the $20,000 into the court and asked that the court require all claimants to establish their claims against the driver of the truck in this single proceeding and in no other. State Farm (P) named Greyhound, the bus driver, the driver of the truck, the owner of the truck, and each of the prospective claimants as defendants. Tashire (D) moved to have this action dismissed and, in the alternative, for a change of venue to the Northern District of California. The court refused to dismiss the action and granted the injunction that State Farm (P) had wanted, which provided that all suits against the driver of the pickup truck, State Farm (P), Greyhound, and the bus driver be prosecuted in the interpleader proceeding. On interlocutory appeal, the Ninth Circuit Court of Appeals reversed the district court's decision. They ruled that an insurance company may not invoke the federal interpleader until the claims against it have been reduced to judgment. The case was then appealed to the Supreme Court.

ISSUE: Can insurance companies invoke the federal interpleader before the claims against them have been reduced to judgment?

HOLDING AND DECISION: (Fortas, J.) Yes. The Supreme Court ruled that the 1948 revision of the Judicial Code made clear that insurance companies do not have to wait until claims against them have been reduced to judgment before making use of the federal interpleader. Even though State Farm (P) had properly invoked the federal interpleader, it was not entitled to an injunction enjoining prosecution of suits against it outside the confines of the interpleader proceeding and also extending the same protection to its insured, the alleged tortfeasor. Greyhound (D) was even less entitled to have the order expanded to require all actions to be brought against it and its driver to be brought in the interpleader proceeding. State Farm's (P) interest in this case is protected when the court restrains claimants from seeking to enforce against the insurance company any judgment obtained against its insured, except in the interpleader proceeding itself. State Farm (P) shouldn't be allowed to determine where dozens of tort plaintiffs must bring their claims. The interpleader was not made to force all the litigants in multiparty litigation to bring their actions in a particular court. Interpleader is to control the allocation of a fund among successful tort plaintiffs and not to control the underlying litigation against alleged tortfeasors. The decision of the court of appeals was reversed, and the district court was to modify the injunction prohibiting the bringing of all other actions connected with the accident in any court except the interpleader proceedings. The injunction should only restrain claimants from seeking to enforce against the insurance company any judgment obtained against its insured, except in the interpleader proceeding itself. Remanded to modify the injunction consistent with the Court's opinion.

▶ ANALYSIS

This case points up the general nature of federal interpleader. Generally, the interpleader device allows a party to join all adverse claimants asserting several mutually exclusive claims (regarding the same property or debt) against him and require them to litigate to determine their own interests. Note that there are two types of federal interpleader. Rule 22 interpleader, limited by normal federal jurisdiction (e.g., federal question greater than $10,000,

Continued on next page.

diversity of citizenship) venue and procedure require-ments, is available to any so qualified parties who may be exposed to multiple liability if not permitted to interplead. 28 U.S.C. § 1335 interpleader (statutory) is more liberal as to jurisdiction than most federal rules and requires: (1) diversity of citizenship; (2) greater than only $500 be in-volved; and (3) payment into the court of bond. Perhaps the greatest advantage of § 1335 interpleader, however, is "nationwide service of process."

■═■

Quicknotes

INTERPLEADER An equitable proceeding whereby a per-son holding property, which is subject to the claims of multiple parties, may require such parties to resolve the matter through litigation.

SERVICE OF PROCESS The communication of reasonable notice of a court proceeding to a defendant in order to provide him with an opportunity to be heard.

■═■

Natural Resources Defense Council, Inc. v. United States Nuclear Regulatory Commission

Public interest group (P) v. Federal agency (D)

578 F.2d 1341 (10th Cir. 1978).

NATURE OF CASE: Appeal of denial of motion to intervene.

FACT SUMMARY: The American Mining Congress (AMC) and Kerr-McGee (KM) appealed the denial of their motion to intervene in an action brought by the Natural Resources Defense Council (NRDC) (P) against the Nuclear Regulatory Commission (NRC) (D) seeking a declaration that state-granted nuclear power operation licenses are subject to the requirement of filing an environmental impact statement and seeking to enjoin the grant of one such license by the New Mexico Environmental Improvement Agency (NMEIA).

RULE OF LAW

A party may intervene in an action under Fed. R. Civ. P. 24(a)(2) if he has an interest upon which the disposition of that action will have a significant legal effect.

FACTS: The Nuclear Regulatory Commission (NRC) (D) was permitted by federal law to give the several states the power to grant licenses to operate nuclear power facilities. The NRC (D) was also empowered to grant such licenses subject to a requirement that such "major federal action" be preceded by the preparation of an environmental impact statement. The NRC (D) entered into an agreement with the New Mexico Environmental Improvement Agency (NMEIA) permitting it to issue a license, which it did, to United Nuclear without preparing an impact statement. The Natural Resources Defense Council (NRDC) (P) brought this action, seeking a declaration that state-granted licenses are the product of "major federal action" and subject to the statement requirement and seeking an injunction against the issuance of the license. United Nuclear intervened without objection. Kerr-McGee (KM), a potential recipient of an NMEIA license, and MAC, a public interest group, sought to intervene, but their motions were denied. Both appealed.

ISSUE: May a party intervene in an action under Fed. R. Civ. P. 24(a)(2) if he has an interest upon which the disposition of that action will have a significant legal effect?

HOLDING AND DECISION: (Doyle, J.) Yes. Fed. R. Civ. P. 24(a)(2) gives a party the right to intervene when he has a sufficiently protectable interest related to the property or transaction which is the subject of the action and the disposition will "as a practical matter, impair or impede his ability to protect that interest." The argument that the effect upon the movant's right must be a res judicata effect is unpersuasive. The effect must "as a practical matter"

impair or impede the ability to protect the right. A party may thus intervene in an action under Fed. R. Civ. P. 24(a)(2) if he has an interest upon which the disposition of that action will have a significant legal effect. It need not be a strictly legal effect. KM and MAC each have rights, not protected by other parties to the litigation, which will be thus effected, and they must be allowed to intervene. Reversed and remanded.

ANALYSIS

Fed. R. Civ. P. 24(a) covers the intervention of right, while Rule 24(b) sets forth criteria for permissive intervention. Intervention is permissive if there is a common question of law or fact or if a statute gives a conditional right to intervene. In either case, an intervenor has the same status in the litigation as an original party, but he cannot raise any new issues. Ancillary jurisdiction attaches over the intervenor.

■■■

Quicknotes

ANCILLARY JURISDICTION Authority of a federal court to hear and determine issues related to a case over which it has jurisdiction, but over which it would not have jurisdiction if such claims were brought independently.

■■■

Hansberry v. Lee

Black landowner (D) v. Covenant holder (P)

311 U.S. 32 (1940).

NATURE OF CASE: A class action to enforce a racially restrictive covenant.

FACT SUMMARY: Lee (P) sought to enjoin a sale of land to Hansberry (D) on the grounds that the sale violated a racially restrictive covenant.

🏛 RULE OF LAW
There must be adequate representation of the members of a class action or the judgment is not binding on the parties not adequately represented.

FACTS: Hansberry (D), who was black, purchased land from a party who had signed a restrictive covenant forbidding the sale of the land to people who were black. Lee (P), one of the parties who signed the covenant, sought to have the sale enjoined because it breached the covenant, contending that the validity of the covenant was established in a prior case in which one of the parties was a class of landowners involved with the covenant. To be valid, 95 percent of the landowners had to sign the covenant. The defendant in the prior case stipulated that 95 percent of the landowners had signed the covenant. That case was appealed, and the Illinois Supreme Court upheld the decision, even though it found that 95 percent of the landowners had not signed the covenant, but it held that since it was a class action, all members of the class would be bound by the decision of the court. The trial court found that the decision in the prior case was binding on the person who sold Hansberry (D) the property and the Illinois Supreme Court affirmed. Otherwise, its decision was still binding. The case was appealed to the U.S. Supreme Court.

ISSUE: For a judgment in a class action to be binding, must all of the members of the class be adequately represented by parties with similar interests?

HOLDING AND DECISION: (Stone, J.) Yes. It is not necessary that all members of a class be present as parties to the litigation to be bound by the judgment if they are adequately represented by parties who are present. In regular cases, to be bound by the judgment the party must receive notice and an opportunity to be heard. If due process isn't afforded the individual, then the judgment is not binding. The class action is an exception to the general rule. Because of the numbers involved in class actions, it is enough that the party be adequately represented by a member of the class with a similar interest. Hansberry (D) was not adequately represented by the class of landowners. Their interests were not similar enough to even be considered members of the same class. Lee (P) and the landowners were trying to restrict black people from buying any of the land, and Hansberry (D) was a black man attempting to purchase land. When there is such a conflicting interest between members of a class, there is most likely not adequate representation of one of the members of the class. There must be a similarity of interest before there can even be a class. Since there was no similarity of interests between Lee (P) and Hansberry (D), Hansberry (D) could not be considered a member of the class and so the prior judgment was not binding on Hansberry (D). Hansberry (D) was not afforded due process because of the lack of adequate representation. Reversed.

▶ *ANALYSIS*

Rule 23(c)(3) requires that the court describe those whom the court finds to be members of the class. The court is to note those to whom notice was provided and also those who had not requested exclusion. These members are considered members of the class and are bound by the decision of the court, whether it is in their favor or not. The federal rules allow a member of the class to request exclusion from the class, and that party will not be bound by the decision of the court. Since a party must receive notice of the class action before he can request exclusion from the class, the court must determine if a party received sufficient notice of the action or if sufficient effort was made to notify him of the action. The rules state that if the court finds that the party did have sufficient notice and was considered a member of the class, he is bound by the decision.

■=■

Quicknotes

CLASS ACTION A suit commenced by a representative on behalf of an ascertainable group that is too large to appear in court, who shares a commonality of interests and who will benefit from a successful result.

NOTICE Communication of information to a person by an authorized person or an otherwise proper source.

RESTRICTIVE COVENANT A promise contained in a deed to limit the uses to which the property will be made.

■=■

Walters v. Reno

Class representative of aliens (P) v. U.S. Attorney General (D)

145 F.3d 1032 (9th Cir. 1998).

NATURE OF CASE: Appeal from class certification and grant of summary judgment.

FACT SUMMARY: Plaintiffs were granted class certification and summary judgment as aliens subject to deportation under § 274C of the Immigration and Naturalization Act and allegedly deprived of due process because the INS notices under § 274C did not adequately inform the aliens of their rights. The government argues that the class should not have been certified because of the factual differences among the aliens' cases and that summary judgment was error.

🏛 RULE OF LAW
Aliens are constitutionally entitled to adequate notice under § 274C of the Immigration and Naturalization Act before deportation may occur, and aliens receiving constitutionally defective notice may be certified as a class.

FACTS: An alien accused of document fraud receives two notices from the INS acting under § 274C of the Immigration and Naturalization Act. To avoid an unappealable final order of deportation, an alien so accused must request in writing a hearing within 60 days. The forms of the notices, however, are written in dense legalese and confusing to most aliens. Nearly all aliens accused of document fraud are deported or subject to deportation.

A group of affected aliens sought class certification and filed a complaint against the INS to seek an injunction against further deportations. The judge certified the class and granted summary judgment to the plaintiffs. The government appealed, claiming that the factual differences of the aliens' cases were sufficient to defeat class certification and also summary judgment.

ISSUE: Are aliens constitutionally entitled to adequate notice under § 274C of the Immigration and Naturalization Act before deportation may occur, and are they certifiable as a class?

HOLDING AND DECISION: (Reinhardt, J.) Yes. Aliens are constitutionally entitled to adequate notice under § 274C of the Immigration and Naturalization Act before deportation may occur, and aliens receiving constitutionally defective notice may be certified as a class. The government argues that the aliens' due process rights are not violated because the forms are not required to be written in any particular manner, and that no prejudice had resulted. It will be no hardship for the INS to slightly alter the forms to make them more understandable to affected aliens. The prejudice that results from nearly incomprehensible notice is as great as the consequence of deportation.

The government points out that two class representatives admitted under a grant of immunity that they were guilty of document fraud. The plaintiffs need only show plausible grounds for relief, not that relief would definitely be granted. For class certification under Rule 23(a), the class should meet the following prerequisites: (1) numerosity, (2) commonality, (3) typicality, and (4) adequate representation. Two alternative prerequisites must be met under Rule 23(b). The government argues that the aliens have not satisfied commonality or adequacy of representation under Rule 23(b). The government claims that the different factual circumstances of each alien makes their argument insufficiently similar to meet the prerequisite of commonality. Additionally, the § 274C proceedings may be individualized, which means that the INS may not use the forms as notice in each case. The government may not avoid responsibility by claiming that it might not follow its own rules and procedures in each case, nor does each alien's circumstances need to be exactly the same for class purposes. The government next argues that the admission of guilt by some of the aliens results in inadequate representation for the rest of the class. Again, the factual differences among some of the aliens' cases do not prohibit certification as a class. The government's fear of increased individual proceedings is understandable, but certification as a class prevents the need for individual cases revolving around the constitutionality of the INS' forms. Thus, the government's contention that Rule 23(b)(2) is not satisfied fails. Finally, the district court's remedy of a permanent injunction is appropriate, even though broad, because each alien who received the notice forms received constitutionally defective notice. Affirmed and remanded.

▶ ANALYSIS

The class members in *Walters* could not opt out because the injunction applied to the entire class, so proper certification is a key. A loose affiliation of persons with somewhat similar claims is not sufficient under Rule 23. A moving step by step through the prerequisites of class certification results in fairness to all potential class members similarly situated.

■■■■

Quicknotes

SUMMARY JUDGMENT Judgment rendered by a court in response to a motion made by one of the parties, claiming that the lack of a question of material fact in respect to an issue warrants disposition of the issue without consideration by the jury.

■■■■

Castano v. American Tobacco Co.

Nicotine addicts (P) v. Tobacco company (D)

84 F.3d 734 (5th Cir. 1996).

NATURE OF CASE: Appeal from class certification in a mass tort action.

FACT SUMMARY: Castano (P) brought a class action suit against American Tobacco Co. (ATC) (D), seeking compensation for nicotine addiction.

🏛 RULE OF LAW
Class actions may be certified under Fed. R. Civ. P. 23(b)(3) only if the requirements of predominance and superiority are met.

FACTS: Castano (P) filed a class action against ATC (D) for the injury of nicotine addiction. Castano (P) sought class action certification under Fed. R. Civ. P. 23(b)(3), claiming the class consisted of all nicotine-dependent persons in the United States and numerous entities related to them. The district court certified the class conditionally on the issues of core liability and punitive damages. ATC (D) appealed the certification.

ISSUE: May class actions be certified under Fed. R. Civ. P. 23(b)(3) only if the requirements of predominance and superiority are met?

HOLDING AND DECISION: (Smith, J.) Yes. Class actions may be certified under Fed. R. Civ. P. 23(b)(3) only if the requirements of predominance and superiority are met. Here, Castano (P) has not met his burden for class certification because he has not considered the effect that variations in state laws will have on the issues of predominance and superiority. The district court only gave a cursory glance at the variations in state law and did not weigh whether such variations would make a class action unmanageable. Furthermore, the court did not consider how the plaintiffs' actions would be tried individually or on a class basis, and thus did not adequately address the predominance requirement; it merely assumed that because common issues would be involved in every trial, they would be significant. That is not enough to satisfy the predominance requirement, which denies certification unless common questions predominate over individual questions. It is also questionable whether a class action would be better for the parties than would individual actions, thereby obviating the requirement that the class action be superior to individual adjudication. Fairness demands that immature mass torts, i.e., those with few prior verdicts, should first be litigated in individual actions until new theories of liability become established. Accordingly, class certification is reversed.

▶ ANALYSIS

Class actions are becoming an effective tool in today's litigious society. The objective of class actions is to preserve judicial resources, while ensuring fairness for all of the parties involved. For example, without class certification, the parties who sue first may deplete the resources of a defendant, so that parties who sue later will have nothing to recover.

■■■■

Quicknotes

CLASS ACTION A suit commenced by a representative on behalf of an ascertainable group that is too large to appear in court, who shares a commonality of interests and who will benefit from a successful result.

■■■■

CHAPTER 5

Obtaining Information for Trial

Quick Reference Rules of Law

In Re Convergent Technologies Securities Litigation

Recipient of interrogatories (P) v. Court (D)

108 F.R.D. 328 (N.D. Cal. 1985).

NATURE OF CASE: Motion to compel responses to interrogations in civil securities litigation.

FACT SUMMARY: Unable to agree on the propriety of certain interrogatories, the litigants sought judicial oversight and relief.

🏛 RULE OF LAW
The pretrial discovery process should be self-executing and have minimum judicial intervention.

FACTS: In a large securities litigation, over 1,000 contention interrogatories were served upon the plaintiff. The dispute as to their propriety became bitter, and a motion to compel was filed.

ISSUE: Should the pretrial discovery process be self-executing and have minimum judicial intervention?

HOLDING AND DECISION: (Brazil, Mag.) Yes. The pretrial discovery process should be self-executing and have minimum judicial intervention. It has always been the spirit of civil discovery that parties are to cooperate as fully as possible in exchanging discovery. The judicial system is completely incapable of refereeing more than a minuscule number of such disputes. The 1983 amendments to Fed. R. Civ. P. 26 make it clear that discovery should only be served when it is reasonably calculated to lead to the discovery of evidence both admissible and sufficiently significant to justify the burdens on both the serving and responding parties. This requires analysis and cooperation on the part of all parties involved, which should make judicial oversight unnecessary. [The court went on to hold most of the interrogatories to be premature and denied the motion in the greater part.]

▶ ANALYSIS

The scope of discovery has always been broad. The 1983 amendments to Fed. R. Civ. P. 26 tightened the scope a bit. Besides being calculated to lead to admissible evidence, discovery had to lead to useful evidence as well. Despite the changes, discovery remains, as a policy matter, expansively construed.

■═■

Quicknotes

DISCOVERY The pretrial procedure during which one party makes certain information available to the other.

■═■

Davis v. Ross

Alleged libel victim (P) v. Former employer (D)

107 F.R.D. 326 (S.D.N.Y. 1985).

NATURE OF CASE: Cross-motions to compel responses to discovery in action for damages for libel.

FACT SUMMARY: Davis (P), a former employee of Ross (D) who sued Ross (D) for libel, sought information on Ross's (D) net worth and annual income; fees paid to Ross's (D) attorneys, one of whom would be a witness in the case; and the names of other employees who had complained about Ross (D). Ross (D), in turn, sought to compel discovery on Davis's (P) psychiatric treatment.

RULE OF LAW

(1) Where a plaintiff is seeking punitive damages, he may not discover information on a defendant's net worth and income through pretrial discovery even though he is otherwise bound by a confidentiality order.

(2) Legal fees paid by a client to an attorney may not be discovered for the purpose of determining the attorney's bias and credibility where the attorney is to be a witness in a case in which the client is a defendant.

(3) In a libel case brought by a former employee against a former employer, the names of other employees who have complained about the employer may not be discovered for the purpose of determining if there has been defamation or for casting doubt on the employer's credibility.

(4) A plaintiff's psychiatric treatment may be discovered where the plaintiff has claimed mental anguish and pain.

FACTS: Davis (P), who had worked for Ross (D), sued Ross (D) for libel, on the basis of a letter in which Ross (D) had indicated that the work or personal habits of several former employees, including those of Davis (P), were not acceptable to Ross (D) and that Ross (D) would not "recommend these people." Davis (P) sought compensatory and punitive damages. Davis (P) propounded discovery, seeking three sets of data. First, Davis (P) sought information on Ross's (D) net worth and annual income, claiming that because she was bound by a confidentiality order, concerns for Ross's (D) privacy did not require waiting for this data until a jury had returned a punitive damages award. Second, Davis (P) sought information on billings by Ross's law firm and Frankenheimer, an attorney in the firm who would be a witness in the case, on the grounds that the amount of fees paid by Ross (D) to Frankenheimer and his firm would be relevant to the issue of his bias and credibility. Third, Davis (P) sought to discover the names of other employees who had complained about Ross (D), on the

theory that if Ross (D) was a bad or unpopular boss, this would show that Ross (D) lied about Davis (P). Ross (D) refused to divulge such information, and Davis (P) moved to compel. Ross (P), in turn, moved to compel discovery of Davis's (P) treatment by a psychiatrist during the period that Davis (P) worked for Ross (D) since Davis (P) sued to recover for "mental pain and anguish."

ISSUE:

(1) Where a plaintiff is seeking punitive damages, may he discover information on a defendant's net worth and income through pretrial discovery even though he is otherwise bound by a confidentiality order?

(2) May legal fees paid by a client to an attorney be discovered for the purpose of determining the attorney's bias and credibility where the attorney is to be a witness in a case in which the client is a defendant?

(3) In a libel case brought by a former employee against a former employer, may the names of other employees who have complained about the employer be discovered for the purpose of determining if there has been defamation or for casting doubt on the employer's credibility?

(4) May a plaintiff's psychiatric treatment be discovered, where the plaintiff has claimed mental anguish and pain?

HOLDING AND DECISION: (Carter, J.)

(1) No. Where a plaintiff is seeking punitive damages, he may not discover information on a defendant's net worth and income through pretrial discovery even though he is otherwise bound by a confidentiality order. Information on a defendant's net worth may not be discovered until a verdict awarding punitive damages is made. When punitive damages are alleged, a defendant's net worth is relevant as to the appropriate damages amount. However, the law recognizes the confidential nature of a person's finances. This, plus the relative ease of alleging punitives, has led to the rule that information regarding a defendant's net wealth may not be forcibly disclosed until a jury has decided that punitives would in fact be awarded. Here, the action has not reached this stage, so disclosure cannot be compelled. Even though Davis (P) is bound by a confidentiality order, this does not change the general rule, since Ross (D) should not be compelled to disclose this private data to anyone, even one bound by a confidentiality order, until a jury has determined punitives are appropriate. Motion to compel discovery of Ross's (D) wealth and income is denied.

Continued on next page.

(2) No. Legal fees paid by a client to an attorney may not be discovered for the purpose of determining the attorney's bias and credibility where the attorney is to be a witness in a case in which the client is a defendant. While Davis (P) may probe for bias by inquiring into the nature of the relationship between Frankenheimer and Ross (D), the amount of fees earned, without more, does not tend to prove bias. Even where a witness has earned his entire livelihood from a single employer on whose behalf he will testify, bias may not be inferred from this fact alone. Further, given that the attorney-client relationship should not be unduly burdened, Davis's motion to compel discovery of legal fees is denied.

(3) No. In a libel case brought by a former employee against a former employer, the names of other employees who have complained about the employer may not be discovered for the purpose of determining if there has been defamation or for casting doubt on the employer's credibility. Davis (P) claims that the truth of Ross's (D) statement that Davis's (P) work or personal habits were objectively unacceptable will be an issue at trial, and from this argues that if it was Ross's (D) personality that was a problem, a jury could infer that there was nothing objectionable about Davis's (P) personality and that Ross (D) was, therefore, liable for defamation. This logic is weak. First, whether Ross (D) was a bad or unpopular boss is not probative of whether Davis's (P) personal or work habits were objectively satisfactory. Second, there is no connection between what kind of boss Ross (D) was and her capacity for telling the truth. Therefore, the information sought is irrelevant to any material issue. Davis's (P) motion to compel discovery of the names of complaining employees and the nature of their complaints is dismissed.

(4) Yes. A plaintiff's psychiatric treatment may be discovered where the plaintiff has claimed mental anguish and pain. This material is relevant and the physician-client privilege has been waived by Davis's (P) suing to recover for mental anguish and pain; Davis (P) has put her mental condition in issue. Where compensation is sought for personal injury, the health of the plaintiff before and after the accident may be inquired into. This is equally true for physical and mental injury. Davis (P) argues that for a libel case of the kind she is bringing, damages are presumed, so that it is unnecessary for her to prove either the existence or the amount of damages. Ross (D) counters that the rule permitting recovery for presumed damages in libel cases has been overruled. However, even if Davis's (P) view of the law is correct, it does not mean that information relating to the existence or amount of damages is irrelevant or not discoverable. While general damages may be presumed, the defendant still may be able to rebut the presumption. Also, the amount of damages is always an issue. Motion to compel discovery of plaintiff's treatment by a psychiatrist is granted.

▶ ANALYSIS

At the heart of all the court's rulings in this case—against Davis (P) and for Ross (D)—is the court's determination of whether the discovery requests were relevant to material issues and would lead to admissible evidence. After this case was decided, Fed. R. Civ. P. Rule 26(b)(1) was amended to authorize discovery of information "relevant to any party's claim or defense." Under the court's approach in this case, as well as under Rule 26, the notion of relevancy is extremely broad and contemplates liberal discovery. Nevertheless, as the case illustrates, some discovery requests will be denied where the court determines that the information sought to be discovered is irrelevant.

■■■■

Quicknotes

DISCOVERY The pretrial procedure during which one party makes certain information available to the other.

PUNITIVE DAMAGES Damages exceeding the actual injury suffered for the purposes of punishment, deterrence and comfort to plaintiff.

■■■■

Kozlowski v. Sears, Roebuck & Co.

Burned pajamas owner (P) v. Department store (D)

73 F.R.D. 73 (D. Mass. 1976).

NATURE OF CASE: Motion to set aside default entry.

FACT SUMMARY: Sears, Roebuck & Co. (D) refused to produce records because it claimed it was impossible to locate them.

RULE OF LAW
If difficulty in locating records is the fault of the party requested to produce, production will not be excused.

FACTS: Kozlowski (P) was burned when a pair of pajamas purchased from Sears, Roebuck & Co. (Sears) (D) caught fire. Kozlowski (P) demanded production of all reports of similar occurrences. Sears (D) refused. A court ordered production. Sears (D) did not comply. Upon motion, Sears's (D) default was entered. Sears (D) moved to set aside the default, contending that Sears's (D) complaint indexing system was by name, not occurrence, making compliance impossibly burdensome.

ISSUE: If difficulty in locating records is the fault of the party requested to produce, will production be excused?

HOLDING AND DECISION: (Julian, Sr. J.) No. If difficulty in locating records is the fault of the party requested to produce, production will not be excused. Under Fed. R. Civ. P. 34, the party from whom discovery is sought has the burden of showing some sufficient reason why discovery should not be allowed once it has been shown that the items sought are within the scope of discovery. While burdensomeness may be a reason, it will not be so considered if it is the responding party's own actions or inaction that created the burden. Here, Sears (D) employed an indexing system making compliance difficult. The indexing system was created and controlled by Sears (D). This being so, no good excuse for not mandating discovery exists. Motion denied.

ANALYSIS

Sears (D) offered to open its records warehouse doors to let Kozlowski's (P) attorney search for the records. The court held this insufficient, considering it a thinly disguised attempt to shift the burden of the request onto Kozlowski (P).

■━■

Quicknotes

DISCOVERY The pretrial procedure during which one party makes certain information available to the other.

■━■

McPeek v. Ashcroft

Employee (P) v. Federal government (D)

202 F.R.D. 31 (D.D.C. 2001).

NATURE OF CASE: Motion to compel discovery.

FACT SUMMARY: McPeek (P), an employee of the Department of Justice (DOJ) (D), attempted to force defendant agency to search computer hard-drive backup tapes for possibly relevant evidence. The DOJ argued that the potential costs of the search far outweighed the utility, and attempted to avoid compliance.

RULE OF LAW
The "marginal utility" approach to electronic discovery is the most appropriate because the more it is that an electronic record contains relevant information, the fairer it is that the party in possession of the record searches at its own expense.

FACTS: Steven McPeek (P) filed a sexual harassment suit against his superior at a federal government agency. Contrary to the terms of the resulting Settlement Agreement, other employees learned of the suit and allegedly began retaliating against McPeek (P). McPeek (P) by then had transferred to a new agency within the Department of Justice (DOJ) (D). McPeek (P) filed a complaint, alleging that the employees of the DOJ (D) engaged in retaliatory acts against him. McPeek's (P) discovery requests demanded a search of the backup electronic data of the DOJ (D). The DOJ (D) argues that such a search would be prohibitively expensive and would not likely result in the production of any relevant testimony.

ISSUE: Is the "marginal utility" approach to electronic discovery the most appropriate?

HOLDING AND DECISION: (Facciola, Mag. J.) Yes. The "marginal utility" approach to electronic discovery is the most appropriate because the more it is that an electronic record contains relevant information, the fairer it is that the party in possession of the record searches at its own expense. The defendants have used three operating systems during the relevant period with no system in place designed to access the hard drives. The backup systems were intended merely to prevent the catastrophic loss of an entire day's documents should the operating system fail. The backup tapes could yield absolutely nothing of relevance or they could yield documents directly bearing on a claim or defense. The Government (D) argues that the cost of a search of the backup tapes in terms of dollars and reassigned employees is prohibitive. Two potential solutions are to make the requesting party pay for the search, or to maintain the present rule of having the producing party pay for it. Neither approach is ideal because a requesting party does not have to pay for a paper search, and if the producing party has to pay for the electronic search, then that party will be reluctant to install any backup systems at all. In the case of the Government (D), a downed operating system without a backup could result in a shutdown of government agencies. The only reasonable approach is the marginal utility approach. In this case, one year's worth of backup drives should be searched for any relevant e-mails. The year chosen reflects the time surrounding the initial e-mail concerning the retaliatory actions. Once this information has been produced, the court will hear further arguments on the cost benefit of such a search.

ANALYSIS

The court notes that attorneys may request significantly fewer documents if the requesting party has to pay for the search. While that seems like an enticing solution, the client may suffer when relevant evidence is overlooked due to financial constraints. Cost-shifting would necessarily be to the detriment of private individuals seeking discovery from large corporations. Requiring a good-faith basis before requesting production of difficult-to-produce documents, especially in digital format, seems to be a proper compromise.

Quicknotes

DISCOVERY The pretrial procedure during which one party makes certain information available to the other.

Hickman v. Taylor

Representative (P) v. Tug owner (D)

329 U.S. 495 (1947).

NATURE OF CASE: Action for damages for wrongful death.

FACT SUMMARY: Five crew members drowned when a tug sank. In anticipation of litigation, the attorney for Taylor (D), the tug owner, interviewed the survivors. Hickman (P), as representative of one of the deceased, brought this action and tried by means of discovery to obtain copies of the statements Taylor's (D) attorney obtained from the survivors.

🏛 **RULE OF LAW**
Material obtained by counsel in preparation of litigation is the work product of the lawyer, and while such material is not protected by the attorney-client privilege, it is not discoverable on mere demand without a showing of necessity or justification.

FACTS: Five of the nine crew members drowned when a tug sank. A public hearing was held at which the four survivors were examined. Their testimony was recorded and was made available to all interested parties. A short time later, the attorney for Taylor (D), the tug owner, interviewed the survivors in preparation for possible litigation. He also interviewed other persons believed to have information on the accident. Ultimately, claims were brought by representatives of all five of the deceased. Four were settled. Hickman (P), the fifth claimant, brought this action. He filed interrogatories asking for any statements taken from crew members, as well as any oral or written statements, records, reports, or other memoranda made concerning any salvaging and repair of the tug and the death of the deceased. Taylor (D) refused to summarize or set forth the material on the ground that it was protected by the attorney-client privilege.

ISSUE: Does a party seeking to discover material obtained by an adverse party's counsel in preparation for possible litigation have a burden to show a justification for such production?

HOLDING AND DECISION: (Murphy, J.) Yes. The deposition-discovery rules are to be accorded a broad and liberal treatment, since mutual knowledge of all the relevant facts gathered by both parties is essential to proper litigation. But discovery does have ultimate and necessary boundaries. Limitations arise upon a showing of bad faith or harassment or when the inquiry seeks material which is irrelevant or privileged. In this case, the material sought by Hickman (P) is not protected by the attorney-client privilege. However, such material as that sought here does constitute the work product of the lawyer. The general policy against invading the privacy of an attorney in performing his various duties is so well recognized and so essential to the orderly working of our legal system that the party seeking the work product material has a burden to show reasons to justify such production. Interviews, statements, memoranda, correspondence, briefs, mental impressions, etc., obtained in the course of preparation for possible or anticipated litigation fall within the work product. Such material is not free from discovery in all cases. Where relevant and nonprivileged facts remain hidden in an attorney's file and where production of those facts is essential to the preparation of one's case, discovery may be had. But there must be a showing of necessity and justification. In this case, Hickman (P) seeks discovery of oral and written statements of witnesses whose identities are well known and whose availability to Hickman (P) appears unimpaired. Here, no attempt was made to show why it was necessary that Taylor's (D) attorney produce the material. No reasons were given to justify this invasion of the attorney's privacy. Hickman's (P) counsel admitted that he wanted the statements only to help him prepare for trial. That is insufficient to warrant an exception to the policy of protecting the privacy of an attorney's professional activities. Affirmed.

CONCURRENCE: (Jackson, J.) The primary effect of the practice advocated would be to require attorneys to act as witnesses.

▌ *ANALYSIS*

The *Hickman* decision left open a number of questions as to the scope of the work product doctrine and the showing needed to discover work product material. In 1970, Fed. R. Civ. P. 26(b)(3) was added to deal with the discovery of work product material. It provides that documents and tangible things which were prepared in anticipation of litigation or for trial are discoverable only upon a showing that the party seeking such material has substantial need of them and that he is unable without undue hardship to obtain the substantial equivalent of the material by other means. The Rule states that mental impressions, conclusions, opinions, or legal theories of an attorney or other representative of a party, are to be protected against disclosure.

■=■

Quicknotes

ATTORNEY-CLIENT PRIVILEGE A doctrine precluding the admission into evidence of confidential communications

Continued on next page.

between an attorney and his client made in the course of obtaining professional assistance.

DISCOVERY The pretrial procedure during which one party makes certain information available to the other.

WRONGFUL DEATH An action brought by the beneficiaries of a deceased person, claiming that the deceased's death was the result of wrongful conduct by the defendant.

■▬■

Upjohn Co. v. United States

Multinational company (D) v. Federal government (P)

449 U.S. 383 (1981).

NATURE OF CASE: Appeal from order to produce documents.

FACT SUMMARY: Upjohn Co. (D) contended that certain questionnaires prepared as part of an internal company investigation were protected from disclosure by the attorney-client privilege.

🏛 RULE OF LAW
The attorney-client privilege may be applied to communications between all corporate employees and corporate counsel.

FACTS: In January 1976, independent accountants conducting an audit of one of Upjohn Co.'s (D) foreign subsidiaries discovered that the subsidiary made payments to, or for the benefit of, foreign government officials in order to secure government business. The accountants so informed Thomas, Upjohn's (D) general counsel, who subsequently undertook an internal investigation of these activities. As part of this investigation, Upjohn's (D) attorneys prepared a questionnaire, which was sent to all foreign general and area managers, regarding the alleged payments. On March 26, 1976, Upjohn (D) voluntarily submitted a preliminary report to the Securities and Exchange Commission disclosing certain questionable payments. After a copy of the report was sent to the Internal Revenue Service, the Service issued a summons demanding production of all files relative to the investigation. Upjohn (D) declined to produce the documents specified in the summons on the grounds that they were protected from disclosure by the attorney-client privilege and constituted the work product of attorneys prepared in anticipation of litigation. After the Government (P) filed a petition seeking enforcement of the summons, the court of appeals held that only senior management personnel were protected by the privilege. Upjohn (D) appealed, contending that the privilege applied to all corporate personnel who answered the questionnaire.

ISSUE: May the attorney-client privilege be applied to communications between all corporate employees and corporate counsel?

HOLDING AND DECISION: (Rehnquist, J.) Yes. The attorney-client privilege may be applied to communications between all corporate employees and corporate counsel. The privilege exists to protect not only the giving of professional advice to those who can act on it but also the giving of information to the lawyer to enable him to give sound and informed advice. Middle- and lower-level employees can, by actions within the scope of their employment, embroil the corporation in serious legal difficulties, and it is only natural that these employees would have the relevant information needed by corporate counsel if he is adequately to advise the client with respect to such actual or potential difficulties. The control group test adopted by the court of appeals frustrates the very purpose of the privilege by discouraging the communication of relevant information by employees of the client to attorneys seeking to render legal advice to the client corporation. Here, because the privilege does not protect the disclosure of the underlying facts by those who communicated with the attorney, the Government (P) was free to question the employees who communicated with Thomas as a means of conducting discovery. Reversed.

▶ ANALYSIS

As the Court notes in its opinion, the attorney-client privilege is the oldest of the privileges for confidential communications known to the common law. Its purpose is to encourage full and frank communication between attorneys and their clients and to thereby promote broader public interests in the observance of law and administration of justice.

■=■

Quicknotes

ATTORNEY-CLIENT PRIVILEGE A doctrine precluding the admission into evidence of confidential communications between an attorney and his client made in the course of obtaining professional assistance.

DISCOVERY The pretrial procedure during which one party makes certain information available to the other.

■=■

In Re Shell Oil Refinery

Petroleum company (D) v. Legal committee (P)

132 F.R.D. 437 (E.D. La. 1990).

NATURE OF CASE: Motion for reconsideration of the court's ruling on plaintiffs' request for discovery of defendant's experts.

FACT SUMMARY: During pretrial discovery, the court denied discovery motions by which the Plaintiffs' Legal Committee (P) sought the results of tests conducted by Shell Oil Refinery (Shell) (D) after an explosion at its refinery and leave of court to depose Shell's (D) in-house experts, even though Shell (D) did not intend to use them at trial.

> **⬛ RULE OF LAW**
> The facts known and opinions held by nontestifying experts who are retained or specially employed in anticipation of litigation or preparation for trial are subject to discovery only in exceptional circumstances.

FACTS: After an explosion at a Shell Oil Refinery (D), several suits ultimately certified as a class action were filed. In preparation for the litigation, Shell (D) conducted certain tests. Its legal department and outside counsel requested that two of Shell's (D) in-house experts, present at the tests, prepare preliminary reports and help the investigation team defend the lawsuits. The Plaintiffs' Legal Committee (PLC) (P) sought the results of Shell's (D) tests and also sought to depose the two in-house experts. Shell (D) stated that it did not intend to call its in-house experts at trial or to use their preliminary reports. On these facts, the court ruled against the PLC's (P) motions for expert discovery. The PLC (P) filed a motion for reconsideration.

ISSUE: Are the facts known and opinions held by nontestifying experts who are retained or specially employed in anticipation of litigation or preparation for trial subject to discovery only in exceptional circumstances?

HOLDING AND DECISION: (Mentz, J.) Yes. The facts known and opinions held by nontestifying experts who are retained or specially employed in anticipation of litigation or preparation for trial are subject to discovery only in exceptional circumstances. Although Shell's (D) in-house experts might have studied the cause of the explosion regardless of litigation, their usual duties did not include litigation assistance. Thus, they were retained or specially employed by Shell (D) in preparation for trial. The PLC (P) had access to the materials tested by Shell (D) and can conduct its own expert tests. The parties could also discover the basis for each other's expert's conclusions during the period set aside for expert discovery. Thus, the PLC (P) has failed to show exceptional circumstances.

▶ ANALYSIS

Neither Fed. R. Civ. P. 26(b)(4)(A), which the court applied here, nor the Advisory Committee Notes explain when a general employee may become retained or specially employed. If their work was in anticipation of litigation, then discovery must be analyzed under the work product doctrine of Rule 26(b)(3). The exceptional circumstances requirement has been interpreted by the courts to mean an inability to obtain equivalent information from other sources.

⬛═⬛

Quicknotes

DISCOVERY The pretrial procedure during which one party makes certain information available to the other.

WORK PRODUCT DOCTRINE A doctrine excluding from discovery work performed by an attorney in preparation of litigation.

⬛═⬛

Cine Forty-Second Street Theatre Corp. v. Allied Artists Pictures Corp.

Movie theater operator (P) v. Competitors (D)

602 F.2d 1062 (2d Cir. 1979).

NATURE OF CASE: Action seeking damages and injunctive relief for anticompetitive practices.

FACT SUMMARY: The magistrate concluded that Cine Forty-Second Street Theatre Corp. (P) had engaged in repeated and willful noncompliance with the court's orders regarding answering Allied Artists Pictures Corp.'s (D) interrogatories on the issue of damages, with the result that the magistrate recommended to the trial court that Cine (P) be precluded from introducing evidence on that issue.

🏛 RULE OF LAW
A grossly negligent failure to obey an order compelling discovery is sufficient to justify the severest disciplinary measures available under Fed. R. Civ. P. 37.

FACTS: Cine Forty-Second Street Theatre Corp. (Cine) (P) brought an action charging Allied Artists Pictures Corp. (Allied) (D) and others operating competing movie theatres with engaging in a conspiracy with motion picture distributors to cut off its access to first-run, quality films. It sought treble damages under the antitrust laws and injunctive relief. Allied (D) proposed interrogatories on the issue of damages, which Cine (P) repeatedly failed to answer adequately or on time, although given several extensions. Finally, the magistrate held that Cine (P) acted willfully in not complying with the court's orders concerning discovery as to the issue of damages and precluded Cine (P) from introducing evidence on that issue. This effectively amounted to a dismissal of the damage claim, leaving only the claim for injunctive relief. The district judge, to whom the order was submitted for approval, felt Cine (P) had been grossly negligent and no more and that this was insufficient to impose the severest sanctions of Fed. R. Civ. P. 37. Being unsure of the law, however, he certified an interlocutory appeal on his own motion.

ISSUE: Is gross negligence in failing to obey discovery orders sufficient to justify the severest disciplinary measures available under Fed. R. Civ. P. 37?

HOLDING AND DECISION: (Kaufman, C.J.) Yes. A grossly negligent failure to obey an order compelling discovery is sufficient to justify the severest disciplinary measures available under Fed. R. Civ. P. 37. Negligent, no less than intentional, wrongs are fit subjects for general deterrence. Gross professional incompetence no less than deliberate tactical intransigence may be responsible for the interminable delays and costs which plague modern complex lawsuits. In fact, Cine (P) has, by its gross negligence, frozen this litigation in the discovery phase for nearly four years. There is simply no reason to avoid imposing harsh sanctions in such a situation. Reversed.

▶ ANALYSIS

Under Fed. R. Civ. P. 37, a party who willfully disobeys a court order pertaining to discovery can be held in contempt and imprisoned or fined. On the other hand, the court may strike or dismiss any or all of that party's claim or defense, preclude the introduction of evidence in support of such, or hold certain facts to be established.

■══■

Quicknotes

FED. R. CIV. P. 37 Provides a spectrum of sanctions to ensure that a party will not profit from its own failure to comply with discovery orders.

■══■

Adjudication Before Trial: Summary Judgment

Quick Reference Rules of Law

Adickes v. S.H. Kress & Co.

Restaurant patron (P) v. Restaurant owner (D)

398 U.S. 144 (1970).

NATURE OF CASE: Appeal of summary judgment denying damages for civil rights violation.

FACT SUMMARY: In a civil rights action in which a conspiracy between the police and a store was alleged, summary judgment was granted when Adickes (P) could not produce evidence to support a conspiracy.

RULE OF LAW
In an action based on conspiracy, summary judgment may not be granted unless a defendant can show that no evidence thereof exists.

FACTS: Adickes (P) was refused service at a restaurant owned by S.H. Kress & Co. (Kress) (D) and was arrested for loitering. She then brought an action seeking damages under § 1983, alleging a conspiracy between Kress (D) and the police. Under the circumstances of the case, a conspiracy could have existed only if police had been present at the store before the arrest. When Adickes (P) could not show that police had been present, Kress (D) moved for summary judgment. This was granted and affirmed on appeal. Adickes (P) appealed to the Supreme Court.

ISSUE: In an action based on conspiracy, may summary judgment be granted if a defendant has not shown that no evidence thereof exists?

HOLDING AND DECISION: (Harlan, J.) No. In an action based on conspiracy, summary judgment may not be granted unless a defendant can show that no evidence thereof exists. In a motion for summary judgment, the burden is on the moving party to affirmatively show the absence of a genuine issue as to any material fact. The fact that the burden would be on the other party on the same fact at trial is of no matter. Here, while at trial, Adickes (P) would have to prove the presence of police earlier in the day; at the summary judgment level, the burden was on Kress (D) to prove they were not. This it did not do. Reversed.

▶ ANALYSIS

The present case's rule was modified by the Court 16 years later in *Celotex Corp. v. Catrett*, 477 U.S. 317 (1986). The Court there liberalized the burden on a moving party, holding that such a party, on an issue the opposing party has the ultimate burden of proving, could prevail on the basis that the nonmoving party could not produce evidence on the issue. This has made summary judgment a much easier procedure to obtain in federal courts than in most state courts, as most states' procedural rules are similar to that announced in the present action.

■≡■

Quicknotes

CONSPIRACY Concerted action by two or more persons to accomplish some unlawful purpose.

MATERIAL FACT A fact without the existence of which a contract would not have been entered.

SUMMARY JUDGMENT Judgment rendered by a court in response to a motion by one of the parties, claiming that the lack of a question of material fact in respect to an issue warrants disposition of the issue without consideration by the jury.

■≡■

Celotex Corp. v. Catrett

Asbestos products manufacturer (D) v. Wife of decedent (P)

477 U.S. 317 (1986).

NATURE OF CASE: Appeal from reversal of summary judgment denying damages for asbestos exposure.

FACT SUMMARY: In Catrett's (P) action against Celotex Corp. (D) for the death of her husband as a result of his exposure to asbestos manufactured by Celotex (D), Celotex (D) moved for summary judgment, contending that Catrett (P) had failed to identify, in answering interrogatories specifically requesting such information, any witnesses who could testify about the decedent's exposure to Celotex's (D) asbestos.

🏛 RULE OF LAW
The plain language of Federal Rule of Civil Procedure 56(c) mandates the entry of summary judgment, after adequate time for discovery, against a party who fails to make a showing sufficient to establish the existence of an element essential to that party's case.

FACTS: Catrett (P) sued Celotex Corp. (D), alleging that the death of her husband resulted from his exposure to products containing asbestos manufactured by Celotex (D). At trial, Celotex (D) moved for summary judgment, contending that Catrett (P) had failed to identify, in answering interrogatories specifically requesting such information, any witnesses who could testify about the decedent's exposure to Celotex's (D) asbestos products. The district court granted Celotex's (D) motion because there was no showing that the decedent was exposed to Celotex's (D) products within the statutory period. Catrett (P) appealed and the court of appeals reversed.

ISSUE: Does the plain language of Federal Rule of Civil Procedure 56(c) mandate the entry of summary judgment, after adequate time for discovery, against a party who fails to make a showing sufficient to establish the existence of an element essential to that party's case?

HOLDING AND DECISION: (Rehnquist, J.) Yes. The plain language of Federal Rule of Civil Procedure 56(c) mandates the entry of summary judgment, after adequate time for discovery, against a party who fails to make a showing sufficient to establish the existence of an element essential to that party's case. In such a situation, there can be "no genuine issue as to any material fact," since a complete failure of proof concerning an essential element of the nonmoving party's case necessarily renders all other facts immaterial. Here, Catrett (P) failed to identify any witnesses who could testify about her husband's exposure to Celotex's (D) asbestos products. There was also no showing that the decedent was exposed to Celotex's (D) products within the statutory period. Catrett's (P) failure to show sufficient evidence to establish essential elements of her case makes summary judgment proper. Reversed and remanded.

CONCURRENCE: (White, J.) If respondent Catrett (P) had named a witness to support her claim, summary judgment could not have been granted without Celotex (D) somehow showing that the named witness's testimony raised no genuine issue of material fact.

DISSENT: (Brennan, J.) The nonmoving party may defeat a motion for summary judgment that asserts that the nonmoving party has no evidence by calling the court's attention to the supporting evidence in the record that was overlooked by the moving party.

▌ *ANALYSIS*

Celotex is an important case in two ways. First, it integrates the burden of proof borne by the parties at trial with the corresponding burdens on a summary judgment motion. Second, it hints at a larger, more significant role for summary judgment in deciding cases.

■=■

Quicknotes

MATERIAL FACT A fact without the existence of which a contract would not have been entered.

SUMMARY JUDGMENT Judgment rendered by a court in response to a motion by one of the parties, claiming that the lack of a question of material fact in respect to an issue warrants disposition of the issue without consideration by the jury.

■=■

Arnstein v. Porter

Songwriter (P) v. Alleged plagiarist (D)

154 F.2d 464 (2d Cir. 1946).

NATURE OF CASE: Appeal from summary judgment in an action for infringement of copyright.

FACT SUMMARY: Arnstein (P) appealed summary judgment for Porter (D), who, Arnstein (P) alleged, had stolen tunes for several popular songs Arnstein (P) had written.

🏛 RULE OF LAW
Where credibility of the parties is crucial, summary judgment is improper and a trial indispensable.

FACTS: Arnstein (P), a songwriter, alleged that Porter (D), a songwriter, infringed copyrights to several of Arnstein's (P) songs. While not all of Arnstein's (P) songs had been published, copies had been distributed to bands and radio stations. Arnstein (P) claimed that Porter (D) had "stooges" watching him and stealing from him, even though many of the songs had been publicly sung. Porter (D) categorically denied every allegation and was granted summary judgment on grounds of vexatiousness. Arnstein (P) appealed on grounds that there were triable issues of fact and that he was denied a jury trial.

ISSUE: Where credibility of the parties is crucial, is summary judgment improper and a trial indispensable?

HOLDING AND DECISION: (Frank, J.) Yes. Where credibility of the parties is crucial, summary judgment is improper and a trial indispensable. If there is the slightest doubt regarding the facts, a trial is necessary. In copyright infringement cases, there are two separate elements: (1) that defendant has copied from plaintiff's work and (2) if proved, that the copying went so far as to be an improper appropriation. If there is evidence of similarities and access, the court must determine if there was copying. Here, enough similarities in the songs existed so that a jury could infer that no coincidence was involved. Arnstein's (P) songs, being public, provide the opportunity for access. Thus, a jury should hear each side of the story. A witness's demeanor at trial is an important aid to the jury in settling the matter. While it is not denied that Arnstein's (P) allegations are "fantastic," the decision must be reversed and remanded.

DISSENT: (Clark, J.) It is error to deny a trial when there is a genuine issue as to material facts, but it is just as erroneous to deny summary judgment when there is no such issue. There was none here.

▶ ANALYSIS

At trial, Arnstein (P) failed to win his action for copyright infringement, 158 F.2d 795 (2d Cir. 1947). Note that while a copyright infringement case involves two elements, had one element—access—not been shown in the pleadings, then clearly summary judgment could have been granted. In that case, with no access, no copying could have occurred.

■=■

Quicknotes

CREDIBILITY Believability; plausibility; whether or not a witness's testimony is believable.

MATERIAL FACT A fact without the existence of which a contract would not have been entered.

SUMMARY JUDGMENT Judgment rendered by a court in response to a motion by one of the parties, claiming that the lack of a question of material fact in respect to an issue warrants disposition of the issue without consideration by the jury.

■=■

Dyer v. MacDougall

Complainant (P) v. Alleged slanderer (D)

201 F.2d 265 (2d Cir. 1952).

NATURE OF CASE: Appeal from summary dismissal of two counts of complaint for libel and slander.

FACT SUMMARY: Dyer (P) filed a complaint with four counts alleging slander and libel. MacDougall (D) submitted affidavits of purported witnesses to the slander and libel in which the witnesses denied making or hearing the utterances. Two of the four counts were thus dismissed, and Dyer (P) appealed, arguing he could still bring demeanor evidence before the jury.

🏛 RULE OF LAW
A directed verdict against a plaintiff is appropriate where all of plaintiff's witnesses deny the allegations of the complaint.

FACTS: Dyer (P) filed a complaint with four counts against Albert MacDougall (D). All four counts concerned slander and libel, but the last two counts involved witnesses making or hearing the supposed utterances. MacDougall (D) filed a motion to dismiss, along with affidavits of the witnesses involved, stating that they did not make or hear the utterances. The court provided Dyer (P) additional time to conduct depositions of the witnesses, but Dyer (P) did not take the depositions. The court then summarily dismissed counts three and four of the complaint on the grounds that at trial Dyer (P) would have no evidence to support the alleged slander.

ISSUE: Is a directed verdict against a plaintiff appropriate where all of plaintiff's witnesses deny the allegations of the complaint?

HOLDING AND DECISION: (Hand, J.) Yes. A directed verdict against a plaintiff is appropriate where all of plaintiff's witnesses deny the allegations of the complaint. The jury could return a verdict for Dyer (P) based on the demeanor of the testifying witnesses, but no appropriate record would exist for appellate review. The appellate court would only have the testimony denying the allegations and the trial judge's belief that the denials were countered by the witnesses' demeanor. This would result in the trial judge being the final arbiter of the case. Dyer (P) did not take advantage of the opportunity to learn if the witnesses would change their statements during a deposition. It is possible that they may have continued the denials during their depositions and then changed their stories at trial, but that is a tenuous argument. Affirmed.

▌ANALYSIS

Demeanor evidence is troublesome. Nervous people may exhibit characteristics stereotypically associated with people who are lying. Nothing in the law says, however, that juries are not entitled to lend credence to characteristics of testifying witnesses. In fact, a jury is expected to take into consideration all the sense impressions they get from a witness.

Quicknotes

DIRECTED VERDICT A verdict ordered by the court in a jury trial.

LIBEL A false or malicious publication subjecting a person to scorn, hatred or ridicule, or injuring him or her in relation to his or her occupation or business.

SLANDER Defamatory statement communicated orally.

CHAPTER 7

Judicial Supervision of Pretrial and Promotion of Settlement

Quick Reference Rules of Law

G. Heileman Brewing Co. v. Joseph Oat Corp.

Brewery (P) v. Supplier (D)

871 F.2d 648 (7th Cir. 1989).

NATURE OF CASE: Appeal from order sanctioning a party of failure to obey a court order.

FACT SUMMARY: Joseph Oat Corp. (D), represented by counsel, disobeyed a court order to send a corporate representative to a court hearing, and was sanctioned therefor.

> 🏛 **RULE OF LAW**
> A district court may order litigants represented by counsel to appear at a pretrial conference to discuss settlement.

FACTS: In an action between G. Heileman Brewing Co. (P) and Joseph Oat Corp. (Oat) (D), the court ordered the parties to send employees with full settlement authority to a pretrial conference it had set. Oat (D) did not comply. The court issued $5,860.01 in sanctions against Oat (D). Oat (D) appealed, contending that the court lacked the power to compel represented parties to personally appear at conferences.

ISSUE: May a district court order litigants represented by counsel to appear at a pretrial conference to discuss settlement?

HOLDING AND DECISION: (Kanne, J.) Yes. A district court may order litigants represented by counsel to appear at a pretrial conference to discuss settlement. Fed. R. Civ. P. 16 authorizes district courts to compel counsel and pro se litigants to appear before it at status conferences. Oat (D) argued that because Rule 16 does not extend to represented parties, courts cannot compel their attendance. However, the Federal Rules of Civil Procedure are not the exclusive source of district courts' powers. The courts have inherent power to manage their affairs and docket. The Federal Rules explicitly provide that they exist to promote the speedy, just, and inexpensive resolution of actions. When a court issues orders that are consistent with this purpose and are not explicitly prohibited by the Rules, the inherent power of the courts authorizes the order. Here, Rule 16 exists to allow a court to promote expeditious resolution of cases by allowing courts to use pretrial conferences, and ordering represented parties to appear is not inconsistent with the Rule's purposes. Affirmed.

DISSENT: (Posner, J.) Giving district courts much latitude to go beyond their powers under the Rules encourages judicial arrogance.

DISSENT: (Coffey, J.) The terms of Rule 16 are clear and unambiguous, and the court's authority should not go beyond that prescribed by it.

DISSENT: (Easterbrook, J.) Why a court should be able to order an "employee" rather than a representative to attend is puzzling, as an employee is simply another type of representative.

▶ *ANALYSIS*

The traditional image of the courts in this country is that of the neutral forum, where adversaries resolve their disputes. This image, if ever it was true, is no longer so today, particularly in the federal judiciary. Judges sometimes take such an active part in case management and litigation that attorneys often complain that the judge, not his opponent, is the true adversary.

■═■

Quicknotes

FED. R. CIV. P. 16 Addresses the use of pretrial conferences to formulate and narrow issues for trial and discuss means for dispsing of the need for litigation.

■═■

Marek v. Chesny

Offeror (D) v. Settlement offeree (P)

473 U.S. 1 (1985).

NATURE OF CASE: Appeal of denial of award of attorney fees.

FACT SUMMARY: Chesny (P) refused a settlement offer in a § 1983 action and was awarded less at trial.

🏛 RULE OF LAW
Attorney fees incurred by a plaintiff subsequent to an offer of settlement will not be paid when the plaintiff recovers less than the offer.

FACTS: Chesny (P) sued Marek (D) under 42 U.S.C. § 1983. Prior to trial, Marek (D) and the other defendants offered $100,000 to settle. Chesny (P) refused and was awarded $60,000 at trial. The court awarded Chesny (P) $32,000 in costs and fees incurred before the offer but refused to award costs and fees subsequent to the offer, per Fed. R. Civ. P. 68, which shifts to the plaintiff all costs incurred subsequent to an offer of judgment not exceeded by the ultimate recovery. The district court held that fees recoverable by a plaintiff in a § 1983 action were considered costs for purposes of Fed. R. Civ. P. 68. The Seventh Circuit disagreed and reversed. The Supreme Court granted certiorari.

ISSUE: Will attorney fees incurred by a plaintiff subsequent to an offer of settlement be paid when the plaintiff recovers less than the offer?

HOLDING AND DECISION: (Burger, C.J.) No. Attorney fees incurred by a plaintiff subsequent to an offer of settlement will not be paid when the plaintiff recovers less than the offer. Legislative history shows that when Fed. R. Civ. P. 68 was drafted, attorney fees were considered part of costs. When 42 U.S.C. § 1988 was enacted, enabling successful plaintiffs to recover costs and fees, Congress was aware that Fed. R. Civ. P. 68 included fees in its operation, and it could have exempted plaintiffs in § 1983 actions from the force of Fed. R. Civ. P. 68, but it did not do so. In the absence of this, the salutary effect of Fed. R. Civ. P. 68, the encouragement of settlement, should not be hindered. Reversed.

DISSENT: (Brennan, J.) The Court's reasoning is wholly inconsistent with the history and structure of the Federal Rules. Its application to the over 100 attorney fees statutes enacted by Congress will produce absurd variations in Rule 68's operation among the statutes. This is contrary to the purpose of the Federal Rules, which is a uniform procedure in federal courts.

▶ ANALYSIS

42 U.S.C. § 1988 was enacted in 1976. As the Court states, it provides that prevailing plaintiffs in § 1983 actions will be awarded costs and fees. The purpose of the section was to ensure that civil rights plaintiffs obtained effective access to the judicial process.

■■■

Quicknotes

CERTIORARI A discretionary writ issued by a superior court to an inferior court in order to review the lower court's decisions; the Supreme Court's writ ordering such review.

SETTLEMENT OFFER An offer made by one party to a lawsuit to the other agreeing upon the determination of rights and issues between them, thus disposing of the need for judicial determination.

■■■

Trial

Quick Reference Rules of Law

Beacon Theatres, Inc. v. Westover

Theatre company (D) v. Theatre company (P)

359 U.S. 500 (1959).

NATURE OF CASE: Petition for a writ of mandamus to compel district court to vacate orders allegedly depriving petitioner of a jury trial.

FACT SUMMARY: Fox Theatres (Fox) (P) filed an equitable claim, and in the same action, Beacon Theatres, Inc. (Beacon) (D), filed a legal cross-claim. The trial court permitted Fox (P) to try its case first, even though this might deny Beacon (D) its right to a jury trial in the subsequent case.

🏛 RULE OF LAW
Where a plaintiff files a claim either in law or equity, and the defendant, by way of a defense or counterclaim, raises the opposing kind of claim, the legal claim must be tried first so as to preserve the right to a jury trial.

FACTS: Fox Theatres (Fox) (P) had long been exhibiting films under contract with movie producers in San Bernardino. These contracts gave Fox (P) the exclusive right to exhibit these pictures for a period of time during which no other theater could show the same pictures. Beacon Theatres, Inc. (Beacon) (D) opened a theater in the same area, notified Fox (P) that it considered Fox's (P) contracts as being in violation of federal antitrust law, and threatened Fox (P) with damage suits against it and its distributors. Fox (P) brought an action in federal court, praying both for a declaration that its contracts were not in violation of the antitrust law, and for an injunction to prevent Beacon (D) from instituting an antitrust suit. Beacon (D) filed a counterclaim against Fox (P), alleging a violation of the antitrust laws. Because the right to a jury trial is preserved only in legal, and not equity, actions, Beacon (D) might have been collaterally estopped from challenging the claims in its subsequent trial on the legal issues involved. Therefore, Beacon (D) moved the court to try the legal issues first, and thus preserve its right to a jury trial. The district court, ruling that Fox's (P) claims were essentially equitable, held that a party who is entitled to maintain a suit in equity for an injunction may have all the issues in his suit determined by the judge without a jury regardless of whether legal rights are involved and so denied Beacon's (D) motion. Beacon (D) petitioned the appellate courts for a writ of mandamus.

ISSUE: In hybrid actions, involving an equitable claim by the plaintiff and a legal defense or counterclaim by the defendant, must the legal claim be tried first?

HOLDING AND DECISION: (Black, J.) Yes. Only under the most imperative circumstances, where irreparable harm to the plaintiff can result from any delay in having his equitable claims tried first, can the right to a jury trial of legal issues be lost through a prior determination of equitable claims. A legal remedy is only deemed inadequate when a subsequent legal action, though providing an opportunity to try a case to a jury, might not protect the right of the equity plaintiff to a fair and orderly adjudication of the controversy. Such does not appear to be the case here. Any defenses, equitable or legal, Fox (P) may have to charges of antitrust violations can be raised either in its suit for declaratory relief—a legal claim—or in answer to Beacon's (D) counterclaim. Beacon (D) should not therefore be required to split his antitrust case, trying part to a judge and then part to a jury. The writ of mandamus will issue. Reversed.

DISSENT: (Stewart, J.) When declaratory relief is sought, the right to trial by jury depends upon the basic context in which the issues are presented. Fox's (P) complaint went well beyond a mere defense to any subsequent action at law. Fox (P) sought protection against Beacon's (D) allegedly unlawful interference with its business relationship with the movie producers. A declaratory judgment, unsupplemented by equitable relief, might not have afforded full protection. Beacon (D) is thus permitted by the majority, in this decision, to force Fox (P) to respond to its legal claims first rather than to present its own case.

▶ ANALYSIS

Where a plaintiff, in a single proceeding, prays for separate equitable and legal relief, most states permit a court, sitting in equity, to award damages or other legal relief so long as it is incidental to the main equitable claim. However, in federal courts, notwithstanding that any legal relief is only incidental to the main equitable claim, the plaintiff may demand a jury trial on all issues upon which the right to legal relief is dependent.

■=■

Quicknotes

COUNTERCLAIM An independent cause of action brought by a defendant to a lawsuit in order to oppose or deduct from the plaintiff's claim.

WRIT OF MANDAMUS A court order issued commanding a public or private entity, or an official thereof, to perform a duty required by law.

■=■

Ross v. Bernhard

Shareholder (P) v. Broker (D)

396 U.S. 531 (1970).

NATURE OF CASE: Shareholder's derivative suit for damages.

FACT SUMMARY: Ross (P) brought a derivative suit on behalf of Lehman Corporation for damages resulting from breaches of fiduciary duty and negligence by Lehman Brothers (D), who controlled the corporation.

⚖ RULE OF LAW
The right to a jury trial is available in a shareholder's derivative suit.

FACTS: Lehman Brothers (D) were brokers for Lehman Corporation and controlled the corporation through an illegally large representation on the board of directors. Ross (P), a shareholder in the corporation, brought a derivative action for damages resulting from Lehman Brothers' (D) negligence and breach of fiduciary duties. Ross (P) demanded a jury trial on the issue of the claims made on behalf of the corporation.

ISSUE: Is the right to jury trial available in a shareholder's derivative suit?

HOLDING AND DECISION: (White, J.) Yes. The Seventh Amendment preserved the right to jury trials, not only in suits at common law but in all those dealing with legal rights. At common law, a corporation could sue and be sued, but a shareholder of the corporation could not bring the action on behalf of the corporation, such shareholder suit being recognized only in equity. The first case in which the issue of jury trials in derivative suits arose was in *Fleitmann v. Welsbach Street Lighting*, 240 U.S. 27 (1916), an antitrust action seeking treble damages. There, Justice Holmes noted that *Fleitmann*'s only remedy was at law, and the defendant should not have been denied a jury trial because the plaintiff was unable to get the corporation to sue. Since, however, the decision there was based on antitrust statutes it could not extend to this case. However, the Federal Rules of Civil Procedure and a Ninth Circuit case, *Depinto v. Provident Life Ins. Co.*, 323 F.2d 826 (1963), indicate that jury trials are proper in derivative suits. *Depinto* applied the reasoning of previous cases, that when there are both legal and equitable claims, a jury trial should be granted on the legal issues. Thus, where the derivative suit deals with legal issues on behalf of the corporation, it would require a jury trial since equity is available only when no adequate remedy at law exists. Under the Federal Rules of Civil Procedure, there is only one action, the distinction between legal and equitable actions having merged. Thus, the court must first determine if the plaintiff can sue on behalf of the corporation, and, if so, a jury trial is required. The federal rules, by merging law and equity, did away with the necessity of having a corporation's claims presented only by the corporation's directors and not by one of its shareholders. Reversed.

DISSENT: (Stewart, J.) The Seventh Amendment preserves jury trials only in those actions in which the right existed at common law. Since the federal rules only grant jury trials as required by the Seventh Amendment, the two taken together cannot extend jury trials to actions where there was no right at common law.

▶ ANALYSIS

The merger of law and equity, although providing easier forms of pleading, raises serious problems in regard to the extent to which defenses and rights recognized at law will be upheld or discarded when the action is equitable in nature. As the *Ross* case indicates, the question of the right to a jury trial depends more on the issue to be tried, rather than the general character of the entire action. In making this determination, however, a court is forced to ignore the merger of law and equity and first consider whether, in premerger custom, the issue is legal in nature. If so, and if the remedy is one available at law, then, if practical, the issue should be given to a jury. Yet, given the type of analysis required to determine if the issue is basically legal, a plaintiff can virtually dictate his choice for a jury by framing his complaint around legal issues. Other than cases like derivative suits, where a plaintiff has no real choice as to his status and the claims he must make, the merger of law and equity has apparently extended a right to jury trial in cases which essentially involve equitable claims.

■━■

Quicknotes

RIGHT TO JURY TRIAL The right guaranteed by the Sixth Amendment to the federal Constitution that in all criminal prosecutions the accused has a right to a trial by an impartial jury of the state and district in which the crime was allegedly committed.

SHAREHOLDER'S DERIVATIVE ACTION Action asserted by a shareholder in order to enforce a cause of action on behalf of the corporation.

■━■

Curtis v. Loether

African-American woman (P) v. White landlord (D)

415 U.S. 189 (1974).

NATURE OF CASE: On writ of certiorari in action for injunctive relief and damages for violation of fair housing provisions.

FACT SUMMARY: The Loethers (D), who are white, having been charged with racial discrimination in violation of the 1968 Civil Rights Act for failure to rent an apartment to Curtis (P), an African-American, sought a jury trial under the Seventh Amendment.

🏛 RULE OF LAW

The Seventh Amendment of the Constitution applies to actions enforcing statutory rights and requires a jury trial on demand if the statute creates legal rights and remedies enforceable in an action for damages in the ordinary courts of law.

FACTS: Curtis (P), an African-American woman, brought an action under § 812 of the 1968 Civil Rights Act, claiming that the Loethers (D), who are white, refused to rent an apartment to her because of her race, in violation of Title VIII of the fair housing provisions of the Act. Following the voluntary dissolution of a preliminary injunction, the case was tried on the issues of actual and punitive damages. The Loethers (D) made a timely request for a jury trial, which the district court denied, holding that a jury trial was authorized neither by Title VIII nor by the Seventh Amendment. The district court then found that the Loethers (D) had, in fact, racially discriminated against Curtis (P). No actual damage was found, but $250 in punitive damages was awarded. The court of appeals reversed on the issue of the right to jury trial, holding that it was guaranteed by the Seventh Amendment. Curtis (P) appealed, arguing that the Seventh Amendment is inapplicable to new causes of action created by congressional enactment.

ISSUE: Are jury trials required under the Seventh Amendment in actions enforcing statutory rights if the statute creates legal rights and remedies enforceable in an action for damages in the ordinary courts of law?

HOLDING AND DECISION: (Marshall, J.) Yes. Although from a review of the legislative history of Title VIII, the question of whether jury trials were intended can be susceptible to arguments for and against; it is clear that the Seventh Amendment entitles either party to demand a jury trial in an action for damages in the federal courts under § 812 of the 1968 Civil Rights Act. It has long been settled that the Seventh Amendment right to jury trials extends beyond the common law actions existing when the Amendment was framed. As Justice Story pointed out in *Parsons v. Bedford*, 2 U.S. 433, 3 Pet. 433, 7 L. Ed. 732 (1830), the Amendment may be construed to cover all suits, of whatever form, dealing with legal rights as distinct from equity and admiralty jurisdiction. The applicability of the constitutional right to a jury trial in actions enforcing statutory rights has been regarded as a matter too obvious to be doubted. To dispel any further doubt, the Court holds that the Seventh Amendment does apply to actions enforcing statutory rights and requires a jury trial upon demand, if the statute creates legal rights and remedies enforceable in an action for damages in the ordinary courts of law. Curtis (P) relied on *NLRB v. Jones and Laughlin Steel*, 301 U.S. 1 (1937), but those cases merely stand for the proposition that the Seventh Amendment is inapplicable to administrative proceedings since jury trials would be incompatible with the concept of administrative adjudication. *Katchen v. Landry*, 382 U.S. 323 (1966), also relied on by Curtis (P), was also inapplicable since it dealt with a bankruptcy proceeding, which is regarded as a matter of equity. However, the instant action was a damages action, sounding in tort and enforcing legal rights, and when Congress provided for the civil enforcement of statutory rights involving rights and remedies of the sort typically enforced in actions at law, a jury trial must be available. Affirmed.

▶ ANALYSIS

If a legal claim is joined with an equitable claim, the right to jury trial on the legal claim, including all issues common to both claims, remains intact, and the right cannot be abridged by characterizing the legal claim as "incidental to the equitable relief sought." The above case illustrates another instance in which the Seventh Amendment's guarantee of right to jury trial is applicable. Others include (1) declaratory actions presenting traditional common law issues; (2) actions for the recovery and possession of land; (3) proceedings in rem for the confiscation of goods on land; (4) stockholders' derivative actions for damages; and (5) civil rights actions to recover damages. Examples of cases in which the Seventh Amendment has been held applicable to statutory rights include (1) trademarks, (2) immigration cases, and (3) antitrust actions. Note, finally, that even if the preliminary injunction here had not been dissolved before trial, the fact that a damages action was involved here would make the Seventh Amendment applicable.

■═■

Continued on next page.

Quicknotes

JURY TRIAL Trial of a matter or a cause before a jury as opposed to one before a judge.

SEVENTH AMENDMENT Provides that no fact tried by a jury shall be otherwise re-examined in any court of the United States, other than according to the rules of the common law.

■━━■

Teamsters Local No. 391 v. Terry

Union (D) v. Truck driver (P)

494 U.S. 558 (1990).

NATURE OF CASE: Appeal from denial of a defendant's motion to strike a jury demand in an action for breach of a union's duty of fair representation.

FACT SUMMARY: Terry (P) and other truck drivers (P) covered by a collective-bargaining agreement between the Union (D) and their employer brought this action against the Union (D) for allegedly breaching its duty of fair representation, seeking compensatory damages and requesting a jury trial.

> 🏛 **RULE OF LAW**
> An employee who seeks relief in the form of back pay for a union's alleged breach of its duty of fair representation has a right to trial by jury.

FACTS: Terry (P) and others (P) who were truck drivers for McLean Trucking (D) were covered by a collective-bargaining agreement between McLean (D) and the Teamsters Union (D). When the Union (D) refused to refer a grievance to the grievance committee, Terry (P) and the other truck drivers (P) filed an action in the district court, seeking, among other things, compensatory damages for lost wages and health benefits. They alleged that McLean (D) had breached the collective-bargaining agreement in violation of § 301 of the Labor Management Relations Act and that the Union (D) had violated its duty of fair representation. McLean (D) was voluntarily dropped from the suit after filing for bankruptcy. Terry (P) and the others (P) requested a jury trial. The Union (D) moved to strike the jury demand. The district court denied the motion, and the court of appeals affirmed. This appeal followed.

ISSUE: Does an employee who seeks relief in the form of back pay for a union's alleged breach of its duty of fair representation have a right to trial by jury?

HOLDING AND DECISION: (Marshall, J.) Yes. An employee who seeks relief in the form of back pay for a union's alleged breach of its duty of fair representation has a right to trial by jury. This action against the Union (D) encompasses both equitable and legal issues. Congress specifically characterized back pay under Title VII as a form of equitable relief but made no similar pronouncement regarding the duty of fair representation. Back pay sought from an employer under Title VII would generally be restitutionary in nature, in contrast to the damages sought here. Moreover, the fact that Title VII's back pay provision may have been modeled on a provision in the National Labor Relations Act concerning remedies for unfair labor practices does not require that the back pay remedy available here be considered equitable. The money damages sought are the type of relief usually awarded by courts of law. Affirmed.

CONCURRENCE: (Brennan, J.) The constitutional right to a jury trial should be decided on the basis of the relief sought. If the relief is legal in nature, the parties have a constitutional right to a trial by jury, unless Congress has permissibly delegated the particular dispute to a non-Article III decision-maker and jury trials would frustrate Congress's purposes in enacting a particular statutory scheme. Historically, jurisdictional lines between law and equity were primarily a matter of remedy.

CONCURRENCE: (Stevens, J.) Duty of fair representation suits are for the most part ordinary civil actions involving the stuff of contract and malpractice disputes. There is, accordingly, no ground for excluding these actions from the jury right.

DISSENT: (Kennedy, J.) The presence of monetary damages in this duty of fair representation action does not make it more analogous to a legal action than an equitable action. The trust analogy is the controlling one here, and a breach of trust historically carries no right of trial by jury. Furthermore, the Seventh Amendment right to a jury trial in civil cases, a right existing in 1791, cannot be preserved without looking to history to identify it.

▶ **ANALYSIS**

Part III-A of the majority opinion contained a two-part historical test customarily applied by the Court in deciding the right to a jury trial. The historical test first compared the statutory action to eighteenth-century actions brought in the courts of England prior to the merger of the courts of law and equity. Second, the test examined the remedy sought to determine whether it was legal or equitable in nature, with the second inquiry given more weight than the first. The Justices differed as to whether or not this historical test should now be abandoned.

■■■

Quicknotes

COMPENSATORY DAMAGES Measure of damages necessary to compensate victim for actual injuries suffered.

EQUITABLE RELIEF A remedy that is based upon principles of fairness as opposed to rules of law.

JURY TRIAL Trial of a matter or a cause before a jury as opposed to one before a judge.

■■■

Galloway v. United States

Disabled veteran (P) v. Federal government (D)

319 U.S. 372 (1943).

NATURE OF CASE: Appeal of directed defense verdict denying military disability pay.

FACT SUMMARY: In Galloway's (P) action to obtain military disability pay, the court directed a defense verdict.

🏛 RULE OF LAW

A directed verdict does not violate the Seventh Amendment.

FACTS: Galloway (P) served in World War I. During his stay in Europe, he demonstrated several episodes of bizarre behavior. Upon his return, his behavior became increasingly erratic. By 1930, he was diagnosed as psychotic and was put under the care of a guardian (whom he later married). In 1934, he filed a claim for military disability benefits. To qualify therefor, he had to have been mentally ill no later than 1919. His claim was denied, and he filed an action to obtain the benefits. At trial, he introduced virtually no evidence of his condition from 1923 to 1930. The trial court, finding that the lack of evidence for this period made an insufficient showing of mental disability, ordered a directed verdict for the Government (D). The court of appeals affirmed. The Supreme Court granted review.

ISSUE: Does a directed verdict violate the Seventh Amendment?

HOLDING AND DECISION: (Rutledge, J.) No. A directed verdict does not violate the Seventh Amendment. The Amendment preserves the right to jury trial in common law actions. However, the power of juries over the factual issues of a civil action had never been absolute. Further, at different times in the history of the common law, courts had exercised different levels of control over juries. It appears that the true purpose of the Seventh Amendment was to preserve the jury trial as a basic institution and to preserve its most fundamental elements. Judicial control by such procedural mechanisms as the directed verdict is permitted, when appropriate. Here, the evidence presented by Galloway (P) had such large gaps that any award in his favor could only have been based on speculation, an impermissible basis. Affirmed.

DISSENT: (Black, J.) The founders of our government thought that trial by jury was an essential bulwark of liberty. The language of the Seventh Amendment is clear, and the concept of the directed verdict constitutes an improper departure from the Amendment.

▶ ANALYSIS

The Court did not really need to address the issue it did. The present action was based on a statutory right not existing at common law. Statutory actions carry no right to jury trial. The Court acknowledged this but went ahead with its analysis anyway.

■■■

Quicknotes

DIRECTED VERDICT A verdict ordered by the court in a jury trial.

SEVENTH AMENDMENT Provides that no fact tried by a jury shall be otherwise re-examined in any court of the United States, other than according to the rules of the common law.

■■■

Lavender v. Kurn

Estate administrator (P) v. Railway representative (D)

327 U.S. 645 (1946).

NATURE OF CASE: Action under Federal Employer's Liability Act.

FACT SUMMARY: Haney was killed while working for the St. Louis-San Francisco Railway Co. (D) and the Illinois Central Railroad (D) due to head injuries suffered on the job.

RULE OF LAW

An appellate court's function in reviewing a jury verdict is exhausted as soon as it determines that there is an evidentiary basis for the jury's verdict, and only when it finds a complete absence of probative facts to support a verdict may the court reverse it as clearly erroneous.

FACTS: Lavender (P), as administrator of the estate of Haney, sued Kurn (D), as representative of the St. Louis-San Francisco Railway Co. (D) and the Illinois Central Railroad (Railroad) (D), under the Federal Employer's Liability Act. Haney died from head injuries suffered on his job while working as a switch-tender for the Railroad (D). At trial, Lavender (P) attempted to prove that Haney had been killed by a mail hook protruding from a moving train (i.e., negligence). This theory depended upon the jury's finding that Haney was standing exactly at one certain spot on a mound near the tracks so that the hook would have hit him at exactly 63 inches above the ground. The Railroad's (D) defense was that Haney was murdered. The jury entered judgment for Haney. On appeal, the Missouri Supreme Court reversed the jury, stating, "it would be mere speculation and conjecture to say that Haney was struck by the mail hook," and such was not sufficient to sustain a verdict. Lavender (P) appealed.

ISSUE: May an appellate court reverse a jury verdict as erroneous merely because the jury may have engaged in "speculation and conjecture" in reaching its verdict?

HOLDING AND DECISION: (Murphy, J.) No. An appellate court's function in reviewing a jury verdict is exhausted as soon as it determines that there is an evidentiary basis for the jury's verdict, and only when it finds a complete absence of probative facts to support a verdict may the court reverse it as clearly erroneous. The jury is free to discard or disbelieve whatever facts are inconsistent with its conclusion. Whenever facts are in dispute or evidence is such that fair-minded men might draw different inferences, a measure of speculation and conjecture is required on the part of the jury, whose duty it is to choose the most reasonable inference. The appellate court was unjustified in reversing on such grounds. The judgment of the Missouri Supreme Court is reversed and the case remanded.

ANALYSIS

The standard is that the court will not interfere with the judgment of the trier of fact unless it is "clearly erroneous." The jury is to be controlled only where its actions are so clearly out of line ("clearly erroneous") that justice cannot be served in any manner other than reversal. Compare this to the procedure "judgment n.o.v."

Quicknotes

JUDGMENT N.O.V. A judgment entered by the trial judge reversing a jury verdict if the jury's determination has no basis in law or fact.

JURY TRIAL Trial of a matter or a cause before a jury as opposed to one before a judge.

Guenther v. Armstrong Rubber Co.

Mechanic (P) v. Tire manufacturer (D)

406 F.2d 1315 (3d Cir. 1969).

NATURE OF CASE: Appeal of directed verdict in personal injury action.

FACT SUMMARY: In a personal injury action based on an allegedly defective tire, a directed defense award was made when Guenther (P) and his expert disagreed over the identity of the tire.

🏛 RULE OF LAW
Whether or not a crucial piece of evidence is authentic is a jury issue.

FACTS: Guenther (P), a mechanic, was injured when a tire allegedly manufactured by Armstrong Rubber Co. (Armstrong) (D) exploded. He filed a personal injury claim. At trial, disagreement arose between Guenther (P) and his expert as to the identity of the allegedly offending tire. The trial court entered a defense award, based on a failure to authenticate the tire. Guenther (P) appealed.

ISSUE: Is it a jury issue as to whether or not a crucial piece of evidence is authentic?

HOLDING AND DECISION: (McLaughlin, J.) Yes. Whether or not a crucial piece of evidence is authentic is a jury issue. Where an issue of fact as to authentication exists, it is the jury's function to decide whether a proffered piece of evidence is that which it is claimed to be. Here, dispute exists as to whether the tire offered as evidence was in fact the same one that injured the plaintiff. This was an issue the jury could consider. Reversed and remanded.

▶ ANALYSIS

Guenther (P), in support of his offer of proof, noted that 80–85 percent of the tires sold at the store at which he was hurt were manufactured by Armstrong (D). The court rejected this as a basis for authentication. Any conclusion based on this said the court would be speculation.

■■■

Quicknotes

JURY TRIAL Trial of a matter or a cause before a jury as opposed to one before a judge.

■■■

Ahern v. Scholz

Manager (P) v. Musician (D)

85 F.3d 774 (1st Cir. 1996).

NATURE OF CASE: Appeal from final judgment in breach of contract case.

FACT SUMMARY: Scholz (D) sought review of the district court's denial of his motion for a new trial on the basis that the district court erred in not concluding that the jury's verdict in a breach of contract suit was against the clear weight of the evidence.

🏛 RULE OF LAW
A district court's decision not to grant a motion for a new trial may only be overturned upon a finding that the district court's decision constituted a clear abuse of discretion in determining the jury verdict was not against the great weight of the evidence.

FACTS: Scholz (D), a musician and member of the group BOSTON, entered into three agreements with Ahern (P), a promoter and manager of music groups. The first was a recording agreement, the second was a management agreement and the third required Scholz (D) to furnish his exclusive songwriting services for a five-year period. In 1976 CBS and Ahern (P) entered into an agreement for the exclusive recording services of BOSTON. The group's first album sold 11 million copies and the group's second release sold 6 million copies. The group entered into a modification agreement with Ahern (P) in 1978 and another in May 1981. Ahern (P) then ceased managing Scholz (D). CBS cut off royalty payments from the first two albums and brought suit against Scholz (D), Ahern (P), and BOSTON for failure to timely deliver albums. While the litigation was pending, BOSTON released a third album that sold over 4 million copies. The jury found Scholz (D) was not in breach of contract. Ahern (P) then brought this suit against Scholz (D) for breach of the further modification agreement (FMA) claiming failure to pay royalties for the third album. The jury found that Scholz (D) breached § 5.2.1 of the FMA, which required payment to Ahern (P) of royalties from the third album and that Ahern (P) did not breach the agreement to pay Scholtz (D) royalties from the first and second albums. It awarded Ahern (P) $547,007 in damages in addition to $265,000 in attorney's fees and $135,000 in costs. The district court denied Scholz's (D) motions for a new trial, to amend the court's memorandum and order and judgment, and to admit new evidence. Scholz (D) appealed, arguing the court erred in denying the motion for a new trial under Fed. R. Civ. P. 59(a).

ISSUE: May a district court's decision not to grant a motion for a new trial only be overturned upon a finding that the district court's decision constituted a clear abuse of discretion in determining the jury verdict was not against the great weight of the evidence?

HOLDING AND DECISION: (Torruella, C.J.) Yes. A district court's decision not to grant a motion for a new trial may only be overturned upon a finding that the district court's decision constituted a clear abuse of discretion in determining the jury verdict was not against the great weight of the evidence. Scholz (D) argued that Ahern (P) breached his duties under the FMA to account for and pay to Scholz (D) his share of royalties from the first and second albums. The jury and trial court found that Ahern's (P) breach was not material. The issue is whether the district court abused its discretion in holding the jury's decision was not against the weight of the evidence. There was no abuse of discretion in the district court's decision. Scholz (D) argued the breach was material; however, Ahern (P) demonstrated that the agreement only required him to send letters of direction to various entities directing them to send Scholz (D) his share of the royalties once collected. Having done so, he satisfied his obligations under the FMA. Scholz (D) also argued that Ahern's (P) failure to pay was a separate, material breach. The court in reviewing the decision of a lower court does not weight the evidence, but determines whether there was a clear abuse of discretion in determining the jury verdict was not against the weight of the evidence. Here, the jury's finding was not against the clear weight of the evidence and the district court did not abuse its discretion. "Reversed on other grounds and remanded for retrial."

▶ ANALYSIS

Note that the standard for setting aside a verdict and ordering a new trial is whether the verdict in the lower court is against the clear weight of the evidence, based upon false evidence, or would result in a clear injustice. The district court in reviewing the trial court's decision cannot vacate a verdict merely because it would have decided the matter differently. Thus the court of appeals will only vacate the district court's decision where there is a clear abuse of discretion.

■=■

Quicknotes

ABUSE OF DISCRETION A determination by an appellate court that a lower court's decision was based on an error of law.

Continued on next page.

BREACH OF CONTRACT Unlawful failure by a party to perform its obligations pursuant to contract.

MATERIAL BREACH Breach of a contract's terms by one party that is so substantial as to relieve the other party from its obligations pursuant thereto.

■■■

Dimick v. Schiedt

Accident victim (P) v. Driver (D)

293 U.S. 474 (1935).

NATURE OF CASE: Writ of certiorari in action for negligence damages.

FACT SUMMARY: Dimick (P) claimed that the court's increase of his damages award without his consent and consequent denial of his motion for a new trial was a denial of his Seventh Amendment right to a jury trial.

🏛 RULE OF LAW
Although the damages awarded by the jury may be deemed inadequate, the court has no power to increase them even though the defendant consents to such an increase.

FACTS: Dimick (P) sued Schiedt (D) for damages for personal injury allegedly caused by Schiedt's (D) negligent operation of an automobile. The jury returned a verdict for Dimick (P) for $500. Dimick (P) moved for a new trial. One of his arguments was that the damages allowed were inadequate. The trial court ordered a new trial unless Schiedt (D) would consent to an increase in damages to the sum of $1,500. Schiedt (D) consented, and the motion for a new trial was then automatically denied. Dimick (P) appealed, charging that he had not consented to the increase and that he had been denied his Seventh Amendment right to a jury trial. The appellate court reversed.

ISSUE: Where the verdict of the jury is deemed inadequate, can the court deny the plaintiff's motion for a new trial upon the defendant's consenting to pay greater damages than the jury awarded?

HOLDING AND DECISION: (Sutherland, J.) No. In order to determine the intent of the Seventh Amendment, it is necessary to examine the common law existing at the time of its adoption. A review of English law in that period shows that, while the practice of remitting excessive damages awarded by juries (i.e., remittitur) was mildly disapproved of in English law, increasing them (i.e., additur) was expressly prohibited. Without giving any real explanation, our courts have accepted remittitur since 1822. It is notable that they have never—in spite of numerous contrary arguments—granted an increase in damages. This would indicate a lack of judicial belief in the existence of the power to increase damages. A rational foundation can be found for remittitur since it does not consist of eliminating the jury verdict but of merely lopping off an increment when that verdict is excessive. However, when the verdict is too small, an increase by the court is an addition which in no sense can be found in the jury verdict. There is consequently a deprivation of the constitutional guarantee of trial by jury. What we are dealing with here is not merely the court's power to declare and effectuate an adaptation of common law but rather the question of the court's changing the Constitution. This the court cannot do. Therefore, even if the defendant should consent to an increase in damages, the court has no power to increase damages when the amount awarded by the jury is deemed inadequate. Affirmed.

DISSENT: (Stone, J.) First, the Court should not be limited by the fact that, by the time the Seventh Amendment was adopted, no English judge had denied a motion for a new trial in actions at law. The trial court's action here is not a procedure which would curtail the jury's essential function of deciding questions of fact. It is unquestionably within the discretion of the trial judge to deny the motion for a new trial without intruding on the province of the jury to decide questions of fact. Then surely he may also exercise his discretion in denying it when he knows the plaintiff will suffer no harm since he will receive a proper recovery and the defendant will suffer no harm since he consented to it.

▌ *ANALYSIS*

Additur occurs when the court grants a new trial but conditions its order by providing that if the defendant will consent to an increase in the amount of the verdict to a specified sum, then the motion for a new trial will be denied. Additur is not presently allowed in federal courts. In the above case, the Court rejected additur as violative of the plaintiff's right to a second jury trial on the issue of damages if the first award is inadequate. The position seems untenable since remittitur involves the same impairment of the right to jury trial and its constitutionality is not questioned. In any event, additur is permitted under various state statutes. Note that in some of these jurisdictions, the defendant need not be required to consent before a judge can increase the amount of a legally inadequate jury award.

■=■

Quicknotes

ADDITUR Authority of a court to increase a jury's award of damages.

JURY TRIAL Trial of a matter or a cause before a jury as opposed to one before a judge.

REMITTITUR The authority of the court to reduce the amount of damages awarded by the jury.

Continued on next page.

SEVENTH AMENDMENT Provides that no fact tried by a jury shall be otherwise re-examined in any court of the United States, other than according to the rules of the common law.

■═■

Whitlock v. Jackson

Estate administrator (P) v. Police representative (D)

754 F. Supp. 1394 (S.D. Ind. 1991).

NATURE OF CASE: Motion for a new trial on personal injury/civil rights action.

FACT SUMMARY: The estate administrator (P) for Gaisor, who had died in police custody, sought a new trial on the basis that the jury's answers to special interrogatories were inconsistent.

🏛 **RULE OF LAW**
A jury's answers to interrogatories will not be a basis for overturning a verdict if any means of reconciling them with the verdict exists.

FACTS: Gaisor died of a brain aneurysm after an arrest in which he had been struck several times. Whitlock (P), his estate administrator, filed an action alleging wrongful death and assault and battery, as well as constitutional violations. The jury returned a special verdict finding liability for battery on the part of the officers (D), but no constitutional violations. It also found that the officers' (D) conduct had not proximately caused Gaisor's death. The jury awarded $29,700 collectively against the arresting officers (D) in the form of compensatory and punitive damages. Whitlock (P) moved for a new trial, contending that the verdict was internally inconsistent since if it awarded punitive damages, it had to have found a civil rights violation.

ISSUE: Will a jury's answers to interrogatories be a basis for overturning a verdict if any means of reconciling them with the verdict exists?

HOLDING AND DECISION: (McKinney, J.) No. A jury's answers to interrogatories will not be a basis for overturning a verdict if any means of reconciling them with the verdict exists. There will often be more than one way to view what a jury is saying when it renders a verdict, and if any one way is consistent with the law, the verdict will stand. Here, the jury found that the officers (D) battered Gaisor and awarded punitive damages but did not find the officers (D) used excessive force or denied medical treatment—both torts of constitutional magnitude. Contrary to Whitlock's (P) contentions, this is not inconsistent. Punitive damages can be awarded to deter other officers from battering suspects without finding that the conduct of the officers (D) here was constitutionally protected. Not every example of police battery rises to the level of a civil rights violation. The jury here apparently found that the police officers (D) had neither caused Gaisor's death nor violated his due process rights, but that they

had been too liberal in the use of force. This was a legally acceptable verdict. Motion denied.

▶ **ANALYSIS**

Far and away the most common form of verdict in jury trials is the general verdict whereby the jury does not disclose any grounds for its final decision. However, in order to save appellate time that would otherwise be spent determining whether a jury decided its verdict based on inadmissible evidence, the Federal Rules provide for two additional forms of verdict: a special verdict where the jury answers certain factual questions and the judge then enters a judgment accordingly (Rule 49(a)); and a general verdict accompanied by written interrogatories (Rule 49(b)). The distinction between the two special verdicts was highlighted in the case above, since Rule 49(b) expressly provides that a plaintiff's failure to object to inconsistent jury answers constitutes waiver of the objection, while Rule 49(a) does not contain this waiver principle.

■■■

Quicknotes

COMPENSATORY DAMAGES Measure of damages necessary to compensate victim for actual injuries suffered.

INTERROGATORY A method of pretrial discovery in which written questions are provided by one party to another who must respond in writing under oath.

JURY TRIAL Trial of a matter or a cause before a jury as opposed to one before a judge.

PUNITIVE DAMAGES Damages exceeding the actual injury suffered for the purposes of punishment, deterrence and comfort to plaintiff.

■■■

People v. Hutchinson

State (P) v. Drug user (D)

Cal. Sup. Ct., 455 P.2d 132 (1969).

NATURE OF CASE: Appeal of denial of motion for new trial.

FACT SUMMARY: A trial court refused to consider a juror's affidavit of improper remarks by a bailiff to the jury trying Hutchinson (D).

🏛 RULE OF LAW
Jurors may testify as to objective facts to impeach a verdict.

FACTS: Hutchinson (D) was prosecuted for and convicted of drug possession. Subsequently, in support of a motion for a new trial, Hutchinson (D) produced an affidavit from a juror to the effect that the bailiff had made remarks tending to pressure the jury into a guilty verdict. The trial court refused to consider the affidavit, ruling that a juror cannot impeach the verdict. The motion was denied. The court of appeal affirmed. The State Supreme Court granted review.

ISSUE: May jurors testify as to objective facts to impeach a verdict?

HOLDING AND DECISION: (Traynor, C.J.) Yes. Jurors may testify as to objective facts to impeach a verdict. The old rule to the contrary was based on an English maxim that one cannot impeach. In recent times, the justification for such a rule has been the discouragement of instability of verdicts, as well as fraud. This has been seen as more important a policy than prevention of the occasional injustice resulting from the rule. However, this court is of the view that individuals suffering such instances of injustice are entitled to more consideration. When a juror testifies as to matters capable of objective verification, the possibility of fraud is minimal. Therefore, jurors should be able to impeach a verdict when the grounds for impeachment are objectively verifiable. Here, the alleged remarks of the bailiff were verifiable, so the juror's affidavit should have been considered. Reversed and remanded.

▌ *ANALYSIS*

Jury verdicts are seldom overturned for misconduct. Generally speaking, only misconduct by forces extrinsic to the jury itself will lead to overturning a verdict. For instance, a verdict was upheld in *Tanner v. United States*, 483 U.S. 107 (1987), despite evidence of heavy alcohol and drug use during the trial by several jurors.

Quicknotes

AFFIDAVIT A declaration of facts written and affirmed before a witness.

JURY TRIAL Trial of a matter or a cause before a jury as opposed to one before a judge.

Choosing the Forum

Quick Reference Rules of Law

Pennoyer v. Neff

Land purchaser (D) v. Nonresident property owner (P)

95 U.S. (5 OTTO) 714 (1877).

NATURE OF CASE: Action to recover possession of land.

FACT SUMMARY: Neff (P) alleged that Pennoyer's (D) deed from a sheriff's sale was invalid because the court ordering the sale had never obtained personal jurisdiction over Neff (P).

🏛 RULE OF LAW
Where the object of the action is to determine the personal rights and obligations of the parties, service by publication against nonresidents is ineffective to confer jurisdiction on the court.

FACTS: Neff (P) owned real property in Oregon. Mitchell brought suit in Oregon to recover legal fees allegedly owed him by Neff (P). Neff (P), a nonresident, was served by publication, and Mitchell obtained a default judgment. The court ordered Neff's (P) land sold at a sheriff's sale to satisfy the judgment. Pennoyer (D) purchased the property. Neff (P) subsequently learned of the sale and brought suit in Oregon to recover possession of his property. Neff (P) alleged that the court ordering the sale had never acquired in personam jurisdiction over him. Therefore, the court could not adjudicate the personal rights and obligations between Neff (P) and Mitchell, and the default judgment had been improperly entered.

ISSUE: Where an action involves the adjudication of personal rights and obligations of the parties, is service by publication against a nonresident sufficient to confer jurisdiction?

HOLDING AND DECISION: (Field, J.) No. Every state possesses exclusive jurisdiction and sovereignty over persons and property within its territory. Following from this, no state can exercise direct jurisdiction and authority over persons or property outside of its territory. These are two well-established principles of public law respecting the jurisdiction of an independent state over persons and property. However, the exercise of jurisdiction which every state possesses over persons and property within it will often affect persons and property outside of it. A state may compel persons domiciled within it to execute, in pursuance of their contracts respecting property situated elsewhere, instruments transferring title. Likewise, a state may subject property situated within it which is owned by nonresidents to the payment of the demands of its own citizens. Substituted service by publication or by other authorized means may be sufficient to inform the parties of the proceedings where the property is brought under the control of the court or where the judgment is sought as a means of reaching such property or effectuating some interest therein. That is, such service is effectual in proceedings in rem. The law assumes that property is always in the possession of its owner or an agent. It proceeds upon the theory that a seizure of the property will inform the owner that he must look to any proceedings upon such seizure for the property's condemnation or sale. But where the entire object of the action is to determine personal rights and obligations, the action is in personam and service by publication is ineffectual to confer jurisdiction over the nonresident defendant upon the court. Process sent out of state to a nonresident is equally ineffective to confer personal jurisdiction. In an action to determine a defendant's personal liability, he must be brought within the court's jurisdiction by service of process within the state or by his voluntary appearance. Without jurisdiction, due process requirements are not satisfied. In the case herein, Neff (P) was not personally served, and he never appeared. Hence, the personal judgment obtained against Neff (P) was not valid, and the property could not be sold.

▶ ANALYSIS

This is the leading case on the extent of the court's power to compel a defendant's attendance. At common law, the presence of the defendant within the jurisdiction, plus service while there, were the indispensable ingredients for the acquisition of jurisdiction of the person of the defendant. It still remains the basic method of acquiring jurisdiction over the defendant. It does not matter how transient the defendant's presence is if she is served within the jurisdiction. One case held that service on a defendant while he was in an airplane passing over a state is sufficient. Of course, a voluntary appearance by a defendant also gives the court jurisdiction over her.

━■━■

Quicknotes

JURISDICTION The authority of a court to hear and declare judgment in respect to a particular matter.

SERVICE BY PUBLICATION A means of serving process pursuant to statute upon a defendant, upon whom service of process cannot be accomplished personally, by publication of a summons as an advertisement in a newspaper specified by the court.

━■━■

International Shoe Co. v. Washington

Corporation (D) v. Commissioner (P)

326 U.S. 310 (1945).

NATURE OF CASE: Proceedings to recover unemployment contributions.

FACT SUMMARY: A state statute authorized the mailing of notice of assessment of delinquent contributions for unemployment compensation to nonresident employers. International Shoe Co. (International) (D) was a nonresident corporation. Notice of assessment was served on one of its salespersons within the state and was mailed to International's (D) office.

RULE OF LAW

For a state to subject a nonresident defendant to in personam jurisdiction, due process requires that the defendant have certain minimum contacts with the state such that the maintenance of the suit does not offend traditional notions of fair play and substantial justice.

FACTS: A Washington statute set up a scheme of unemployment compensation that required contributions by employers. The statute authorized the commissioner of revenue (P), to issue an order and notice of assessment of delinquent contributions by mailing the notice to nonresident employers. International Shoe Co. (International) (D), a Delaware corporation having its principal place of business in Missouri, employed 11 to 13 salespersons under the supervision of managers in Missouri. These salespeople resided in Washington and did most of their work there. They had no authority to enter into contracts or make collections. International (D) did not have any office in Washington and made no contracts there. Notice of assessment was served upon one of International's (D) Washington salespersons, and a copy of the notice was sent by registered mail to International's (D) Missouri address.

ISSUE: For a state to subject a nonresident defendant to in personam jurisdiction, does due process require only that the defendant have certain minimum contacts with the state such that the maintenance of the suit does not offend notions of fair play and substantial justice?

HOLDING AND DECISION: (Stone, C.J.) Yes. Historically, the jurisdiction of courts to render judgment in personam is grounded on their power over the defendant's person, and his presence within the territorial jurisdiction of a court was necessary for a valid judgment. But now, due process requires only that in order to subject a defendant to a judgment in personam, if the defendant is not present within the territorial jurisdiction, the defendant has certain minimum contacts with the territory such that

the maintenance of the suit does not offend traditional notions of fair play and substantial justice. The contacts must be such as to make it reasonable, in the context of our federal system, to require a defendant corporation to defend the suit brought there. An estimate of the inconveniences which would result to the corporation from a trial away from its "home" is relevant. To require a corporation to defend a suit away from home where its contact has been casual or isolated has been thought to lay too unreasonable a burden on it. However, even single or occasional acts may, because of their nature, quality, and circumstances, be deemed sufficient to render a corporation liable to suit. Hence, the criteria to determine whether jurisdiction is justified, is not simply mechanical or quantitative. Satisfaction of due process depends on the quality and nature of the activity in relation to the fair and orderly administration of the laws. In this case, International's (D) activities were neither irregular nor casual. Rather, they were systematic and continuous. The obligation sued upon here arose out of these activities. They were sufficient to establish sufficient contacts or ties to make it reasonable to permit Washington (P) to enforce the obligations International (D) incurred there. Affirmed.

DISSENT: (Black, J.) The U.S. Constitution leaves to each state the power to tax and to open the doors of its courts for its citizens to sue corporations who do business in the state. It is a judicial deprivation to condition the exercise of this power on this Court's notion of "fair play."

▶ ANALYSIS

Before this decision, three theories had evolved to provide for suits by and against foreign corporations. The first was the consent theory. It rested on the proposition that since a foreign corporation could not carry on its business within a state without the permission of that state, the state could require a corporation to appoint an agent to receive service of process within the state. However, it soon became established law that a foreign corporation could not be prevented by a state from carrying on interstate commerce within its borders. The presence doctrine required that the corporation was "doing business" and "present" in the state. The third theory used either the present or consent doctrine, and it was necessary to determine whether the corporation was doing business within the state to decide whether its consent could properly be implied or to discover whether the corporation was present.

Continued on next page.

Quicknotes

IN PERSONAM JURISDICTION The jurisdiction of a court over a person as opposed to his interest in property.

MINIMUM CONTACTS The minimum degree of contact necessary in order to sustain a cause of action within a particular forum, consistent with the requirements of due process.

World-Wide Volkswagen Corp. v. Woodson

Automobile distributor (P) v. Court (D)

444 U.S. 286 (1980).

NATURE OF CASE: Petition for a writ prohibiting the exercise of in personam jurisdiction.

FACT SUMMARY: World-Wide Volkswagen Corp. (P) sought a writ of prohibition to keep district court Judge Woodson (D) from exercising in personam jurisdiction over it, alleging it did not have sufficient "contacts" with the forum state of Oklahoma to render it subject to such jurisdiction.

RULE OF LAW

A state court may exercise personal jurisdiction over a nonresident defendant only so long as there exist sufficient "minimum contacts" between him and the forum state such that maintenance of the suit does not offend "traditional notions of fair play and substantial justice."

FACTS: World-Wide Volkswagen Corp. (World-Wide) (P) was the regional distributor of Audi automobiles for the tristate area of New York, New Jersey, and Connecticut. It was the distributor of the particular Audi that the Robinsons purchased from a New York dealer and drove to Oklahoma, where three family members were severely burned when another car struck their Audi in the rear. The Robinsons brought a products liability action in an Oklahoma district court, suing the New York dealership and World-Wide (P) (a New York corporation). Claiming that no evidence showed it had any connection with Oklahoma whatsoever, World-Wide (P) sought a writ of prohibition to keep district court Judge Woodson (D) from exercising in personam jurisdiction. It argued that a lack of sufficient contacts with the forum state made assertion of such jurisdiction improper under the Due Process Clause. The Supreme Court of Oklahoma denied the writ, noting that World-Wide (P) could foresee that the automobiles it sold would be taken into other states, including Oklahoma. The United States Supreme Court granted certiorari.

ISSUE: Must a defendant have "minimum contacts" with the forum state before it can exercise in personam jurisdiction over him?

HOLDING AND DECISION: (White, J.) Yes. Under the Due Process Clause, the exercise of in personam jurisdiction over a defendant is not constitutional unless he has sufficient "minimum contacts" with the forum state so that maintenance of the suit does not offend "traditional notions of fair play and substantial justice." Here, World-Wide (P) had no "contacts, ties, or relations" with Oklahoma, so personal jurisdiction could not be exercised. As for the notion that it was foreseeable that cars sold in New York would wind up in Oklahoma, the foreseeability

that is critical to due process analysis is not the mere likelihood that a product will find its way into the forum state. Rather, it is that the defendant's conduct and connection with the forum state are such that he should reasonably anticipate being haled into court there. Such conduct and connection are simply missing in this case. Reversed.

DISSENT: (Marshall, J.) The consumer's intended use may provide jurisdiction to the State, especially when considering that the intended use of an automobile is to travel from place to place. It is reasonable that an interstate car dealer should expect that his cars may be involved in accidents in other states and he should be made to answer there. Unlike *Kulko*, 436 U.S. 84 (1978), this case involved commercial transactions, which are more likely than family issues, to involve other states. The Constitution allows for a balancing of all factors to determine the fairness in bringing a defendant before a State court and this case should have required petitioners to defend in Oklahoma.

DISSENT: (Brennan, J.) The automobile is designed specifically to facilitate travel from place to place, and the sale of one purposefully injects it into the stream of interstate commerce. Thus, this case is not unlike those where in personam jurisdiction is properly exercised over one who purposefully places his product into the stream of interstate commerce with the expectation it will be purchased by consumers in other states. Furthermore, a large part of the value of automobiles is the extensive, nationwide network of highways. State maintenance of such roads contributes to the value of World-Wide's (P) business. World-Wide (P) also participates in a network of related dealerships with nationwide service facilities. Having such facilities in Oklahoma also adds to the value of World-Wide's (P) business. Thus, it has the required minimum contacts with Oklahoma to render this exercise of personal jurisdiction constitutional.

ANALYSIS

Over the years, modern transportation and communication have made foreign state suits much less of a burden to defendants. This resulted in a relaxing of the due process limits placed on state jurisdiction down to the "minimum contacts" concept. However, even if there were no inconvenience to the defendant, a state could not exercise personal jurisdiction over him if he had no "contacts, ties, or relations." This is true even if that state had a strong interest in applying its law to the controversy; it was the

Continued on next page.

most convenient location for litigation, etc. The reason is that the Due Process Clause serves two distinct functions: The first is as a guarantor against inconvenient litigation, but the second is as a guardian of interstate federalism. It is in this second capacity that the Due Process Clause would prevent assumption of jurisdiction in the aforementioned instance by recognizing the "territorial limitations on the power of the respective states."

Quicknotes

IN PERSONAM JURISDICTION The jurisdiction of a court over a person as opposed to his interest in property.

MINIMUM CONTACTS The minimum degree of contact necessary in order to sustain a cause of action within a particular forum, consistent with the requirements of due process.

WRIT OF PROHIBITION A writ issued by a superior court prohibiting a lower court from exceeding its jurisdiction or from usurping jurisdiction beyond that authorized by law.

Burger King Corp. v. Rudzewicz

Fast food corporation (P) v. Franchisee (D)

471 U.S. 462 (1985).

NATURE OF CASE: Appeal from decision reversing assertion of personal jurisdiction over nonresident in action for breach of contract.

FACT SUMMARY: Burger King Corporation (P) appealed a decision of the court of appeals finding that the district court erred in asserting personal jurisdiction over Rudzewicz (D) without reasonable notice of the prospect of franchise litigation in Florida and thus violated due process fairness concerns.

🏛 RULE OF LAW
Where the circumstances establish a substantial and continuing relationship with a forum state and indicate that there was a fair notice that a nonresident might be subject to suit in the forum state, the assertion of personal jurisdiction over the nonresident by the forum state, if otherwise fair, does not offend due process.

FACTS: Burger King Corporation (BKC) (P) oversaw its franchise operations through a two-tiered administrative structure. Governing contracts provided that franchise relationships were established in Miami and they were governed by Florida law. All fees were paid to the Miami office, where BKC (P), a Florida corporation, was headquartered. Major problems were resolved through the Miami office. The day-to-day monitoring of the franchises, which were subject to exacting regulation and supervision by BKC (P) under the franchising contracts, was conducted through a network of offices. Rudzewicz (D), a Michigan resident, and MacShara applied at the regional office in Michigan for a franchise, and the application was forwarded to the Miami office. A preliminary agreement was entered into by BKC (P); it was decided that Rudzewicz (D) and MacShara would take over an existing facility in Drayton Plains, Michigan. They purchased restaurant equipment from a division of BKC (P) in Miami, and MacShara attended required management courses in Miami. Disputes arose, with Rudzewicz (D) and MacShara negotiating with both the regional and the Miami offices. Operations were begun in June 1979, with Rudzewicz (D) personally becoming liable for over $1 million in payments over the 20-year franchise relationship. Rudzewicz (D) and MacShara fell behind in their payments, and an extended period of negotiations between them, the regional office, and the Miami office ensued. BKC (P) eventually terminated the franchise, but Rudzewicz (D) refused to vacate the premises, continuing to operate the restaurant as a Burger King. Florida's long-arm statute extended jurisdiction over nonresidents resulting from breaches of contract formed in

Florida. BKC (P) brought suit in the Southern District of Florida, and Rudzewicz (D) made a special appearance, contending that since they were nonresidents and the claim did not arise within the Southern District of Florida, the district court lacked personal jurisdiction. The district court disagreed, and after trial judgment was entered in favor of BKC (P). On appeal, the court of appeals reversed, stating that the assertion of jurisdiction was unfair under the circumstances since Rudzewicz (D) was bereft of notice of the prospect of franchise litigation in Florida. From this decision, BKC (P) appealed.

ISSUE: Where the circumstances establish a substantial and continuing relationship with a forum state and indicate that there was fair notice that a nonresident might be subject to suit in the forum state, does the assertion of personal jurisdiction over the nonresident by the forum state, if otherwise fair, offend due process?

HOLDING AND DECISION: (Brennan, J.) No. Where the circumstances establish a substantial and continuing relationship with the forum state and indicate that there was fair notice that a nonresident might be subject to suit in the forum state, the assertion of personal jurisdiction over the nonresident by the forum state, if otherwise fair, does not offend due process. When determining whether it is fair to determine that a nonresident reasonably could anticipate out-of-state litigation, a court should look to see if the nonresident purposefully availed himself of the benefits and privileges of conducting activities within that state. Once minimum contacts are established, other factors that may make the assertion of jurisdiction unfair can be considered in order to comport with fundamental fairness and substantial justice. Substantial evidence exists to support a finding of jurisdiction in the present case. The existence of the contract with BKC (P), a Florida corporation, is not sufficient to support the assertion of Florida jurisdiction over Rudzewicz (D). The prior negotiation of the contract, the terms of the contract itself, the consequences of the contract, and the parties' actual course of dealings must all be evaluated to determine whether a nonresident has established minimum contacts with the forum state. Rudzewicz (D), in the present case, entered into a highly structured 20-year relationship with BKC (P) involving continuing and wide-reaching contacts with Burger King (P) in Florida. Negotiations were made with the Miami office, not the regional office. His actions in refusing to vacate the premises and continuing to use the Burger King (P) trademarks after termination caused foreseeable injuries to BKC (P). Surely, Rudzewicz's (D) connection

Continued on next page.

with Florida cannot be seen as "random, fortuitous, or attenuated." Further, the contract specified that the agreements were made in and enforced from Miami, and the negotiations which led to the litigation came from the Miami office. Choice of law analysis is distinct from minimum contacts jurisdiction analysis, and to hold that such choice should be ignored in determining whether a nonresident has purposefully availed himself of the benefits of the state confuses the two. Rudzewicz (D) has not pointed to any other factors that outweigh the considerations favoring a finding of jurisdiction and certainly no factors establishing the unconstitutionality of the Florida long-arm statute. All parties involved were experienced in business, and there is no indication that Rudzewicz (D) was under any economic duress. No mechanical rule can be applied in these cases, and each case must be scrutinized individually. Here, jurisdiction was properly asserted pursuant to the Florida long-arm statute. Reversed and remanded.

DISSENT: (Stevens, J.) Rudzewicz's (D) only contacts with BKC (P) were conducted through the regional Michigan office. He only did business in Michigan. There is nothing in the record to establish that he purposefully availed himself of the benefits and protections of Florida law. His activities gave him no notice of the possibility of franchise litigation in Florida for which he was financially unprepared. The unequal bargaining positions of the parties further accentuate the unfairness of hauling Rudzewicz (D) into Florida courts.

▶ ANALYSIS

There is some question among the Circuits as to what extent a choice of law provision in a contract also implies a choice of forum. Even though it is clear that mechanical tests will not be applied in making these determinations, the contrasting factual viewpoints of the majority and the dissent in the present case make it quite likely that future opinions in this area will be inconsistent.

∎≡∎

Quicknotes

FORESEEABILITY A reasonable expectation that an act or omission would result in injury.

FORUM STATE The state in which a court, or other location in which a legal remedy may be sought, is located.

PERSONAL JURISDICTION The court's authority over a person or parties to a lawsuit.

PROCEDURAL DUE PROCESS The constitutional mandate that if the state or federal government acts so as to deny a citizen of a life, liberty or property interest the individual is first entitled to notice and the right to be heard.

∎≡∎

Asahi Metal Industry Co. v. Superior Court

Tire valve assembly manufacturer (P) v. Municipality (D)

480 U.S. 102 (1987).

NATURE OF CASE: Appeal from discharge of writ quashing service of summons.

FACT SUMMARY: Asahi Metal Industry Co. (Asahi) (P) appealed from a decision of the California Supreme Court discharging a peremptory writ issued by the appeals court quashing service of summons in Cheng Shin's indemnity action, contending that there did not exist minimum contacts between California and Asahi (P) sufficient to sustain jurisdiction.

RULE OF LAW

Minimum contacts sufficient to sustain jurisdiction are not satisfied simply by the placement of a product into the stream of commerce coupled with awareness that its product would reach the forum state.

FACTS: Asahi (P), a Japanese corporation, manufactured tire valve assemblies in Japan, selling some of them to Cheng Shin, a Taiwanese company who incorporated them into the motorcycle tires it manufactured. Zurcher was seriously injured in a motorcycle accident, and a companion was killed. He sued Cheng Shin in California, alleging the motorcycle tire, manufactured by Cheng Shin was defective. Cheng Shin sought indemnity from Asahi (P), and the main action settled. Asahi (P) moved to quash service of summons, contending that jurisdiction could not be maintained by California, the state in which Zurcher filed his action, consistent with the Due Process Clause of the Fourteenth Amendment. The evidence indicated Asahi's (P) sales to Cheng Shin took place in Taiwan, and shipments went from Japan to Taiwan. Cheng Shin purchased valve assemblies from other manufacturers. Sales to Cheng Shin never amounted to more than 1.5 percent of Asahi's (P) income. Approximately 20 percent of Cheng Shin's sales in the United States are in California. In declaration, an attorney for Cheng Shin stated he made an informal examination of tires in a bike shop in Solano County, where Zurcher was injured, finding approximately 20 percent of the tires with Asahi's (P) trademark (25 percent of the tires manufactured by Cheng Shin). The Superior Court (D) denied the motion to quash, finding it reasonable that Asahi (P) defend its claim of defect in its product. The court of appeals issued a peremptory writ commanding the Superior Court (D) to quash service of summons. The California Supreme Court reversed and discharged the writ, finding that Asahi's (P) awareness that some of its product would reach California by placing it in the stream of commerce satisfied minimum contacts sufficient to sustain jurisdiction. From this decision, Asahi (P) appealed.

ISSUE: Are minimum contacts sufficient to sustain jurisdiction satisfied by the placement of a product into the stream of commerce, coupled with the awareness that its product would reach the forum state?

HOLDING AND DECISION: (O'Connor, J.) No. Minimum contacts sufficient to sustain jurisdiction are not satisfied by the placement of a product in the stream of commerce, coupled with the awareness that its product would reach the forum state. To satisfy minimum contacts, there must be some act by which the defendant purposefully avails itself of the privilege of conducting activities within the forum state. Although the courts that have squarely addressed this issue have been divided, the better view is that the defendant must do more than place a product in the stream of commerce. The unilateral act of a consumer's bringing the product to the forum state is not sufficient. Asahi (P) has not purposefully availed itself of the California market. It does not do business in the state, conduct activities, maintain offices or agents, or advertise. Nor did it have anything to do with Cheng Shin's distribution system, which brought the tire valve assembly to California. Assertion of jurisdiction based on these facts exceeds the limits of due process. [The Court went on to consider the burden of defense on Asahi (P) and the slight interests of the state and Zurcher, finding the assertion of jurisdiction unreasonable and unfair.] Reversed.

CONCURRENCE: (Brennan, J.) The California Supreme Court correctly concluded that the stream of commerce theory, without more, has satisfied minimum contacts in most courts which have addressed the issue, and it has been preserved in the decision of this Court.

CONCURRENCE: (Stevens, J.) The minimum contacts analysis is unnecessary; the Court has found by weighing the appropriate factors that jurisdiction under these facts is unreasonable and unfair.

ANALYSIS

The Brennan concurrence is quite on point in criticizing the plurality for its characterization that this case involves the act of a consumer in bringing the product within the forum state. The argument presented in *World-Wide Volkswagen Corp. v. Woodson*, 444 U.S. 286 (1980), cited by the plurality, seems more applicable to distributors and retailers than to manufacturers of component parts.

Continued on next page.

Quicknotes

MINIMUM CONTACTS The minimum degree of contact necessary in order to sustain a cause of action within a particular forum, consistent with the requirements of due process.

PEREMPTORY WRIT Writ directing the sheriff to have the defendant appear before the court so long as the plaintiff has provided adequate security in order to prosecute the action.

QUASH To vacate, annul, void.

■━━■

Pavlovich v. Superior Court

Web site creator (P) v. Superior Court (D)

Cal. Sup. Ct., 58 P.3d 2 (2002).

NATURE OF CASE: Appeal of finding of personal jurisdiction over defendant.

FACT SUMMARY: When the trial court found specific personal jurisdiction over Pavlovich (P) based solely on his passive Internet Web site, Pavlovich (P) argued that personal jurisdiction may not be acquired over a defendant simply based on a posting on a passive Internet Web site.

🏛 RULE OF LAW
Personal jurisdiction may not necessarily be acquired over a defendant based on a posting on a passive Internet Web site.

FACTS: Matthew Pavlovich (P), a computer systems and network administrator, was a Texas resident who did not reside or work in California and never had a place of business, telephone listing, or bank account in California, and never owned property in California. Neither Pavlovich (P) nor his company (LiVid) ever solicited any business in California nor had any business contacts in California. Pavlovich (P) opened and operated a single-page passive Web site which only provided information, but did not solicit or transact any business and permitted no interactive exchange of information between its operators and visitors. The site sought to defeat certain DVD technology and enable the decryption and copying of DVDs containing motion pictures. LiVid posted the source code of a program named DeCSS on its Web site to allow users to circumvent the DVD technology and copy motion pictures. Real party in interest, DVD Copy Control Association, brought suit against Pavlovich (P) for posting this proprietary information, and the California Superior Court exercised specific personal jurisdiction over Pavlovich (P) based on his Web site. The California Court of Appeal affirmed the finding of jurisdiction, and Pavlovich (P) appealed.

ISSUE: May personal jurisdiction necessarily be acquired over a defendant based on a posting on a passive Internet Web site?

HOLDING AND DECISION: (Brown, J.) No. Personal jurisdiction may not necessarily be acquired over a defendant based on a posting on a passive Internet Web site. A court may exercise specific jurisdiction over a nonresident defendant only if (1) the defendant has purposefully availed himself of forum benefits, (2) the controversy arises out of the defendant's contacts with the forum, and (3) the assertion of personal jurisdiction would comport with fair play and substantial justice. Here, Pavlovich's (P) sole contact with California was LiVid's posting of a DVD source code containing proprietary information on an Internet Web site accessible to any person

with Internet access. A passive Web site, as here, that does little more than make information available to those who are interested in it is not grounds for the exercise of personal jurisdiction. In such case, the exercise of jurisdiction is determined by examining the level of interactivity and commercial nature of the exchange of information that occurs on the Web site. Here, LiVid's Web site merely posts information and has no interactive features. There is no evidence suggesting that the site targeted California. Indeed, there is no evidence that any California resident ever visited, much less downloaded, the DeCSS source code from the LiVid Web site. Pavlovich's (P) mere knowledge that his tortious conduct may harm industries centered in California, while relevant to the determination of personal jurisdiction, alone is insufficient to establish express aiming at the forum state as required to establish personal jurisdiction in the forum state. Hence, Pavlovich's (P) conduct was not, by itself, sufficient to subject him to California jurisdiction. Reversed.

DISSENT: (Baxter, J.) The intended targets of Pavlovich (P) were entire businesses. He knew at least two of the targets: the movie industry and the computer industry, and both industries were centered in California. Thus, for purposes of specific personal jurisdiction, Pavlovich's (P) intentional act, even if committed outside California, was "expressly aimed" at California. In these particular circumstances, it cannot matter that Pavlovich (P) may not have known or cared about the exact identities or precise locations of each individual target, or that he happened to employ a so-called passive Internet Web site, or whether any California resident visited the site.

▶ ANALYSIS

In *Pavlovich*, the court made clear that creating a Web site, like placing a product into the stream of commerce, may be felt nationwide, or even worldwide, but, without more, is not an act purposely directed toward the forum state. Otherwise, personal jurisdiction in Internet-related cases would almost always be found in any forum in the country. Such a result would violate long-held and inviolate principles of personal jurisdiction.

■=■

Quicknotes

FORUM A court or other location in which a legal remedy may be sought.

PERSONAL JURISDICTION The court's authority over a person or parties to a lawsuit.

■=■

Shaffer v. Heitner

Company (D) v. Shareholder (P)

433 U.S. 186 (1977).

NATURE OF CASE: Appeal from a finding of state jurisdiction.

FACT SUMMARY: Heitner (P) brought a derivative suit against Greyhound (D) directors for antitrust losses it had sustained in Oregon. The suit was brought in Delaware, Greyhound's (D) state of incorporation.

🏛 RULE OF LAW
Jurisdiction cannot be founded on property within a state unless there are sufficient contacts within the meaning of the test developed in *International Shoe.*

FACTS: Heitner (P) owned one share of Greyhound (D) stock. Greyhound (D) had been subjected to a large antitrust judgment in Oregon. Heitner (P), a nonresident of Delaware, brought a derivative suit in Delaware, the state of Greyhound's (D) incorporation. Jurisdiction was based on the presence of Greyhound (D) stock, which was deemed to be located within the state of incorporation. The Delaware sequestration statute allowed property within the state to be seized ex parte to compel the owner to submit to the in personam jurisdiction of the court. None of the stock was actually in Delaware, but a freeze order was placed on the corporate books. Greyhound (D) made a special appearance to challenge the court's jurisdiction to hear the matter. Greyhound (D) argued that the sequestration statute was unconstitutional under the line of cases beginning with *Sniadach,* 395 U.S. 337 (1969). Greyhound (D) also argued that there were insufficient contacts with Delaware to justify an exercise of jurisdiction. The Delaware courts found that the sequestration statute was valid since it was not a per se seizure of the property and was merely invoked to compel out-of-state residents to defend actions within the state. Little or no consideration was given to the "contact" argument based on a finding that the presence of the stock within the state conferred quasi-in-rem jurisdiction.

ISSUE: May a state assume jurisdiction over an issue merely because defendant's property happens to be within the state?

HOLDING AND DECISION: (Marshall, J.) No. Mere presence of property within a state is insufficient to confer jurisdiction on a court absent independent contacts within the meaning of *International Shoe,* which would make acceptance constitutional. The Court expressly rejected that line of cases represented by *Harris v. Balk,* 198 U.S. 215 (1905), which permits jurisdiction merely because the property happens to be within the state. If sufficient contacts do not exist to assume jurisdiction

absent the presence of property within the state, it cannot be invoked on the basis of property within the court's jurisdiction. This decision is based on the fundamental concepts of justice and fair play required under the Due Process and Equal Protection Clauses of the Fourteenth Amendment. Here, the stock is not the subject of the controversy. There is no claim to ownership of it or injury caused by it. The defendants do not reside in Delaware or have any contacts there. The injury occurred in Oregon. No activities complained of were done within the forum. Finally, Heitner (P) is not even a Delaware resident. Jurisdiction was improperly granted. Reversed.

CONCURRENCE: (Powell, J.) The Court errs only in regard to cases involving property permanently within the state, e.g., real property. Such property should confer jurisdiction.

CONCURRENCE: (Stevens, J.) Purchase of stock in the marketplace should not confer in rem jurisdiction in the state of incorporation.

CONCURRENCE AND DISSENT: (Brennan, J.) The Court reasons correctly regarding the use of a minimum contacts test but misapplies it in this case. The Delaware sequestration statute's sole purpose is to force in personam jurisdiction through a quasi-in-rem seizure. The opinion is purely advisory in that if the court finds the statute invalid, the rest of the opinion is not required. Delaware never argued that it was attempting to obtain in rem jurisdiction. Further, a derivative suit may be brought in the state of incorporation. Greyhound's (D) choice of incorporation in Delaware is a prima facie showing of submission to its jurisdiction.

▶ ANALYSIS

While the corporation could be sued in its state of incorporation under the dissent's theory, the suit is against the directors, and neither the site of the wrong nor the residence of a defendant is in Delaware. The decision will only have a major impact in cases such as herein where the state really has no reason to want to adjudicate the issue. Of course, real property would still be treated as an exception.

■■■

Quicknotes

EQUAL PROTECTION CLAUSE A constitutional guarantee that no person should be denied the same protection of the laws enjoyed by other persons in like circumstances.

Continued on next page.

FOURTEENTH AMENDMENT DUE PROCESS CLAUSE Provides that protections mandated by the Constitution and observed by the federal government are equally applicable, and therefore must be observed by the states.

IN PERSONAM JURISDICTION The jurisdiction of a court over a person as opposed to his interest in property.

IN REM JURISDICTION A court's authority over a thing so that its judgment is binding in respect to the rights and interests of all parties in that thing.

MINIMUM CONTACTS The minimum degree of contact necessary in order to sustain a cause of action within a particular forum, consistent with the requirements of due process.

Burnham v. Superior Court

Divorce applicant (P) v. Court (D)

495 U.S. 604 (1990).

NATURE OF CASE: Writ of certiorari from denial of motion to quash service of process in divorce proceeding.

FACT SUMMARY: Burnham (P), a New Jersey resident, was served with divorce papers by his separated wife while he was visiting their children in California.

RULE OF LAW
A defendant who has been personally served with process within the boundaries of a state may not assert that the state lacks personal jurisdiction over him merely because his contacts with the state are minimal or because the lawsuit is unrelated to his activities within the state.

FACTS: Burnham (P) and his wife wanted a divorce. She moved to California with the children and he stayed in New Jersey. He filed for divorce in New Jersey on grounds of "desertion" but did not have a summons issued and did not serve process on his wife. She filed for divorce in California on grounds of "irreconcilable differences" and served him while he was visiting their children in the San Francisco bay area. Burnham (P) made a special appearance in California Superior Court to quash service of summons on the grounds that the court lacked personal jurisdiction over him because his only contacts with California were a few short visits to the state for the purpose of conducting business and visiting his children. The Superior Court (D) denied the motion, and the California Court of Appeal denied Burnham's (P) writ of mandate. The United States Supreme Court granted a writ of certiorari.

ISSUE: May a defendant who has been personally served with process within the boundaries of a state challenge that state's personal jurisdiction over him on the grounds that his contacts with the state are minimal or that the lawsuit is unrelated to his activities within the state?

HOLDING AND DECISION: (Scalia, J.) No. A defendant who has been personally served with process within the boundaries of a state may not challenge that state's personal jurisdiction over him with regard to the relevant litigation on the grounds that his contacts with the state are minimal or that the lawsuit is unrelated to his activities within the state. Personal service upon a physically present defendant suffices in all cases to confer jurisdiction, regardless of whether the defendant was only briefly in the state or whether the cause of action was related to his activities there. Burnham (P) inappropriately attempted to apply the *International Shoe* (326 U.S. 310

(1945)) standard of due process to his own case, but the *International Shoe* standard—which allows jurisdiction over a defendant if the defendant maintains "continuous and systematic" contacts with the forum—applies only if the defendant is absent from the jurisdiction and cannot be physically served with process. Under the *International Shoe* standard, maintenance of suit in a jurisdiction in which an individual or corporation has "minimum contacts" comports with "traditional notions of fair play and substantial justice." That standard was developed by analogy to "physical presence," and operates as a substitute for it; if the defendant is actually served with process while within the jurisdiction, the *International Shoe* standard is never applied. Affirmed.

CONCURRENCE: (White, J.) The rule allowing jurisdiction to be obtained over a non-resident by personal service in the forum state, without more, has been and is so widely accepted throughout this country that it cannot be stricken. There has been no showing that the rule is so arbitrary and lacking in common sense in so many instances that it should be held violative of due process in every case.

CONCURRENCE: (Brennan, J.) No longer must this Court be content to limit jurisdictional analysis to pronouncements that the foundation of jurisdiction is "physical power." Both *International Shoe* and *Shaffer v. Heitner* (433 U.S. 186 (1977)) held that all assertions of state-court jurisdiction (and therefore assertions based on personal service within the forum) must be consistent with "traditional notions of fair play and substantial justice." Therefore, an independent inquiry into the fairness of each prevailing in-state service rule is justified.

CONCURRENCE: (Stevens, J.) This is an easy case, in which Justice Scalia's historical consensus approach, Justice Brennan's fairness approach, and Justice White's commonsense approach, all make sense.

▶ ANALYSIS

By holding that personal service in all cases confers jurisdiction but that "substituted" service under the *International Shoe* "minimum contacts" standard confers jurisdiction only on a case-by-case basis, Justice Scalia held that personal service amounts to a "higher pedigree" of jurisdiction. Scalia justifies this by blind adherence to the word "traditional" in the *International Shoe* phrase "traditional notions of fair play and substantial justice." However, as certain commentators have pointed out, *Inter-*

Continued on next page.

national Shoe did not equate tradition with particular practices of asserting jurisdiction, but rather with a generalized due process concern with fundamental procedural fairness. See, e.g., Redish, Tradition, Fairness, and Personal Jurisdiction: Due Process and Constitutional Theory After *Burnham v. Superior Court*, 22 Rutgers L.J. (1991). Accordingly, Justice Brennan's concurrence seems more in accord with the judicial intent behind *International Shoe*.

■■■

Quicknotes

CERTIORARI A discretionary writ issued by a superior court to an inferior court in order to review the lower court's decisions; the Supreme Court's writ ordering such review.

MINIMUM CONTACTS The minimum degree of contact necessary in order to sustain a cause of action within a particular forum, consistent with the requirements of due process.

SERVICE OF PROCESS The communication of reasonable notice of a court proceeding to a defendant in order to provide him with an opportunity to be heard.

■■■

Bates v. C & S Adjusters, Inc.

Borrower (P) v. Creditor (D)

980 F.2d 865 (2d Cir. 1992).

NATURE OF CASE: Appeal from dismissal of a complaint due to improper venue.

FACT SUMMARY: After Bates (P) received a collection notice, which C & S Adjusters, Inc. (D) had sent to Bates's (P) old address in Pennsylvania but which had been forwarded to his new address in New York, Bates (P) brought this action in New York, alleging violations of the Fair Debt Collection Practices Act.

🏛 RULE OF LAW
Action may be brought in a judicial district in which a substantial part of the events or omissions giving rise to the claim occurred.

FACTS: Bates (P) incurred a debt while he was a resident of the western district of Pennsylvania. The creditor, a corporation with its principal place of business in that district, referred the account to C & S Adjusters, Inc. (C & S) (D), a local collection agency which transacted no regular business in New York. Meanwhile, Bates (P) had moved to the western district of New York. When C & S (D) mailed a collection notice to Bates (P) at his Pennsylvania address, it was forwarded to his new address in New York. When he received the collection notice, Bates (P) filed this action in the western district of New York, alleging violations of the Fair Debt Collection Practices Act. The district court dismissed because of improper venue. Bates (P) appealed.

ISSUE: May an action be brought in a judicial district in which a substantial part of the events or omissions giving rise to the claim occurred?

HOLDING AND DECISION: (Newman, J.) Yes. An action may be brought in a judicial district in which a substantial part of the events or omissions giving rise to the claim occurred. In adopting the Fair Debt Collection Practices Act, Congress was concerned about the harmful effects of abusive debt-collection practices on consumers. The harm does not occur until receipt of the collection notice, which is a substantial part of the events giving rise to a claim under the Act. If the bill collector prefers not to be challenged for its collection practices outside the district of a debtor's original residence, the envelope containing the notice can be marked "do not forward." Here, because C & S Adjusters, Inc. (D) appears not to have marked the notice with instructions not to forward and has not objected to the assertion of personal jurisdiction, trial in the western district of New York would not be unfair. Reversed.

▶ ANALYSIS

Prior to 1966, venue was proper in federal question cases, absent a special venue statute, only in the defendant's state of citizenship. From 1966 to 1990, 28 U.S.C. § 1391 allowed for venue in the judicial district in which the claim arose. This language gave rise to a variety of conflicting interpretations. Before Congress's 1990 amendment of § 1391(b), applied in the instant case, most courts applied at least a form of the weight of contacts test.

■■■

Quicknotes

VENUE The specific geographic location over which a court has jurisdiction to hear a suit.

■■■

Piper Aircraft Co. v. Reyno

Aircraft manufacturer (D) v. Crash victims (P)

454 U.S. 235 (1981).

NATURE OF CASE: Appeal from dismissal on the basis of forum non conveniens.

FACT SUMMARY: Reyno (P), the representative of five victims of an air crash, brought suit in California even though the location of the crash and the homes of the victims were in Scotland.

🏛 RULE OF LAW
A plaintiff may not defeat a motion to dismiss for forum non conveniens merely by showing that the substantive law that would be applied in the alternative forum is less favorable to him than that of the present forum.

FACTS: Reyno (P) was the representative of five air crash victims' estates and brought suit for wrongful death in United States district court in California, even though the accident occurred and all the victims resided in Scotland. After removing the case to federal court in Pennsylvania, Piper Aircraft Co. (D) moved to dismiss for forum non conveniens, contending that Scotland was the proper forum. Reyno (P) opposed the motion on the basis that the Scottish laws were less advantageous to her than American laws. The district court granted the motion, while the court of appeals reversed. The Supreme Court granted certiorari.

ISSUE: May a plaintiff defeat a motion to dismiss for forum non conveniens merely on the basis that the laws of the alternative forum are less advantageous?

HOLDING AND DECISION: (Marshall, J.) No. A plaintiff may not defeat a motion to dismiss for forum non conveniens merely by showing that the substantive law of the alternative forum is less advantageous than that of the present forum. In this case, all the evidence, witnesses, and interests were in Scotland. Thus, the most convenient forum was there. As a result, the motion was properly granted. Reversed.

▶ ANALYSIS

The Court in this case specifically noted that under some circumstances, the fact that the chosen state's laws are less attractive to the defendant could be used to defeat a motion to dismiss for forum non conveniens. If the state chosen by the plaintiff has the only adequate remedy for the wrong alleged, then the motion may be denied.

Quicknotes

FORUM NON CONVENIENS An equitable doctrine permitting a court to refrain from hearing and determining a case when the matter may be more properly and fairly heard in another forum.

FORUM STATE The state in which a court, or other location in which a legal remedy may be sought, is located.

MOTION TO DISMISS Motion to terminate a trial based on the adequacy of the pleadings.

Subject Matter Jurisdiction—State or Federal Court?

Quick Reference Rules of Law

Mas v. Perry

Student couple (P) v. Landlord (D)

489 F.2d 1396 (5th Cir. 1974).

NATURE OF CASE: Jurisdictional appeal of damages awarded for invasion of privacy.

FACT SUMMARY: Judy Mas (P), temporarily in Louisiana with no intention of returning to her home in Mississippi, sued Perry (D), a Louisiana citizen, in the federal district court of Louisiana.

🏛 RULE OF LAW
A party's mere residence in a state, even if the party has no intention of returning to her state of citizenship, will not create citizenship for purposes of federal diversity jurisdiction.

FACTS: Jean Paul Mas (P) was a citizen of France. Judy Mas (P) was a U.S. citizen from Mississippi. They resided in Louisiana while studying. Judy Mas (P) did not intend to return to Mississippi, and did not intend to remain in Louisiana, as the couple was undecided about where they intended to move after their studies were finished. After discovering that Perry (D), their landlord, spied on them through a two-way mirror, they sued in Louisiana district court. Perry (D), a Louisiana citizen, appealed the damages awarded based on a jurisdictional objection, contending that Judy Mas (P) was a citizen of Louisiana.

ISSUE: Will a party's residence in a state, even if the party has no intention of returning to her state of citizenship, create citizenship for purposes of federal diversity jurisdiction?

HOLDING AND DECISION: (Ainsworth, J.) No. A party's mere residence in a state, even if the party has no intention of returning to her state of citizenship, will not create citizenship for purposes of federal diversity jurisdiction. For such purposes, a party is considered a citizen of the state of domicile. "Domicile" means a fixed residence coupled with the intention of remaining. A move from the state of domicile cannot be considered a change of domicile unless an intention to remain exists. Until such an intention is formed, domicile remains in the last state where such an intention existed, even if no intention to return exists. Here, although Judy Mas (P) had no intention of returning to Mississippi, her state of domicile, she had not formed new domiciliary intentions. Consequently, she remained a citizen of Mississippi. Affirmed.

▶ ANALYSIS

Perry (D) also argued that Judy Mas (P) had lost her Mississippi citizenship due to her marriage to a foreign national. Unlike Jean Paul Mas (P), who by statute could sue in district court, Judy (P) would not be able to do so, as she was not an alien. The court rejected this out of hand, noting that one forfeits no citizenship rights by reason of marriage alone.

◼▬◼

Quicknotes

DIVERSITY JURISDICTION The authority of a federal court to hear and determine cases involving $10,000 or more and in which the parties are citizens of different states, or in which one party is an alien.

DOMICILE A person's permanent home or principal establishment to which he has an intention of returning when he is absent therefrom.

◼▬◼

Louisville & Nashville R.R. v. Mottley

Rail company (D) v. Train occupant (P)

211 U.S. 149 (1908).

NATURE OF CASE: Appeal of a decision overruling a demurrer in an action for specific performance of a contract.

FACT SUMMARY: Mottley (P) was injured on a train owned by Louisville & Nashville R.R. (D), which granted Mottley (P) a lifetime free pass which he sought to enforce.

🏛 RULE OF LAW
Alleging an anticipated constitutional defense in the complaint does not give a federal court jurisdiction if there is no diversity of citizenship between the litigants.

FACTS: In 1871, Mottley (P) and his wife were injured while riding on the Louisville & Nashville R.R. (D). The Mottleys (P) released their claims for damages against the Louisville & Nashville R.R. (D) upon receiving a contract granting free transportation during the remainder of their lives. In 1907, the Louisville & Nashville R.R. (D) refused to renew the Mottleys' (P) passes, relying upon an act of Congress which forbade the giving of free passes or free transportation. The Mottleys (P) filed an action in the circuit court of the United States for the western district of Kentucky. The Mottleys (P) and the Louisville & Nashville R.R. (D) were both citizens of Kentucky. Therefore, the Mottleys (P) attempted to establish federal jurisdiction by claiming that the Louisville & Nashville R.R. (D) would raise a constitutional defense in its answer, thus raising a federal question. The Louisville & Nashville R.R. (D) filed a demurrer to the complaint for failing to state a cause of action. The demurrer was denied. On appeal, the Supreme Court did not look at the issue raised by the litigants but on its own motion raised the issue of whether the federal courts had jurisdiction to hear the case.

ISSUE: Does an allegation in the complaint that a constitutional defense will be raised in the answer raise a federal question which would give a federal court jurisdiction if no diversity of citizenship is alleged?

HOLDING AND DECISION: (Moody, J.) No. The Supreme Court reversed the lower court's ruling and remanded the case to that court with instructions to dismiss the suit for want of jurisdiction. Neither party to the litigation alleged that the federal court had jurisdiction in this case, and neither party challenged the jurisdiction of the federal court to hear the case. Because the jurisdiction of the circuit court is defined and limited by statute, the Supreme Court stated that it is their duty to see that such jurisdiction is not exceeded. Both parties to the litigation were citizens of Kentucky, and so there was no diversity of citizenship. The only way that the federal court could have

jurisdiction in this case would be if there was a federal question involved. Mottley (P) did allege in his complaint that the Louisville & Nashville R.R. (D) based its refusal to renew the free pass on a federal statute. Mottley (P) then attempted to allege information that would defeat the defense of the Louisville & Nashville R.R. (D). This is not sufficient. The plaintiff's complaint must be based upon the federal laws of the Constitution to confer jurisdiction on the federal courts. Mottley's (P) cause of action was not based on any federal laws or constitutional privileges; it was based on a contract. Even though it is evident that a federal question will be brought up at the trial, plaintiff's cause of action must be based on a federal statute or the Constitution in order to have a federal question which would grant jurisdiction to the federal courts.

▶ ANALYSIS

If Mottley (P) could have alleged that he was basing his action on a federal right, it would have been enough to have given the federal court jurisdiction. The federal court would have had to exercise jurisdiction at least long enough to determine whether there actually was such a right. If the federal court ultimately concludes that the claimed federal right does not exist, the complaint would be dismissed for failure to state a claim upon which relief can be granted rather than for lack of jurisdiction. The court has the power to determine the issue of subject matter jurisdiction on its own motion as it did in this case. Subject matter jurisdiction can be challenged at any stage of the proceeding.

■■■

Quicknotes

DIVERSITY JURISDICTION The authority of a federal court to hear and determine cases involving $10,000 or more and in which the parties are citizens of different states, or in which one party is an alien.

SUBJECT MATTER JURISDICTION The authority of the court to hear and decide actions involving a particular type of issue or subject.

■■■

Grable & Sons Metal Products, Inc. v.
Darue Engineering & Manufacturing

Former owner of seized property (P) v. New owner (D)

545 U.S. 308 (2005).

NATURE OF CASE: Review of federal appeals court decision.

FACT SUMMARY: Property owned by a company that was delinquent in paying its federal taxes was seized and sold. The company sued the new owner, claiming that the Internal Revenue Service should have provided notice by personal service, according to federal tax law. The new owner removed the case to federal court.

RULE OF LAW

A case involving the interpretation of federal tax law may be removed to federal court from state court.

FACTS: In 1994, the Internal Revenue Service (IRS) seized property owned by Grable & Sons Metal Products, Inc. (Grable) (P) to satisfy Grable's (P) tax debt, and gave Grable (P) notice by certified mail before selling the property to Darue Engineering & Manufacturing (Darue) (D). Grable (P) received the notice. Grable (P) later sued in state court, claiming Darue's (D) title was invalid because federal law required the IRS to give Grable (P) notice of the sale by personal service, not certified mail. Darue (D) removed the case to federal district court, arguing that the case presented a federal question because Grable's (P) claim depended on an interpretation of federal tax law. The district court agreed and ruled for Darue (D). The Sixth Circuit affirmed.

ISSUE: May a case involving the interpretation of federal tax law be removed to federal court from state court?

HOLDING AND DECISION: (Souter, J.) Yes. A case involving the interpretation of federal tax law may be removed to federal court from state court. The case involved a federal question and could thus be removed to federal court. The case implicated serious federal issues. The national interest in providing a federal forum for federal tax litigation warranted removing the case to federal court.

CONCURRENCE: (Thomas, J.) In an appropriate case, limiting § 1331 to cases in which federal law creates the cause of action pleaded by a plaintiff should be considered.

▶ ANALYSIS

The Supreme Court was unanimous in affirming the Third Circuit's decision by holding that the national interest in providing a federal forum for federal tax litigation is suffi-ciently substantial to support the exercise of federal question jurisdiction. The interests of the United States are affected by the case, via the federal tax law. Otherwise, the case would have been a state cause of action.

Quicknotes

SUBJECT MATTER JURISDICTION The authority of the court to hear and decide actions involving a particular type of issue or subject.

United Mine Workers v. Gibbs

Boycotters (D) v. Supervisor (P)

383 U.S. 715 (1966).

NATURE OF CASE: Appeal in action asserting claims under the Labor Management Relations Act (LMRA) and state law. [The procedural posture of the case is not presented in the casebook excerpt.]

FACT SUMMARY: Gibbs (P) brought federal claims against the United Mine Workers (UMW) (D) under § 303 of the Labor Management Relations Act (LMRA) for damages he suffered as the result of an illegal secondary boycott and also sued under state law for intentional interference with advantageous commercial relations. The district court exercised pendent jurisdiction over the state claims.

> **RULE OF LAW**
> (1) Pendent jurisdiction exists where there is a federal question claim and the relationship between that claim and the state claim permits the conclusion that the entire action before the federal court comprises only one "case."
> (2) Where a federal court exercises pendent jurisdiction, its rendering judgment as a matter of law on the federal claims does not deprive it of jurisdiction to enter judgment on the state claims.

FACTS: A coal mine closed and laid off miners belonging to the United Mine Workers (UMW) (D) union. Thereafter, the mine sought to re-open, but hiring only members of a rival union. Gibbs (P) was hired as the supervisor and was given a contract to haul the coal to market. UMW (D) members, upon learning of these facts, conducted a violent assault on the mine. Subsequently, UMW (D) members picketed and kept the mine closed for several months. Gibbs (P) sued UMW (D) under § 303 of the Labor Management Relations Act (LMRA) for damages he suffered as the result of an illegal secondary boycott and also sued under state law for intentional interference with advantageous commercial relations. Because the LMRA had preempted most state tort law grounds for relief (e.g., tort claims for violent activity survived), jurisdiction depended on a finding that the state claims were so related to the federal claim under § 303 as to satisfy the standard for pendent claim jurisdiction, which hitherto meant that that pendent jurisdiction would exist only if the state and federal claims did little more than used different epithets to characterize the same group of circumstances. The district court submitted both the LMRA claim and state law claims to the jury, but granted judgment as a matter of law to UMW (D) on the LMRA claim. The district court entered judgment on the state law claims.

The United States Supreme Court granted certiorari in the case.

ISSUE:
(1) Does pendent jurisdiction exist where there is a federal question claim and the relationship between that claim and the state claim permits the conclusion that the entire action before the federal court comprises only one "case"?
(2) Where a federal court exercises pendent jurisdiction, does its rendering judgment as a matter of law on the federal claims deprive it of jurisdiction to enter judgment on the state claims?

HOLDING AND DECISION: [Judge not stated in casebook excerpt.]
(1) Yes. Pendent jurisdiction exists where there is a federal question claim and the relationship between that claim and the state claim permits the conclusion that the entire action before the federal court comprises only one "case." The prior approach, which permitted pendent jurisdiction only if the federal and nonfederal claims merely used different labels to characterize the same group of circumstances, was too limited and unnecessarily grudging. Instead, it the relationship between the state and federal claims must be analyzed. First, the federal claim must be of sufficient substance to confer subject matter jurisdiction on the federal court. Next, the federal and nonfederal claims must "derive from a common nucleus of operative fact." If the claims would ordinarily be tried in one judicial proceeding (when not taking into account whether they are state or federal claims), the federal court has power to hear all the claims. The federal court, however, has discretion not to exercise such power if it determines that considerations of judicial economy, convenience, and fairness to litigants are not present. Also, other consideration, such as jury confusion, might warrant the separation of the federal and state claims. Where the federal claims are dismissed, the state claims should also be dismissed. If it appears at any point in the proceedings that the state claims predominate, they should be dismissed without prejudice for adjudication by the state courts. While ordinarily the issue of pendent jurisdiction may be resolved on the pleadings, the question remains open throughout the litigation, and, if it turns out subsequent to the pleadings that the state claims predominate, the court should dismiss them.

Continued on next page.

[The Court's disposition of this issue is not indicated in the casebook excerpt.]

(2) No. Where a federal court exercises pendent jurisdiction, its rendering judgment as a matter of law on the federal claims does not deprive it of jurisdiction to enter judgment on the state claims. UMW (D) argues that by granting its motion for judgment as a matter of law on the LMRA claim, the district court was deprived of jurisdiction to enter judgment on the state law claims. This argument is rejected, since the district court's power to adjudicate the whole case had attached at the beginning of the case and the decision to submit both the federal and nonfederal claims to the jury served the interest of convenience and efficiency. That decision also did not constitute an abuse of discretion. [The Court's disposition of this issue is not indicated in the casebook excerpt.]

▶ *ANALYSIS*

The *Gibbs* case is notable for having articulated the formulation of pendent jurisdiction as arising where the federal and nonfederal claims would be part of the same case or controversy if they "derive from a common nucleus of operative fact." As such, it departed from prior practice. In 1990, Congress attempted to codify this "common nucleus" formulation, along with the concept of ancillary jurisdiction, in 28 U.S.C. § 1367, which uses the term "supplemental" jurisdiction to combine both concepts into one.

■══■

Quicknotes

ANCILLARY JURISDICTION Authority of a federal court to hear and determine issues related to a case over which it has jurisdiction, but over which it would not have jurisdiction if such claims were brought independently.

PENDENT JURISDICTION A doctrine granting authority to a federal court to hear a claim that does not invoke diversity jurisdiction if it arises from the same transaction or occurrence as the primary action.

SUPPLEMENTAL JURISDICTION A doctrine granting authority to a federal court to hear a claim that does not invoke diversity jurisdiction if it arises from the same transaction or occurrence as the primary action.

■══■

Owen Equipment & Erection Co. v. Kroger

Crane company (D) v. Wife of electrocuted decedent (P)

437 U.S. 365 (1978).

NATURE OF CASE: Appeal from an action for damages for wrongful death.

FACT SUMMARY: Kroger (P), the widow of decedent, filed a wrongful death action against Omaha Public Power District after her husband was electrocuted when a steel crane hit a power line.

RULE OF LAW
In an action in which federal jurisdiction is based on diversity, a plaintiff may not assert a claim against a third-party defendant when there is no independent basis for federal jurisdiction over that claim.

FACTS: James Kroger was electrocuted when the boom of a steel crane next to which he was walking came too close to a high-tension electric power line. Kroger (P), the decedent's widow, filed a wrongful death action in the U.S. District Court for Nebraska against Omaha Public Power District. Kroger's (P) complaint alleged that Omaha's negligence had caused her husband's death. Federal jurisdiction was based on diversity, since Kroger (P) was a citizen of Iowa and Omaha was a Nebraska corporation. Omaha then filed a third-party complaint pursuant to Rule 14 of the Fed. Rules of Civ. P. against Owen Equipment (D), alleging that the crane was owned and operated by Owen (D) and that Owen's (D) negligence had been the proximate cause of Kroger's (P) death. While a motion for summary judgment on the part of Omaha was pending, Kroger (P) was granted leave to file an amended complaint naming Owen (D) as an additional defendant. Omaha's motion was granted, and the case went to trial between Kroger (P) and Owen (D). At trial, it was disclosed that Owen (D) was an Iowa corporation and not a Nebraska corporation as was alleged and that Kroger (P) and Owen (D) were, thus, both citizens of Iowa. Owen (D) moved to dismiss the complaint for lack of jurisdiction. The court reserved decision on the motion, and the jury returned a verdict in favor of Kroger (P). Then the court denied the motion to dismiss. The judgment was affirmed on appeal. The court of appeals held that the district court had power to adjudicate the claim because it arose from the core of operative facts giving rise to both Kroger's (P) claim against Omaha and Omaha's claim against Owen (D).

ISSUE: In an action in which federal jurisdiction is based on diversity, may the plaintiff assert a claim against a third-party defendant when there is no independent basis for federal jurisdiction over that claim?

HOLDING AND DECISION: [Judge not stated in casebook excerpt.] No. In an action in which federal jurisdiction is based on diversity, the plaintiff may not assert a claim against a third-party defendant when there is no independent basis for federal jurisdiction over that claim. 28 U.S.C. § 1332(a)(1) confers upon federal courts jurisdiction over civil actions where the matter in controversy exceeds the sum of $10,000 and is between citizens of different states. Thus, it is clear that Kroger (P) could not originally have brought suit in federal court naming Owen (D) and Omaha as codefendants, since citizens of Iowa would have been on both sides of the litigation. Yet, the identical lawsuit resulted when Kroger (P) amended her complaint. Complete diversity was destroyed just as surely as if Kroger (P) had sued Owen (D) initially. If, as the court of appeals thought, a common nucleus of operative fact were the only requirement for ancillary jurisdiction in a diversity case, there would be no principled reason why Kroger (P) could not have joined her cause of action against Owen (D) in her original complaint as ancillary to her cause against Omaha. Congress's requirement of complete diversity would thus have been evaded completely. Reversed.

DISSENT: (White, J.) Given the Court's willingness to recognize ancillary jurisdiction over nonfederal claims in situations involving impleader, cross-claims, and counterclaims, despite the requirements of § 1332, there is no justification for the Court's refusal to approve the district court's exercise of ancillary jurisdiction in the present case.

ANALYSIS

The court of appeals relied upon the doctrine of ancillary jurisdiction as enunciated in *Mine Workers v. Gibbs*, 383 U.S. 715. However, the *Gibbs* case differed from this one in that it involved pendent jurisdiction, which concerns the resolution of a plaintiff's federal and state law claims against a single defendant in one action. In this claim, there was no claim based on substantive federal law.

Quicknotes

ANCILLARY JURISDICTION Authority of a federal court to hear and determine issues related to a case over which it has jurisdiction, but over which it would not have jurisdiction if such claims were brought independently.

DIVERSITY The authority of a federal court to hear and determine cases involving $10,000 or more and in which the parties are citizens of different states, or in which one party is an alien.

Exxon Mobil Corp. v. Allapattah Services, Inc.
Rosario Ortega v. Star-Kist Foods, Inc.

Class members (P) v. Corporations (D)

545 U.S. 546 (2005).

NATURE OF CASE: Appeal of judgment regarding supplemental jurisdiction.

FACT SUMMARY: [Only some members of a class met the amount-in-controversy to establish diversity jurisdiction, and the circuit courts were split as to whether each member's claim must meet the requirement in order for their claims to go forward.]

RULE OF LAW
Where one plaintiff's claim satisfies the minimum amount-in-controversy requirement for federal diversity jurisdiction and another plaintiff's related claim does not, 28 U.S.C. § 1367 allows federal courts to exercise supplemental jurisdiction over the claim that is less than the required amount.

FACTS: [These cases were consolidated and the Supreme Court granted certiorari to resolve a circuit split over the federal supplemental jurisdiction statute, 28 U.S.C. § 1367. The plaintiffs in the *Exxon* case are a class of approximately 10,000 gas dealers (P) who claimed that Exxon (D) overcharged them for fuel purchases. The court of appeals affirmed the district court's verdict for the dealers (P), and held that the federal supplemental jurisdiction statute allows a district court in a class-action lawsuit to exercise supplemental jurisdiction over class members whose claims do not meet the jurisdictional minimum amount. In the *Ortega* case, a nine-year-old girl injured her finger on a can of Star-Kist tuna. The girl (P) and her family (P) sued in federal court, on the basis of diversity jurisdiction. The district court dismissed the claims for lack of jurisdiction, holding that the girl's (P) and family members' (P) claims did not meet the minimum amount for jurisdiction. The First Circuit Court of Appeals reversed as to the girl (P), but upheld the district court's conclusion that none of the family members (P) satisfied the amount-in-controversy requirement.]

ISSUE: Where one plaintiff's claim satisfies the minimum amount-in-controversy requirement for federal diversity jurisdiction, and another plaintiff's related claim does not, does 28 U.S.C. § 1367 allow federal courts to exercise supplemental jurisdiction over the claim that is less than the required amount?

HOLDING AND DECISION: (Kennedy, J.) Yes. Where one plaintiff's claim satisfies the minimum amount-in-controversy requirement for federal diversity jurisdiction and another plaintiff's related claim does not, 28 U.S.C. § 1367 allows federal courts to exercise supplemen-

tal jurisdiction over the claim that is less than the required amount. Courts only need to determine whether they have original jurisdiction over one of the claims in a case. If they do, courts can then decide to extend supplemental jurisdiction to the other related claims. The indivisibility and contamination theories are easily dismissed. The indivisibility theory is inconsistent with the whole notion of supplemental jurisdiction, and the contamination theory is inconsistent with the amount-in-controversy requirement. The unambiguous text of the statute indicates that jurisdiction should extend to the other plaintiffs, regardless of legislative history or other extrinsic material. Judgment of the Court of Appeals for the Eleventh Circuit affirmed, and judgment of the Court of Appeals for the First Circuit reversed.

DISSENT: (Stevens, J.) [The majority should have consulted the legislative history of the statute.]

DISSENT: (Ginsburg, J.) The majority's reading of the statute is plausible, but broad. It should be read as instructing that the district court have original jurisdiction over the action first, before supplemental jurisdiction can attach. This would be a less disruptive reading of the statute.

▶ ANALYSIS

The Court's holding greatly expands the limits of diversity jurisdiction. This case overrules *Zahn v. International Paper*, 414 U.S. 291 (1973), which held that in order for a federal court to exercise diversity jurisdiction, all plaintiffs in the case had to satisfy 28 U.S.C. § 1332's amount-in-controversy requirement. The courts of appeal had divided on the question and the Supreme Court had previously failed to resolve the issue in the 2000 case, *Free v. Abbott Laboratories, Inc.*, 529 U.S. 333 (2000).

Quicknotes

AMOUNT IN CONTROVERSY The value of a claim sought by a party to a lawsuit.

CLASS ACTION A suit commenced by a representative on behalf of an ascertainable group that is too large to appear in court, who shares a commonality of interests and who will benefit from a successful result.

DIVERSITY JURISDICTION The authority of a federal court to hear and determine cases involving a statutory sum

Continued on next page.

and in which the parties are citizens of different states, or in which one party is an alien.

ORIGINAL JURISDICTION The power of a court to hear an action upon its commencement.

SUPPLEMENTAL JURISDICTION A doctrine granting authority to a federal court to hear a claim that does not invoke diversity jurisdiction if it arises from the same transaction or occurrence as the primary action.

CHAPTER 1

Choosing the Law to Be Applied in Federal Court

Quick Reference Rules of Law

Swift v. Tyson

Debt holder (P) v. Endorsee (D)

41 U.S. (16 Pet.) 1 (1842).

NATURE OF CASE: Review of action seeking to enforce a bill of exchange.

FACT SUMMARY: The result in a diversity federal action depended upon whether the district court was obligated to follow state decisional precedent.

🏛 RULE OF LAW
Federal courts sitting in diversity are not obligated to follow state decisional precedent.

FACTS: In an action seeking to enforce a bill of exchange, an issue arose as to whether the district court was obligated to follow New York common law or was free to apply general principles of common law. [The casebook excerpt did not state the decision in the district court.]

ISSUE: Are federal courts sitting in diversity obligated to follow state decisional precedent?

HOLDING AND DECISION: (Story, J.) No. Federal courts sitting in diversity are not obligated to follow decisional precedent. The Rules of Decision Act, found at 28 U.S.C. § 1652, mandates that federal courts sitting in diversity follow state law. However, the decisions of courts are not laws; they are interpretations thereof and can be reexamined, qualified, or reversed by courts themselves. Consequently, while federal courts sitting in diversity must follow state statutes, they need not follow state court decisions. [The casebook excerpt did not note how the rule affected the case in question.]

▌ANALYSIS

This decision was reversed almost a century later in *Erie Railroad Co. v. Tompkins*, 304 U.S. 64 (1938). *Swift* was decided purely as a matter of statutory construction. *Erie* found the creation of federal general common law to be unconstitutional.

■══■

Quicknotes

DIVERSITY JURISDICTION The authority of a federal court to hear and determine cases involving $10,000 or more and in which the parties are citizens of different states, or in which one party is an alien.

■══■

Erie Railroad Co. v. Tompkins

Rail company (D) v. Pedestrian (P)

304 U.S. 64 (1938).

NATURE OF CASE: Action to recover damages for personal injury allegedly caused by negligent conduct.

FACT SUMMARY: In a personal injury suit, a federal district court trial judge refused to apply applicable state law because such law was "common law" (judge-made) and not embodied in any statute.

🏛 RULE OF LAW
Although the 1789 Rules of Decision Act left federal courts unfettered to apply their own rules of procedure in common law actions brought in federal court, state law governs substantive issues. State law includes not only statutory law but case law as well.

FACTS: Tompkins (P) was walking in a right-of-way parallel to some railroad tracks when an Erie Railroad (Erie) (D) train came by. Tompkins (P) was struck and injured by what he would, at trial, claim to be an open door extending from one of the railcars. Under Pennsylvania case law (the applicable law since the accident occurred there), state courts would have treated Tompkins (P) as a trespasser in denying him recovery for anything other than wanton or willful misconduct on Erie's (D) part. Under "general" law, recognized in federal courts, Tompkins (P) would have been regarded as a licensee and would only have been obligated to show ordinary negligence. Because Erie (D) was a New York corporation, Tompkins (P) brought suit in a federal district court in New York, where he won a judgment for $30,000. Upon appeal to a federal circuit court, the decision was affirmed.

ISSUE: Was the trial court in error in refusing to recognize state case law as the proper rule of decision in deciding the substantive issue of liability?

HOLDING AND DECISION: (Brandeis, J.) Yes. The Court's opinion is in four parts: (1) *Swift v. Tyson*, 41 U.S. (16 Pet.) 1 (1842), which held that federal courts exercising jurisdiction on the ground of diversity of citizenship need not, in matters of general jurisprudence, apply the unwritten law of the state as declared by its highest court, is overruled. Section 34 of the federal Judiciary Act of 1789, c. 20, 28 U.S.C. § 725, requires that federal courts in all matters except those where some federal law is controlling apply as their rules of decision the law of the state, unwritten as well as written. Up to this time, federal courts had assumed the power to make "general law" statutes. (2) *Swift* had numerous political and social defects. The hoped-for uniformity among state courts had not occurred; there was no satisfactory way to distinguish between local and general law. On the other hand, *Swift* introduced grave discrimination by noncitizens

against citizens. The privilege of selecting the court for resolving disputes rested with the noncitizen, who could pick the more favorable forum. The resulting far-reaching discrimination was due to the broad province accorded "general law" in which many matters of seemingly local concern were included. Furthermore, local citizens could move out of the state and bring suit in a federal court if they were disposed to do so; corporations, similarly, could simply reincorporate in another state. More than statutory relief is involved here; the unconstitutionality of *Swift* is clear. (3) Except in matters governed by the federal Constitution or by acts of Congress, the law to be applied in any case is the law of the state. There is no federal common law. The federal courts have no power derived from the Constitution or by Congress to declare substantive rules of common law applicable in a state whether they be "local" or "general" in nature. (4) The federal district court was bound to follow the Pennsylvania case law, which would have denied recovery to Tompkins (P). Reversed and remanded.

DISSENT: (Butler, J.) Since no constitutional question was presented or argued in the lower court, and a 1937 statute which required notice to the Attorney General whenever the constitutionality of an Act of Congress was raised was not followed, the court's conduct was improper.

CONCURRENCE (IN PART): (Reed, J.) It is unnecessary to go beyond interpreting the meaning of "laws" in the Rules of Decision Act. Article III and the Necessary and Proper Clause of Article I of the Constitution might provide Congress with the power to declare rules of substantive law for federal courts to follow.

▶ ANALYSIS

Erie can fairly be characterized as the most significant and sweeping decision on civil procedure ever handed down by the U.S. Supreme Court. As interpreted in subsequent decisions, *Erie* held that while federal courts may apply their own rules of procedure, issues of substantive law must be decided in accord with the applicable state law—usually the state in which the federal court sits. Note, however, how later Supreme Court decisions have made inroads into the broad doctrine enunciated here.

■=■

Quicknotes

ERIE DOCTRINE Federal courts must apply state substantive law and federal procedural law.

■=■

Guaranty Trust Co. v. York

Trust company (D) v. Note holder (P)

326 U.S. 99 (1945).

NATURE OF CASE: Class action alleging fraud and misrepresentation.

FACT SUMMARY: York (P), barred from filing suit in state court because of the state statute of limitations, brought an equity action in federal court based upon diversity of citizenship jurisdiction.

RULE OF LAW
Where a state statute that would completely bar recovery in state court has significant effect on the outcome determination of the action, even though the suit is brought in equity, the federal court is bound by the state law.

FACTS: Van Swerigen Corporation, in 1930, issued notes and named Guaranty Trust Co. (Guaranty) (D) as trustee with power and obligations to enforce the rights of the note holders in the assets of the corporation and the Van Swerigens. In 1931, when it was apparent that the corporation could not meet its obligations, Guaranty (D) cooperated in a plan for the purchase of the outstanding notes for 50 percent of the notes' face value and an exchange of 20 shares of the corporation's stock for each $1,000 note. In 1934, York (P) received some cash, her donor not having accepted the rate of exchange. In 1940, three accepting note holders sued Guaranty (D), charging fraud and misrepresentation, in state court. York (P) was not allowed to intervene. Summary judgment in favor of Guaranty (D) was affirmed. In 1942, York (P) brought a class-action suit in federal court based on diversity of citizenship and charged Guaranty (D) with breach of trust. Guaranty (D) moved for, and was granted, summary judgment on the basis of the earlier state decision. The court of appeals reversed on the basis that the earlier state decision did not foreclose this federal court action, and held that, even though the state statute of limitations had run, the fact that the action was brought in equity released the federal court from following the state rule.

ISSUE: Does a state statute of limitations, which would bar a suit in state court, also act as a bar to the same action if the suit is brought in equity in federal court, with jurisdiction being based on diversity of citizenship?

HOLDING AND DECISION: (Frankfurter, J.) Yes. *Erie Railroad Co. v. Tompkins*, 304 U.S. 64 (1938), overruled a particular way of looking at law after its inadequacies had been laid bare. Federal courts have traditionally given state-created rights in equity greater respect than rights in law since the former are more frequently defined by legislative enactment. Even though federal equi-

ty may be thought of as a separate legal system, the substantive right is created by the state, and federal courts must respect state law which governs that right. While state law cannot define the remedies which a federal court must give simply because a federal court in diversity jurisdiction is available as an alternative, a federal court may afford an equitable remedy for a substantive right recognized by a state even though a state court cannot give it. Federal courts enforce state-created substantive rights if the mode of proceeding and remedy were consonant with the traditional body of equitable remedies, practice, and procedure. Matters of "substance" and of "procedure" turn on different considerations. Here, since the federal court is adjudicating a state-created right solely because diversity of citizenship of the parties is, in effect, only another court of the state, it cannot afford recovery if the right to recovery is made unavailable by the state. The question is not whether a statute of limitation is "procedural" but whether the statute so affects the result of litigation as to be controlling in state law. It is, therefore, immaterial to make a "substantive-procedure" dichotomy—*Erie Railroad Co. v. Tompkins* was not an endeavor to formulate scientific legal terminology—but rather an expression of a policy that touches the distribution of judicial power between state and federal courts. *Erie* ensures that insofar as legal rules determine the outcome of litigation, the result should not be any different in a federal court extending jurisdiction solely on the basis of diversity of citizenship. Through diversity jurisdiction, Congress meant to afford out-of-state litigants another tribunal and not another body of law. Reversed and remanded.

ANALYSIS

Guaranty Trust, which clarified *Erie*, may itself be in the process of being slowly eroded by modern courts. *Hanna v. Plumer*, 380 U.S. 460 (1965), held that where state law conflicts with the Federal Rules of Civil Procedure, the latter prevails regardless of the effect on outcome of the litigation. And in *Byrd v. Blue Ridge Elec. Cooperative*, 356 U.S. 525 (1958), the Court suggested that some constitutional doctrines (there, the right to a jury trial in federal court) are so important as to be controlling over state law once again, the outcome notwithstanding.

Quicknotes

CLASS ACTION A suit commenced by a representative on behalf of an ascertainable group that is too large to

Continued on next page.

appear in court, who share a commonality of interests and who will benefit from a successful result.

DIVERSITY JURISDICTION The authority of a federal court to hear and determine cases involving $10,000 or more and in which the parties are citizens of different states, or in which one party is an alien.

ERIE DOCTRINE Federal courts must apply state substantive law and federal procedural law.

■=■

- Guaranty - you can't pay us whole amount so just pay 1/2.

   we take half of value and @ same time you give us shares of company (will end up w/ownership in that co).

- trustee buys the notes from Van Swerigen

- Guaranty realized VS corp can't meet obligations of York stockholders - settles class action lawsuit. we should have gotten more $ did r agree SV + Guaranty deal.

Byrd v. Blue Ridge Rural Electric Cooperative, Inc.

Employee (P) v. Public utility (D)

356 U.S. 525 (1958).

NATURE OF CASE: Appeal of reversal of damages awarded for personal injury.

FACT SUMMARY: In a diversity action, a court of appeals felt constrained to apply state law making certain factual determinations the province of the court alone.

RULE OF LAW
A federal court sitting in diversity need not follow state law allocating the fact-finding roles of judge and jury.

FACTS: Byrd (P), injured while working on power lines owned and operated by Blue Ridge Rural Electric Cooperative, Inc. (Blue Ridge) (D), sued Blue Ridge (D) for damages. Blue Ridge (D) claimed that a certain statutory defense applied. The district court, sitting in diversity, rejected its application, and a jury awarded damages. The court of appeals reversed, holding that the defense applied and was, per state law, an issue to be decided by the court. The court held the defense meritorious and entered judgment for Blue Ridge (D). Byrd (P) appealed.

ISSUE: Must a federal court sitting in diversity follow state law allocating the fact-finding roles of judge and jury?

HOLDING AND DECISION: (Brennan, J.) No. A federal court sitting in diversity need not follow state law allocating the fact-finding roles of judge and jury. The precedents of this Court mandate that federal courts sitting in diversity apply the law of the forum state. A major reason for this is to avoid different outcomes in federal and state courts. However, state laws that affect the basic functions of federal courts in how they operate do not require strict adherence. Where the application of state law would greatly upset the basic functions of the federal judiciary, the law should not be applied. Here, the fact-finding roles of the judge and jury are integral to the federal judiciary, in fact implicating the Constitution by virtue of the Seventh Amendment. Therefore, state law making determination of the statutory defense a factual issue for the court should not have been followed. Reversed and remanded.

ANALYSIS

The Court, in a brief passage, mentioned that the fact-finding allocation of the statute was a "form and mode" of enforcing the statutory immunity and was not integral to the rights of the parties. The import of this passage is unclear. Further, the Court did not appear to base its decision on this observation so much as upon the structural argument outlined above.

■==■

Quicknotes

DIVERSITY JURISDICTION The authority of a federal court to hear and determine cases involving $10,000 or more and in which the parties are citizens of different states, or in which one party is an alien.

SEVENTH AMENDMENT Provides that no fact, tried by a jury shall be otherwise re-examined in any court of the United States, other than according to the rules of the common law.

■==■

Hanna v. Plumer

Nonresident accident victim (P) v. Resident executor (D)

380 U.S. 460 (1965).

NATURE OF CASE: Appeal of summary judgment in federal diversity tort action.

FACT SUMMARY: Hanna (P) filed a tort action in federal court in Massachusetts, where Plumer (D) resided, for an auto accident that occurred in South Carolina.

🏛 RULE OF LAW

The *Erie* doctrine mandates that federal courts are to apply state substantive law and federal procedural law, but, where matters fall roughly between the two and are rationally capable of classification as either, the Constitution grants the federal court system the power to regulate its practice and pleading (procedure).

FACTS: Hanna (P), a citizen of Ohio, filed a tort action in federal court in Massachusetts against Plumer (D), the executor of the estate of Louise Plumer Osgood, a Massachusetts citizen. It was alleged that Osgood caused injuries to Hanna (P) in an auto accident in South Carolina. Service on Plumer (D) was accomplished pursuant to Fed. R. Civ. P. 4(d)(1) by leaving copies of the summons with Plumer's (D) wife. At trial, motion for summary judgment by Plumer (D) was granted on the grounds that service should have been accomplished pursuant to Massachusetts law (by the *Erie* doctrine), which required service by hand to the party personally. On appeal, Hanna (P) contended that *Erie* should not affect the application of the Federal Rules of Civil Procedure to this case. Plumer (D), however, contended that (1) a substantive law question under *Erie* is any question in which permitting application of federal law would alter the outcome of the case (the so-called outcome determination test); (2) the application of federal law here (i.e., 4(d)(1)) will necessarily affect the outcome of the case (from a necessary dismissal to litigation); and, so, therefore, (3) *Erie* requires that the state substantive law requirement of service by hand be upheld along with the trial court's summary judgment.

ISSUE: Does the *Erie* doctrine classification of "substantive law questions" extend to embrace questions involving both substantive and procedural considerations merely because such a question might have an effect on the determination of the substantive outcome of the case?

HOLDING AND DECISION: (Warren, C.J.) No. The *Erie* doctrine mandates that federal courts are to apply state substantive law and federal procedural law, and, where matters fall roughly between the two and are rationally capable of classification as either, the Constitution grants the federal court system the power to regulate its practice and pleading (procedure). It is well settled that the Enabling Act for the Federal Rules of Civil Procedure

requires that a procedural effect of any rule on the outcome of a case be shown to actually "abridge, enlarge, or modify" the substantive law in a case for the *Erie* doctrine to come into play. Where, as here, the question only goes to procedural requirements (i.e., service of summons, a dismissal for improper service here would not alter the substantive right of Hanna [P] to serve Plumer [D] personally, and refile or effect the substantive law of negligence in the case), Article III and the Necessary and Proper Clause provide that Congress has a right to provide rules for the federal court system such as Fed. R. Civ. P. 4(d)(1). "Outcome determination analysis was never intended to serve as a talisman" for the *Erie* doctrine. Reversed.

CONCURRENCE: (Harlan, J.) Though the Court was correct to reject the outcome determination test, it was wrong in stating that anything arguably procedural is constitutionally placed within the province of the federal government to regulate. The test for "substantive" would be whether "the choice of rule would substantially affect those primary decisions respecting human conduct which our constitutional system leaves to state regulation."

▶ ANALYSIS

Fed. R. Civ. P. 4(e)(2), as amended December 31, 2007, covers the provisions of old 4(d)(1). This case points out a return to the basic rationales of *Erie Railroad Co. v. Tompkins* 304 U.S. 64 (1938). First, the Court asserts that one important consideration in determining how a particular question should be classified (substantive or procedural) is the avoidance of "forum shopping" (the practice of choosing one forum, such as federal in which to file, in order to gain the advantages of one), which permits jurisdictions to infringe on the substantive law defining powers of each other. Second, the Court seeks to avoid inequitable administration of the laws which would result from allowing jurisdictional considerations to determine substantive rights. Chief Justice Warren here, in rejecting the "outcome determination" test, asserts that any rule must be measured ultimately against the Federal Rules Enabling Act and the Constitution.

▬▬▬

Quicknotes

ERIE DOCTRINE Federal courts must apply state substantive law and federal procedural law.

FORUM-SHOPPING Refers to a situation in which one party to an action seeks to have the matter heard and determined by a court, or in a jurisdiction, that will provide it with the most favorable result.

▬▬▬

Gasperini v. Center for Humanities, Inc.

Photographer (P) v. Educational organization (D)

518 U.S. 415 (1996).

NATURE OF CASE: Review of reversal of award for damages for lost transparencies.

FACT SUMMARY: Gasperini (P) filed suit against The Center for Humanities (D) after it lost several hundred slides that he had loaned the Center (D) for use in an educational film.

RULE OF LAW
The Seventh Amendment does not preclude appellate review of a trial judge's denial of a motion to set aside a jury verdict as excessive.

FACTS: Gasperini (P), a California resident, was a journalist for CBS News and the Christian Science Monitor who spent seven years reporting in Central America. In 1990, Gasperini (P) agreed to supply The Center for Humanities (Center) (D) with 300 original color transparencies for use in an educational videotape. The Center (D) used 110 of the slides in the video, and agreed to return all of the originals to Gasperini (P). Upon completion of the project, the Center (D) could not find the slides. Gasperini (P) filed suit in a New York federal district court, invoking diversity jurisdiction pursuant to 28 U.S.C. § 1332. The Center (D) conceded liability for the lost transparencies, and the jury awarded the photographic community's "industry standard" of $1,500 per slide to Gasperini (P) for a total of $450,000. The Center (D) appealed on the grounds that the award was excessive, and the court of appeals vacated the judgment, citing New York statutory law. The court of appeals concluded that "industry standard" was not the only factor to consider in determining damages, and that the slides' uniqueness and the photographer's earning level should also be considered. The court ordered a new trial unless Gasperini (P) agreed to accept an award of $100,000. Gasperini (P) appealed, arguing that the Seventh Amendment precluded review of such federal court proceedings.

ISSUE: Does the Seventh Amendment preclude appellate review of a trial judge's denial of a motion to set aside a jury verdict as excessive?

HOLDING AND DECISION: (Ginsburg, J.) No. The Seventh Amendment does not preclude appellate review of a trial judge's denial of a motion to set aside a jury verdict as excessive. New York statutory law requires that when appellate review of a money judgment is granted, the court shall determine if the award is excessive or inadequate based upon whether it "materially deviates" from what would be reasonable compensation. A damages award in federal court cannot be significantly larger than the recovery that would be tolerated in state court. Therefore, if a federal court in New York were permitted to

ignore the prescribed New York standard and instead apply the federal "shock the conscience" test, substantial variations between state and federal judgments would result. The Seventh Amendment governs proceedings in federal courts and controls the allocation of trial functions between judge and jury and the allocation of authority to review verdicts. However, the appropriate court to apply New York statutory law as it pertains to a factual determination such as a damage award is the district court, and not the court of appeals, which will have the opportunity on appeal to review for abuse of discretion. Therefore, the court of appeals judgment shall be vacated, and the case shall be remanded to the district court so that the trial judge can apply the "deviates materially" standard. Vacated and remanded.

DISSENT: (Stevens, J.) The majority was correct in most of its reasoning, but not in the disposition of the case. There is no reason that the district court should be required to repeat a task that has already been well-performed by the reviewing appellate court. The judgment of the court of appeals should be affirmed.

DISSENT: (Scalia, J.) The Court has overruled a long-standing and well-reasoned precedent that prohibited federal appellate courts from reviewing refusals by district courts to set aside civil jury awards as contrary to the weight of the evidence. Additionally, the Court's holding that a state practice that relates to division of duties between state judges and juries must be followed by federal courts in diversity cases is directly contrary to prior Supreme Court decisions.

ANALYSIS

The federal court system relies on a premise of fairly strict finality prior to appeal. Judges and jurors traditionally have been granted a high degree of autonomy within the federal system. In fact, the Seventh Amendment's mandate that findings by juries be allowed to stand subject only to certain exceptions, dates back to eighteenth-century common law.

Quicknotes

SEVENTH AMENDMENT Provides that no fact tried by a jury shall be otherwise re-examined in any court of the United States, other than according to the rules of the common law.

28 U.S.C. § 1332 Governs the requirements for diversity jurisdiction.

Mason v. American Emery Wheel Works

Injured worker (P) v. Equipment manufacturer (D)

241 F.2d 906 (1st Cir. 1957).

NATURE OF CASE: Appeal of dismissal of action for damages for personal injury.

FACT SUMMARY: A federal court sitting in diversity held itself obligated to follow an old Mississippi Supreme Court decision regarding standing to sue in a products liability case.

🏛 RULE OF LAW
A state supreme court ruling on an issue need not be followed by a federal court sitting in diversity if that ruling has lost its vitality.

FACTS: Mason (P), injured by an emery wheel manufactured by American Emery Wheel Works (American) (D), sued in federal court, with jurisdiction being based on diversity. Mason (P) had not obtained the wheel directly from American (D). The district court, following a 1928 Mississippi Supreme Court decision holding that privity of contract was necessary to sue a product manufacturer for injuries, granted summary judgment in favor of American (D). Mason (P) appealed.

ISSUE: Must a state supreme court ruling on an issue be followed by a federal court sitting in diversity if that ruling has lost its vitality?

HOLDING AND DECISION: (Magruder, C.J.) No. A state supreme court ruling on an issue need not be followed by a federal court sitting in diversity if that ruling has lost its vitality. There is no question but that a federal court sitting in diversity must follow state law. Generally speaking, a pronouncement of a state supreme court will be final on a given issue. Where, however, the decision appears to have lost its vitality, it is up to the district court to try to decide how the state court would rule on that issue today. Here, there has been a major shift in products liability law since 1928, and it is unlikely that the Mississippi Supreme Court would follow its own precedent. This is borne out by dicta in at least one case indicating dissatisfaction with the 1928 precedent. In light of this, it seems relatively clear that the true state of the law in Mississippi is not to require contractual privity. Reversed and remanded.

CONCURRENCE: (Hartigan, J.) The decision today was made much easier by the dicta to which reference was made in the opinion. It is much less clear how far a federal court in diversity can go in rejecting state supreme court precedent which has not been undercut in subsequent decisions.

▶ ANALYSIS

Obviously, not every issue that comes before a federal court sitting in diversity will have been ruled upon by the state supreme court. When this occurs, the role of a federal court becomes much like a state trial court. It must search through other state precedent to rule on an issue.

Quicknotes

DIVERSITY The authority of a federal court to hear and determine cases involving $10,000 or more and in which the parties are citizens of different states, or in which one party is an alien.

PRIVITY OF CONTRACT A relationship between the parties to a contract that is required in order to bring an action for breach.

Dice v. Akron, Canton & Youngstown R.R.

Fireman (P) v. Railroad company (D)

342 U.S. 359 (1952).

NATURE OF CASE: Negligence action under Federal Employer's Liability Act.

FACT SUMMARY: Dice (P), a railroad fireman, was injured in an accident involving a train of Akron, Canton & Youngstown R.R. (D).

🏛 RULE OF LAW
Though federal claims may be adjudicated by state courts, state laws are never controlling on the question of what the incidents of any federal right may be.

FACTS: Dice (P), a railroad fireman injured when an engine of the Akron, Canton & Youngstown R.R. (Railroad) (D) jumped the track, sued in an Ohio state court under the Federal Employers Liability Act, charging negligence. At trial, the Railroad (D) offered in defense a document signed by Dice (P) which purported to release the Railroad (D) of all liability over and above $924.63, which Dice (P) had already received. Dice (P) contended that he had not read the statement before signing it, relying on fraudulent representations of the Railroad (D) that the document was merely a receipt for the $924.63. The jury found for Dice (P), but the trial court entered judgment n.o.v. for the Railroad (D) on the grounds that under Ohio state law, Dice (P) could not escape responsibility for signing the release. Under Ohio law, he was under a duty to read the document before signing it. The Ohio Court of Appeals reversed the trial judge on the grounds that federal law (that a finding of fraud will preclude the use of a release such as the one in this case) should have been applied. The Ohio Supreme Court reversed again, and this appeal followed.

ISSUE: In adjudicating a claim arising out of federal law may a state court properly apply state law?

HOLDING AND DECISION: (Black, J.) No. Though federal claims may be adjudicated by state courts, state laws are never controlling on the question of what the incidents of any federal right may be. Federal rights according relief to injured railroad employees could be defeated if states were permitted to have the final say as to what defenses could and could not be interposed here. It is true that Ohio normally allows the judge in an action to resolve all issues of fraud in a negligence action, and that, in itself, is a perfectly acceptable procedure. But it is well settled that the federal right to a jury trial is an essential one, which Ohio may not infringe upon. Reversed and remanded.

DISSENT: (Frankfurter, J.) Requiring federal standards for the determination of fraud unconstitutionally invades the state's reserved power to maintain the common law division between law (i.e., negligence determined by a jury) and equity (fraud relieved by a judge).

▶ ANALYSIS

This case points up the general rule for the treatment of federal rights in state courts. In short, they are always governed by federal law. The Seventh Amendment right to a civil jury trial is an exclusively federal right. It is not a fundamental right incorporated in the Fourteenth Amendment and extended to the states. As such, states may properly provide that certain issues are to be determined by judges. When a federal right is involved, however, such discretion ceases. The federal standard of the Seventh Amendment must prevail.

■=■

Quicknotes

FEDERALISM A scheme of government whereby the power to govern is divided between a central and localized governments.

JUDGMENT N.O.V. A judgment entered by the trial judge reversing a jury verdict if the jury's determination has no basis in law or fact.

JURY TRIAL Trial of a matter or a cause before a jury as opposed to one before a judge.

NEGLIGENCE Conduct falling below the standard of care that a reasonable person would demonstrate under similar conditions.

SEVENTH AMENDMENT Provides that no fact tried by a jury shall be otherwise re-examined in any court of the United States, other than according to the rules of the common law.

■=■

Appeals

Quick Reference Rules of Law

Bowles v. Russell

Inmate (P) v. State official (D)

551 U.S. 205 (2007).

NATURE OF CASE: Appeal from denial to hear an appeal of the denial of a habeas corpus petition.

FACT SUMMARY: Bowles (P) contended that the court of appeals had jurisdiction to hear his appeal of the district court's denial of his habeas corpus petition because even though he did not file the notice of appeal within a 14-day period as required by statute, he filed within the 17-day period the district court had granted to him for such filing.

> 🏛 **RULE OF LAW**
> Failure to file a notice of appeal in the period statutorily provided for deprives the appellate court of jurisdiction to hear the appeal, notwithstanding that the appeal has been made within a period granted by the district court.

FACTS: Bowles (P) was convicted of murder. After he failed to challenge his conviction on direct appeal, he filed a federal habeas corpus application, which was also denied. He had 30 days to file a notice of appeal from the habeas denial, but failed to do so. He then moved to reopen the filing period pursuant to Federal Rule of Appellate Procedure 4(a)(6), and 28 U.S.C. § 2107(c), which allow a district court to grant a 14-day extension under certain conditions. The district court granted Bowles's (P) motion but inexplicably gave him 17 days to file his notice of appeal. He filed within the 17 days allowed by the district court, but after the 14-day period allowed by Rule 4(a)(6) and § 2107(c). The court of appeals held that the notice was untimely and that it therefore lacked jurisdiction to hear the case. The United States Supreme Court granted certiorari.

ISSUE: Does failure to file a notice of appeal in the period statutorily provided for deprive the appellate court of jurisdiction to hear the appeal, notwithstanding that the appeal has been made within a period granted by the district court?

HOLDING AND DECISION: (Thomas, J.) Yes. Failure to file a notice of appeal in the period statutorily provided for deprives the appellate court of jurisdiction to hear the appeal, notwithstanding that the appeal has been made within a period granted by the district court. Here, Rule 4(a)(6) and § 2107(c) provided statutory authority for the district court to grant a 14-day extension. The taking of an appeal in a civil case within the time prescribed by statute is "mandatory and jurisdictional," and there is a significant distinction between time limitations set forth in a statute such as § 2107, which limit a court's jurisdiction, and those based on court rules, which do not.

Because Congress decides, within constitutional bounds, whether federal courts can hear cases at all, it can also determine when, and under what conditions, federal courts can hear them, and when an appeal has not been prosecuted in the manner directed, within the time limited by the acts of Congress, it must be dismissed for want of jurisdiction. The resolution of the issue presented here follows naturally from this reasoning. Because Congress specifically limited the amount of time by which district courts can extend the notice-of-appeal period in § 2107(c), Bowles's (P) failure to file in accordance with the statute deprived the court of appeals of jurisdiction. Since his error is one of jurisdictional magnitude, he cannot rely on forfeiture or waiver to excuse his lack of compliance with the statute's time limitations. Rejected, too, is Bowles's (P) contention that his untimely filing should be excused under the "unique circumstances" doctrine, where a time period was permitted to be extended on the basis of the district court's finding of "excusable neglect." Because the Court has no authority to create equitable exceptions to jurisdictional requirements, use of the doctrine is illegitimate, and the cases on which the unique circumstances doctrine are based are overruled to the extent they purport to authorize an exception to a jurisdictional rule. Affirmed.

DISSENT: (Souter, J.) The majority is subjecting Bowles (P) to a judicial "bait and switch" for which there is no technical justification. Until the majority's decision, the "mandatory and jurisdictional" label had been unanimously repudiated by recent cases. Jurisdiction treatment is not automatic when a time limit is statutory, as here, since limits on the reach of federal statutes are only jurisdictional if Congress says they are. If Congress has not indicated that a statutory limitation is jurisdiction, courts should treat the limitation as nonjurisdictional. In this case, Congress did not expressly indicate that the statutory time limit in § 2107(c) was jurisdictional. The label "jurisdictional" attaches to the statutory prescriptions delineating the classes of cases (subject-matter jurisdiction) and persons (personal jurisdiction) within a court's adjudicatory authority. It does not, however, attach to claims-processing rules, such as a filing deadline, unless Congress so indicates. The time limit at issue here, far from defining the set of cases that may be adjudicated, is much more like a statute of limitations, which provides an affirmative defense, is not jurisdictional, and may be waived to alleviate hardship and unfairness. Consistent with this view, and the limited concept of jurisdiction recently developed by the Court's precedent, an exception to the time limit in § 2107(c)

Continued on next page.

should be available when there is a good justification for one. As in the "unique circumstances" cases, which involved district court errors that misled litigants, reasonable reliance on a judge's official word should not be dishonored and Bowles (P) should be permitted to rely on the district court's ruling. The Court, contrary to the majority's stance, has the authority to recognize an equitable exception to the 14-day limit, and that should be done here. Moreover, the district court's error in this case will not cause prejudice to the other party.

ANALYSIS

Some commentators have suggested that the approach taken by the majority in this case was erroneous and that jurisdictional characterization of statutory deadlines may place in doubt the legitimacy of rule-based appellate deadlines.

■═■

Quicknotes

HABEAS CORPUS A proceeding in which a defendant brings a writ to compel a judicial determination of whether he is lawfully being held in custody.

JURISDICTION The authority of a court to hear and declare judgment in respect to a particular matter.

■═■

Quackenbush v. Allstate Insurance Company

Insurance commissioner (P) v. Insurance company (D)

517 U.S. 706 (1996).

NATURE OF CASE: Appeal from remand order on abstention grounds.

FACT SUMMARY: The district court remanded a case to state court on abstention grounds, and Allstate Insurance Company (D) sought an immediate appeal.

🏛 RULE OF LAW
A district court remand order on abstention grounds is immediately appealable as a final order.

FACTS: Quackenbush (P), the Insurance Commissioner of California, was appointed trustee of Mission Insurance Company (Mission) after a liquidation order. Quackenbush (P) filed suit against Allstate Insurance Company (Allstate) (D), alleging that Allstate (D) had breached reinsurance agreements with Mission. Allstate (D) removed the action to federal court on diversity grounds and moved to compel arbitration. Quackenbush (P) requested a remand to state court, arguing that the federal court should abstain because its resolution might interfere with California's regulation of Mission's insolvency. The district court ruled that it should abstain and remanded the case to state court rather than issue a stay order. The Ninth Circuit Court of Appeals vacated the district court order, and Quackenbush (P) appealed to the Supreme Court.

ISSUE: Is a district court remand order on abstention grounds immediately appealable as a final order?

HOLDING AND DECISION: (O'Connor, J.) Yes. A district court remand order on abstention grounds is immediately appealable as a final order. 28 U.S.C. § 1291 confers appellate jurisdiction over appeals from final decisions of district courts. However, 28 U.S.C. § 1447(d) provides that orders remanding a case to state courts from which the case was removed are not reviewable on appeal. Despite this language, this Court has previously ruled that § 1447(d) applies only to remands on the grounds listed in § 1447(c). Abstention-based remands are not listed in § 1447(c). Thus, there is no express bar to appellate review of abstention-based remand order. The only question is whether this is a final decision entitled to appellate review. This Court has acknowledged that a small class of collateral orders are immediately appealable because they conclusively determine a disputed question that is completely separate from the merits of the action, are effectively unreviewable on appeal from final judgment, and are too important to be denied review. In the present case, the remand order effectively puts the litigants out of court. Since we have previously ruled that stay orders based on pending state court actions are reviewable, the remand order in this case is at least as final as a stay order. Thus, the district court's remand order was properly reviewed by the Ninth Circuit. Affirmed.

▶ ANALYSIS

The Court went on to discuss the merits of the abstention-based remand order. The Court agreed with the Ninth Circuit that the district court should not have abstained from the dispute. The Court found that remands cannot be based on abstention principles when the relief sought is not discretionary. Federal courts have the power to dismiss or remand cases based on abstention principles only where the relief sought is equitable or otherwise discretionary.

■■■

Quicknotes

ABSTENTION A doctrine pursuant to which a federal court may decline to assert its authority to hear a case involving a federal question, pending resolution of an issue in the matter in state court involving a question of state law or if the matter seems more appropriately determined by a state court.

REMAND To send back for additional scrutiny or deliberation.

REMOVAL Petition by a defendant to move the case to another court.

■■■

Will v. Hallock

Federal agent (D) v. Tort claimant (P)

546 U.S. 345 (2005).

NATURE OF CASE: Appeal from affirmance of denial of motion to dismiss action for deprivation of due process under the Constitution's Due Process Clause.

FACT SUMMARY: The Hallocks (P), whose property was damaged by federal agents (D), brought an action under the Due Process Clause of the Constitution against the agents (D) after losing a Federal Tort Claims Act (FTCA) case against the government. The agents (D) contended that the suit against them was barred by the judgment bar of the FTCA.

🏛 RULE OF LAW
An order denying the defense of judgment bar under the Federal Tort Claims Act does not confer jurisdiction for immediate appeal of right as a collateral order.

FACTS: The Hallocks (P) operated a software business from their home. Mr. Hallock's (P) credit card was stolen and used to pay for child pornography. U.S. Customs Service agents raided the Hallocks' (P) residence and seized several computers. The Hallocks (P) were cleared of any guilt, and the computers were returned, but were severely damaged, forcing the Hallocks (P) out of business. They sued the government under the Federal Tort Claims Act (FTCA), and, while that action was pending, sued the agents (D) separately for deprivation of due process under the Fifth Amendment's Due Process Clause. The district court dismissed the FTCA case, and the agents (D) then made a motion for dismissal of the due process claims under a provision of the FTCA that bars suits where a judgment on the claim has already been entered. The district court denied the motion. Although the trial had not yet concluded, the court of appeals granted the agents' (D) appeal of the district court's ruling on the motion and affirmed the district court, ruling that since the Hallocks (P) had not properly brought a claim in the original suit, no judgment had been entered. The court of appeals ruled that it had jurisdiction under the collateral order doctrine. The United States Supreme Court granted certiorari.

ISSUE: Does an order denying the defense of judgment bar under the Federal Tort Claims Act confer jurisdiction for immediate appeal of right as a collateral order?

HOLDING AND DECISION: (Souter, J.) No. An order denying the defense of judgment bar under the Federal Tort Claims Act does not confer jurisdiction for immediate appeal of right as a collateral order. The scope of the collateral order doctrine is narrow. Only orders that cannot be effectively reviewed after a final judgment can be appealed before the close of the trial. The interest at stake is essential to this determination. In this case, the agents' (D) interest in appealing the district court's order had no greater importance than the typical defense of claim preclusion and it therefore warranted no immediate appeal of right as a collateral order. Accordingly, the court of appeals did not have jurisdiction to hear the appeal. Vacated and remanded for dismissal for lack of jurisdiction.

▶ ANALYSIS

There are three stringent requirements for collateral order appeal, as follows: that an order (1) conclusively determine the disputed question, (2) resolve an important issue completely separate from the merits of the action, and (3) be effectively unreviewable on appeal from a final judgment. An appeal is permitted only when these conditions are satisfied, and constitutes an exception the general rule that a party is limited to one appeal after final judgment has been entered. These three conditions are sometimes referred to as conclusiveness, separability, and unreviewability.

◼▬◼

Quicknotes

COLLATERAL ORDER Doctrine pursuant to which an appeal from an interlocutory order may be brought in order to hear and determine claims which are collateral to the merits of the case and which could not be granted adequate review on appeal.

SOVEREIGN IMMUNITY Immunity of government from suit without its consent.

◼▬◼

Carson v. American Brands, Inc.

Class of employees (P) v. Employer (D)

450 U.S. 79 (1981).

NATURE OF CASE: Appeal from denial of a motion to enter a consent decree.

FACT SUMMARY: Carson (P) and American Brands (D) made a joint motion for entrance of a consent decree containing injunctive relief and sought to appeal the district court's denial thereof.

🏛 RULE OF LAW
An interlocutory order denying joint motion of the parties to enter a consent decree containing injunctive relief is immediately appealable under 28 U.S.C. § 1292(a)(1) as an interlocutory order "refusing" an injunction.

FACTS: Carson (P) brought a class-action suit under Title VII, alleging job-related discrimination against black employees and applicants. Without conceding any violation, American Brands (D) joined Carson (P) in moving to have a consent decree entered incorporating a negotiated settlement that would have required hiring and seniority preferences for blacks, and further requiring that one-third of all supervisory positions be filled by qualified blacks. Concluding that such a decree would be illegal because it would extend relief to others than those actual victims of past discrimination and accord preferential treatment on the basis of race without the requisite showing of past or present discrimination, the district court denied the joint motion. The court of appeals dismissed an appeal therefrom, holding that the refusal to enter the consent decree was neither a "collateral order" under 28 U.S.C. § 1291, nor an interlocutory order "refusing" an injunction under 28 U.S.C. § 1292(a)(1).

ISSUE: Is an interlocutory order denying a joint motion of the parties to enter a consent decree containing injunctive relief immediately appealable?

HOLDING AND DECISION: (Brennan, J.) Yes. An interlocutory order denying a joint motion of the parties to enter a consent decree containing injunctive relief is immediately appealable under 28 U.S.C. § 1292(a)(1) as an interlocutory order "refusing" an injunction because it has the practical effect of refusing an injunction even if it does not do so by its terms. However, even where, as here, the practical effect is shown, for it to be immediately appealable under § 1292(a)(1), it must be shown that the order might have "serious, perhaps irreparable, consequence" and can be "effectually challenged" only by immediate appeal. Refusal to issue this consent decree might irretrievably deprive Carson (P) of the opportunity to compromise the class claim and obtain the injunctive

benefits of the settlement agreement. Thus, the requisite showing was made, and the decree is appealable. Reversed.

▶ ANALYSIS

In this decision, the Court recognized that settlement agreements are usually predicated on an express or implied condition that the parties would, by their agreement, be able to avoid the costs and uncertainties of litigation. Once the court refuses to adopt the agreement and litigation proceeds, that motivation for agreeing to negotiated relief, is forever destroyed.

Quicknotes

CONSENT DECREE A decree issued by a court of equity ratifying an agreement between the parties to a lawsuit; an agreement by a defendant to cease illegal activity.

Nystrom v. TREX, Inc.

Patent holder (P) v. Alleged patent infringer (D)

339 F.3d 1347 (Fed. Cir. 2003).

NATURE OF CASE: Appeal from judgment of invalidity and non-infringement of patent claims and order denying sanctions.

FACT SUMMARY: Nystrom (P) contended that notwithstanding that some of TREX's (D) counterclaims were pending, the court of appeals had jurisdiction to hear his appeal from various district court decisions in his patent infringement action.

🏛 RULE OF LAW
In a patent dispute, where a district court has ruled on non-infringement and the validity and enforceability of some patent claims, but has stayed counterclaims as to the validity and enforceability of other patent claims, the district court's decisions do not constitute a final judgment within the meaning of 28 U.S.C. § 1295(a)(1) that confers jurisdiction on a court of appeals to hear an appeal from the district court's decisions.

FACTS: Nystrom (P) brought an action against TREX (D) alleging patent infringement of his '831 patent. TREX (D) filed a counterclaim seeking a declaratory judgment of non-infringement, invalidity and unenforceability, as well as antitrust violations. Eventually, TREX (D) dropped its antitrust claims, but Nystrom (P) moved for sanctions, claiming that TREX (D) had multiplied the proceedings "unreasonably and vexatiously" by having brought the antitrust claims. The district court held a claim construction hearing and granted TREX's (D) motion for summary judgment as to the invalidity of some (claims 18-20), but not all, claims (1-17), and denied Nystrom's (P) motion for sanctions. It also entered judgment of non-infringement on all claims. The district court stayed the remainder of TREX's (D) counterclaim as to claims 1-17. Nystrom (P) appealed from the district court's rulings, but the court of appeal determined that due to the pendency of the counterclaims, the judgment appealed was not final within the meaning of 28 U.S.C. § 1295(a)(1), and that it lacked jurisdiction to hear the appeal—even though the parties stated that they considered the district court's actions to have finally disposed of the case for purposes of appeal. The court of appeals ruled that the case was dismissed and adjourned the proceeding without entertaining argument on the merits. The court of appeals then explained its decision.

ISSUE: In a patent dispute, where a district court has ruled on non-infringement and the validity and enforceability of some patent claims, but has stayed counterclaims as to the validity and enforceability of other patent claims,

do the district court's decisions constitute a final judgment within the meaning of 28 U.S.C. § 1295(a)(1) that confers jurisdiction on a court of appeals to hear an appeal from the district court's decisions?

HOLDING AND DECISION: (Linn, J.) No. In a patent dispute, where a district court has ruled on non-infringement and the validity and enforceability of some patent claims, but has stayed counterclaims as to the validity and enforceability of other patent claims, the district court's decisions do not constitute a final judgment within the meaning of 28 U.S.C. § 1295(a)(1) that confers jurisdiction on a court of appeals to hear an appeal from the district court's decisions. Even though the parties have not raised any objection to the court of appeals' jurisdiction, the court is obligated to satisfy itself of its own jurisdiction. The final judgment rule that the court must follow in patent disputes is set forth in 28 U.S.C. § 1295(a)(1). Under that rule, parties may appeal only a final decision of a district court. If a case is not fully adjudicated as to all claims for all parties and there is no express determination that there is no just reason for delay or express direction for entry of judgment as to fewer than all of the parties or claims, there is no "final decision" and therefore no jurisdiction. This avoids piecemeal disposition on appeals of what is essentially a single controversy. There is no exception to the final judgment rule for patent disputes, and piecemeal litigation is as strictly precluded by the rule of finality for patent cases as it is for any other case. The parties identified—and the district court could have taken—several avenues that would have provided appeal as a matter of right. The district court chose none of these approaches. Instead, the district court kept the invalidity and unenforceability counterclaim as to claims 1-17 in the case pending appeal, expressly reserving the counterclaim as a stayed claim. Stay orders generally are not final for purposes of 28 U.S.C. § 1295. Moreover, a judgment that does not dispose of pending counterclaims is not a final judgment. Without finality at the district court, the court of appeals may not entertain the present appeal. Accordingly, the appeal is dismissed for lack of jurisdiction. Dismissed.

▶ *ANALYSIS*

The avenues the district court could have taken that would have permitted an appeal included: (1) entering a judgment on the decided issues under Fed. R. Civ. P. 54(b); (2) dismissing TREX's (D) counterclaim without prejudice; (3) certifying an interlocutory order under 28 U.S.C. § 1292(c);

Continued on next page.

or (4) proceeding to trial on the counterclaim remaining after a ruling on the fully briefed motion for partial summary judgment of invalidity of claims 18-20, or otherwise disposing of the issue on the merits.

■══■

Quicknotes

FINAL JUDGMENT A decision by the court settling a dispute between the parties on its merits and which is appealable to a higher court.

JURISDICTION The authority of a court to hear and declare judgment in respect to a particular matter.

■══■

Will v. United States

Judge (D) v. Federal government (P)

389 U.S. 90 (1967).

NATURE OF CASE: On writ of certiorari in a criminal tax evasion case.

FACT SUMMARY: The Government (P) requested a writ of mandamus ordering District Judge Will (D) to vacate his order that the Government (P) furnish information to a defendant in an income tax evasion case.

🏛 RULE OF LAW
Appellate review, except in certain narrowly defined circumstances, should be postponed until after final judgment has been rendered by the court, and, therefore, a higher court should not grant appellate review by the extraordinary remedy of mandamus against a lower court where there is nothing in the record to demonstrate that the case is a really extraordinary one amounting to a judicial usurpation of power.

FACTS: In a motion for a bill of particulars, the defendant in a criminal tax evasion case in the U.S. District Court for the Northern District of Illinois requested certain information concerning oral statements by him which were being relied upon by the Government (P). The requested information included the names and addresses of the persons to whom the statements were made as well as the times and places at which they were made. Judge Will (D), the district judge, ordered the Government (P) to furnish this information, but it refused to comply with the order. Judge Will (D) then indicated his intention to dismiss the indictment because of the Government's (P) refusal to comply with his order. The circuit court of appeals then granted the Government's (P) application for a stay of proceedings and subsequently issued a writ of mandamus directing Judge Will (D) to vacate his order requiring the Government (P) to furnish the requested information.

ISSUE: When there is nothing in the record to demonstrate that a case is truly extraordinary, should the court grant appellate review by the extraordinary means of a writ of mandamus against a lower court?

HOLDING AND DECISION: (Warren, C.J.) No. The peremptory writ of mandamus has traditionally been used in the federal courts only "to confine an inferior court to the lawful exercise of its authority when it is its duty to do so." It is basic that appellate review, except in certain narrowly defined circumstances, should be postponed until after final judgment has been rendered by the court, and, therefore, a higher court should not grant appellate review by the extraordinary writ of mandamus against a lower court where there is nothing in the record to demonstrate that the case is really an extraordinary one amounting to

judicial usurpation of power. Examples of writs granted in the past to curtail abuses are where unwarranted judicial action threatened to embarrass the execution aim of the government in conducting foreign relations and where a judicial judge displayed a persistent disregard for the Rules of Civil Procedure promulgated by this Court. The general policy against piecemeal appeals takes on added weight in criminal charges where the defendant is entitled to a speedy resolution of the charges against him. While the writ of mandamus may—in some circumstances—be used to review procedural orders in criminal cases, this Court has never approved its use to review an interlocutory procedural order in a criminal case which did not have the effect of dismissal. The Constitution not only grants a man the right to a speedy trial but also forbids that he be placed twice in jeopardy for the same offense. There is nothing in the record to reflect that Judge Will (D)—as the Government (P) suggested—adopted a policy of deliberate disregard for the criminal discovery rules or that his policies were disruptive of justice. The case does not, therefore, fall into the category of one demanding this extraordinary writ. Hence, the writ is vacated, and the cause is remanded to the court of appeals for further proceedings not inconsistent with this opinion.

▶ ANALYSIS

There persists in our judicial system an antipathy to governmental right of review in criminal cases, and appeal by the government is unusual and not favored. Piecemeal appeals are generally not permitted, and those statutory exceptions are addressed either in terms or by necessity solely to civil actions. The extraordinary writ has never been approved or used by the court to control a procedural order in a criminal case, within the district court's jurisdiction, which did not deprive the prosecution of its right to trial permitted by law or to the results of a proper conviction. The authority to issue the writ has been sparingly used to confine an inferior court to a lawful exercise of its prescribed jurisdiction or to compel it to exercise its authority where it is its duty to do so.

■═■

Quicknotes

WRIT OF MANDAMUS A court order issued commanding a public or private entity, or an official thereof, to perform a duty required by law.

■═■

Bose Corporation v. Consumers Union of United States, Inc.

Audio equipment company (P) v. Publisher (D)

466 U.S. 485 (1984).

NATURE OF CASE: Review of reversal of determination of liability in defamation action.

FACT SUMMARY: A court of appeals performed a de novo review of a district court's finding of reckless disregard of truth in a defamation action.

RULE OF LAW

In a defamation action regarding a public figure, an appellate court must perform a de novo review of a district court's finding of reckless disregard of truth.

FACTS: Bose Corporation (Bose) (P) sued Consumers Union of United States, Inc. (Consumers) (D), publisher of "Consumer Reports," for product disparagement. The district court found Bose (P) to be a public figure, thus implicating the First Amendment. The district court found Consumers Union (D) to have published with a reckless disregard of truth, a sufficient finding to establish liability. The court of appeals, performing a de novo review of the facts, reversed. Bose (P) petitioned for review, contending that the proper scope of review was a "clearly erroneous" standard.

ISSUE: In a defamation action regarding a public figure, must an appellate court perform a de novo review of a district court's finding of reckless disregard of truth?

HOLDING AND DECISION: (Stevens, J.) Yes. In a defamation action regarding a public figure, an appellate court must perform a de novo review of a district court's finding of reckless disregard of truth. Generally speaking, under Fed. R. Civ. P. 52(a), a reviewing court must give special deference to the factual findings of a trial court and upset the factual findings only when they are clearly erroneous. However, this Court has established that in actions implicating the First Amendment, appellate courts must exercise a de novo review of the entire record and satisfy themselves that the factual determinations regarding the crucial issues were in fact within constitutional restrictions. Rule 52(a)'s deferential standard will not be applied in defamation actions implicating the First Amendment. This being so, the court of appeals' standard of review here was proper. Affirmed.

DISSENT: (Rehnquist, J.) Appellate courts are ill-equipped to make the sort of mens rea determinations concerning malice that are at issue in defamation actions implicating the First Amendment.

ANALYSIS

The provisions of Fed. R. Civ. P. 52(a) discussed here are in Rule 52(a)(6), with slight revision, per the 2007 amendments to the Rules. "Clearly erroneous" is one of the more deferential standards of review used by appellate courts. Under it, an appellate court may not reverse a trial court merely because it would have reached a contrary result. Rather, it must be clearly convinced that an incorrect result was reached.

Quicknotes

DEFAMATION An intentional false publication, communicated publicly in either oral or written form, subjecting a person to scorn, hatred or ridicule, or injuring him or her in relation to his or her occupation or business.

FIRST AMENDMENT Prohibits Congress from enacting any law respecting an establishment of religion, prohibiting the free exercise of religion, abridging freedom of speech or the press, the right of peaceful assembly and the right to petition for a redress of grievances.

MALICE The intention to commit an unlawful act without justification or excuse.

MENS REA Criminal intent.

PUBLIC FIGURE/OFFICER Any person who is generally known in the community.

RECKLESSNESS The conscious disregard of substantial and justifiable risk.

Preclusive Effects of Judgments

Quick Reference Rules of Law

CHAPTER 13

Manego v. Orleans Board of Trade

Disco owner (P) v. Regulatory board (D)

773 F.2d 1 (1st Cir. 1985).

NATURE OF CASE: Appeal of summary judgment dismissing an antitrust action.

FACT SUMMARY: After losing an action for civil rights violations, Manego (P) filed an antitrust action based on essentially the same facts.

🏛 RULE OF LAW
One may not bring an action subsequent to final judgment in another action which, although based on a different cause of action, involved essentially the same facts.

FACTS: Manego (P) sought and was denied permission to open a disco in the town of Orleans. The denial was based largely upon concerns that such a facility would negatively impact a nearby skating rink used by children and adolescents. Manego (P) sued various individuals and entities involved in the denial. Summary judgment was granted dismissing the action. Subsequent to this, Manego (P) filed an action based on the Sherman Antitrust Act, contending that a conspiracy to prevent him from competing with the rink, which had recently begun catering to adults, existed. The district court, holding the matter was res judicata due to the prior suit, dismissed. Manego (P) appealed.

ISSUE: May one bring an action subsequent to final judgment in another action which, although based on a different cause of action, involved essentially the same facts?

HOLDING AND DECISION: (Bownes, J.) No. One may not bring an action subsequent to final judgment in another action which, although based on a different cause of action, involved essentially the same facts. Under the doctrine of res judicata, a final judgment on the merits of an action precludes the parties or their privies from relitigating issues which were or could have been raised in that action. The standard is transactional. If the second action is based on the same transaction as the first, preclusion will exist. Here, while the causes of action are different, the underlying transaction is the same. Further, it is true that the defendants are not identical. This is of no moment; Manego (P) could have sued these defendants in the prior action, as the antitrust action could have been brought at this time. This being so, the summary judgment was proper. Affirmed.

▶ ANALYSIS

The standard used by the court here was borrowed from the Restatement (Second) of Judgments, which holds that subsequent claims, rights, or remedies which arise out of the same transaction as a prior action are precluded. The Restatement does not give a bright line definition of "transaction" but rather holds that a court should pragmatically weigh factors such as time, space, origin, and motivation.

■━■

Quicknotes

CAUSE OF ACTION A fact or set of facts the occurrence of which entitles a party to seek judicial relief.

FINAL JUDGMENT A decision by the court settling a dispute between the parties on its merits and which is appealable to a higher court.

RES JUDICATA The rule of law that a final judgment by a court precludes subsequent litigation between the parties regarding the same cause of action.

■━■

Federated Department Stores, Inc. v. Moitie

Department store (D) v. Government (P)

452 U.S. 394 (1981).

NATURE OF CASE: Appeal from reversal of dismissal of antitrust action.

FACT SUMMARY: Federated Department Stores, Inc. (D) contended that the doctrine of res judicata barred relitigation of an unappealed adverse judgment where other plaintiffs in similar actions had successfully appealed judgments against them.

> 🏛 **RULE OF LAW**
> Res judicata bars relitigation of an unappealed adverse judgment where other plaintiffs in similar actions against common defendants successfully appealed the judgments against them.

FACTS: The Government (P) brought an antitrust action against Federated Department Stores, Inc. (Federated) (D), alleging that it had violated § 1 of the Sherman Act by agreeing to fix the retail price of women's clothing sold in Northern California. Seven parallel civil actions were subsequently filed by private plaintiffs seeking treble damages on behalf of proposed classes of retail purchasers, including that of Moitie (P) (*Moitie I*) in state court and Brown (P) (*Brown I*) in federal district court. Each of these complaints tracked almost verbatim the allegations of the Government's (P) complaint, although the *Moitie I* complaint referred solely to state law. All of the actions, including *Moitie I*, which was removed to federal court, were assigned to a single federal judge, who dismissed all of the actions because of pleading defects. The plaintiffs in five of the suits appealed that judgment to the federal court of appeals, while the single counsel representing Moitie (P) and Brown (P) chose not to appeal and instead refiled the two actions in state court, *Moitie II* and *Brown II*. Federated (D) removed the new actions to federal district court, where they were dismissed on the grounds of res judicata. However, the court of appeals reversed and Federated (D) appealed.

ISSUE: Does res judicata bar relitigation of an unappealed adverse judgment where other plaintiffs in similar actions against common defendants successfully appealed the judgments against them?

HOLDING AND DECISION: (Rehnquist, J.) Yes. Res judicata bars relitigation of an unappealed adverse judgment where other plaintiffs in similar actions against common defendants successfully appealed the judgments against them. A final judgment on the merits of an action precludes the parties or their privies from relitigating issues that were, or could have been, raised in that action. A judgment merely voidable because it is based upon an

erroneous view of the law is not open to collateral attack but can be corrected only by a direct review and not by bringing another action upon the same cause of action. Here, both *Brown I* and *Moitie I* were final judgments on the merits and involved the same claims and the same parties as *Brown II* and *Moitie II*. Both those parties seek to be the windfall beneficiaries on an appellate reversal procured by other independent parties, and it is further apparent that Brown (P) and Moitie (P) made a calculated choice to forgo their appeals. Reversed and remanded.

CONCURRENCE: (Blackmun, J.) *Brown I* is res judicata on Brown's (P) state law claims. Even if the state and federal claims are distinct, Brown's (P) failure to allege the state claims in *Brown I* manifestly bars their allegation in *Brown II*.

DISSENT: (Brennan, J.) The Court today disregards statutory restrictions on federal court jurisdiction and, in the process, confuses rather than clarifies long-established principles of res judicata.

▶ **ANALYSIS**

The Court, in a footnote, agreed with the court of appeals that at least some of the claims had a sufficient federal character, such as would support removal to the federal court. Both the district court and the court of appeals had found that Brown (P) and Moitie (P) had attempted to avoid removal jurisdiction by artfully casting their essentially federal law claims as state-law claims.

━━━

Quicknotes

FINAL JUDGMENT A decision by the court settling a dispute between the parties on its merits and which is appealable to a higher court.

JUDGMENT ON THE MERITS A determination of the rights of the parties to litigation based on the presentation evidence, barring the party from initiating the same suit again.

REMOVAL Petition by a defendant to move the case to another court.

RES JUDICATA The rule of law that a final judgment by a court precludes subsequent litigation between the parties regarding the same cause of action.

━━━

Rinehart v. Locke

Arrestee (P) v. Officer (D)

454 F.2d 313 (7th Cir. 1971).

NATURE OF CASE: Appeal from dismissal of an action for false arrest based on res judicata.

FACT SUMMARY: Rinehart's (P) action for false arrest was dismissed for failure to allege lack of probable cause. No leave to amend was granted.

🏛 RULE OF LAW
The dismissal of a complaint for failure to state a claim, which does not specify whether it is with prejudice, is res judicata on a subsequent claim alleging the same facts.

FACTS: Rinehart (P) brought suit for an alleged false arrest. The action was dismissed for failure to state a claim since lack of probable cause was not alleged. No leave to amend was granted. Rinehart (P) did not appeal. Instead, a year later, he instituted a new suit based on the same cause of action but this time alleging lack of probable cause. Locke (D) moved to dismiss based on res judicata. The district court dismissed on this basis. Rinehart (P) appealed on the basis that a dismissal for failure to state a claim was not a judgment on the merits and that a dismissal, unless with prejudice, should not bar his claim.

ISSUE: Is a dismissal for failure to state a claim res judicata on a subsequent claim based on the same cause of action?

HOLDING AND DECISION: (Fairchild, J.) Yes. Rule 41(b) states that except for specific listed exceptions, all dismissals are on the merits. Under this rule, a dismissal of a complaint for failure to state a claim is a judgment on the merits and bars a subsequent claim. A plaintiff's only remedy is to request that the dismissal be made "without prejudice" or "with leave to amend." If this is refused, a plaintiff's only remedy is to appeal the decision. Since Rinehart (P) failed to do so the dismissal (even though it was not stated to be "without prejudice") bars his subsequent claim. The decision of the district court is affirmed.

▶ ANALYSIS

It is discretionary with the trial court whether a case may be dismissed "with prejudice" where there is a failure to prosecute or to obey a court order. The reviewing court is somewhat hesitant to allow such a dismissal based upon an attorney's dereliction of duty. It will look for less drastic sanctions. *Industrial Bldg. Materials, Inc. v. Interchemical Corp.*, 437 F.2d 1336 (9th Cir. 1970).

Quicknotes

JUDGMENT ON THE MERITS A determination of the rights of the parties to litigation based on the presentation evidence, barring the party from initiating the same suit again.

MOTION TO DISMISS Motion to terminate a trial based on the adequacy of the pleadings.

PROBABLE CAUSE A reasonable basis for believing that a crime has been committed.

Marrese v. American Academy of Orthopaedic Surgeons

Prospective member (P) v. Professional organization (D)

470 U.S. 373 (1985).

NATURE OF CASE: Appeal of dismissal of federal antitrust action.

FACT SUMMARY: A court of appeals gave preclusive effect to an antitrust action, holding that an earlier state action arising out of the same set of circumstances was res judicata.

> ## 🏛 RULE OF LAW
> A state court judgment's preclusive effect on a federal antitrust claim shall be governed by the law of the state in which the initial judgment was rendered.

FACTS: Marrese (P), denied membership in the American Academy of Orthopaedic Surgeons (Academy) (D), filed an Illinois state court action, alleging various violations of his common law rights. The action was dismissed. Marrese (P) then filed a federal antitrust action. The Academy (D) moved to dismiss on the grounds that the state action constituted res judicata. The district court denied the motion. The Seventh Circuit reversed, holding that as a matter of law the case was res judicata. Marrese (P) appealed.

ISSUE: Shall a state court judgment's preclusive effect on a federal antitrust claim be governed by the law of the state in which the initial judgment was rendered?

HOLDING AND DECISION: (O'Connor, J.) Yes. A state court judgment's preclusive effect on a federal antitrust claim shall be governed by the law of the state in which the judgment was rendered. The preclusive effect of such judgments is generally governed by the full faith and credit statute, 28 U.S.C. § 1738. The statute requires a federal court to look to the law of the state in which a judgment was rendered to determine the preclusive effect of the judgment. Comity and respect for state laws require this. The fact that the antitrust action could not have been brought in state court does not change this analysis. Unless an exception to § 1738 is found in the law upon which federal jurisdiction is predicated, § 1738 rules. Here, on remand, the district court is to apply the Illinois law regarding preclusion to the state action. Reversed.

CONCURRENCE: (Burger, C.J.) Where, as a review of Illinois law in this instance shows to be a possibility, the state law regarding preclusion is unclear, it may be appropriate to formulate a federal rule.

▶ ANALYSIS

The Court largely relied on a prior case, *Kremer v. Chemical Construction Corp.*, 456 U.S. 461 (1982). The particular case enunciated the same rule but only as applied to issue preclusion. The Court extended it here to claim preclusion as well.

■══■

Quicknotes

COMITY A rule pursuant to which courts in one state give deference to the statutes and judicial decisions of another.

FULL FAITH AND CREDIT Doctrine that a judgment by a court of one state shall be given the same effect in another state.

ISSUE PRECLUSION When a particular issue has already been litigated, further litigation of the same issue is barred.

RES JUDICATA The rule of law that a final judgment by a court precludes subsequent litigation between the parties regarding the same cause of action.

■══■

Semtek International, Inc. v. Lockheed Martin Corp.

Injured (P) v. Alleged tortfeasor (D)

531 U.S. 497 (2001).

NATURE OF CASE: Review of dismissal of state action on res judicata grounds.

FACT SUMMARY: When Semtek International, Inc.'s (Semtek) (P) breach of contract and tort claims were barred by California's two-year statute of limitations, Semtek (P) filed the same charges in Maryland, which had a three-year statute of limitations.

🏛 RULE OF LAW
Federal common law governs the claim-preclusive effect of a dismissal by a federal court sitting in diversity.

FACTS: Semtek International, Inc. (P) sued Lockheed Martin Corp. (D) in California state court for breach of contract and tort. After removal to federal court in California, the action was dismissed because it was barred by the two-year statute of limitations. Semtek (P) filed the same claims in Maryland, which had a three-year statute of limitations. The Maryland court dismissed on res judicata grounds and Semtek (P) appealed. The Maryland Court of Special Appeals affirmed, and the U.S. Supreme Court granted certiorari.

ISSUE: Does federal common law govern the claim-preclusive effect of a dismissal by a federal court sitting in diversity?

HOLDING AND DECISION: (Scalia, J.) Yes. Federal common law governs the claim-preclusive effect of a dismissal by a federal court sitting in diversity. Since state, rather than federal law, is at issue here, there is no need for a uniform federal rule. The same claim-preclusive rule should apply, whether the dismissal was ordered by a federal or a state court. Here, there was no conflict between state law and federal interests. Reversed and remanded.

▌ *ANALYSIS*

The dismissal in this case simply barred refiling the same case in the same court. It did not bar refiling in other courts. This holding is in keeping with *Erie Railroad Co. v. Tompkins*, 304 U.S. 64 (1938).

■■■■

Quicknotes

CERTIORARI A discretionary writ issued by a superior court to an inferior court in order to review the lower court's decisions; the Supreme Court's writ ordering such review.

REMOVAL Petition by a defendant to move the case to another court.

RES JUDICATA The rule of law that a final judgment by a court precludes subsequent litigation between the parties regarding the same cause of action.

STATUTE OF LIMITATIONS A law prescribing the period in which a legal action may be commenced.

■■■■

Little v. Blue Goose Motor Coach Co.

Decedent driver (P) v. Bus operator (D)

Ill. Sup. Ct., 346 Ill. 266, 178 N.E. 496 (1931).

NATURE OF CASE: Appeal in an action for damages in tort for personal injuries and wrongful death.

FACT SUMMARY: A judgment was rendered for Blue Goose Motor Coach Co. (Blue Goose) (D) against Little (P) for negligence which became final. Little (P), and later his executrix (P), then sued Blue Goose (D) for personal injuries and wrongful death based on the same transaction.

RULE OF LAW

A previous justice court judgment constitutes estoppel by verdict to a subsequent action, involving the same parties, issues, and transaction.

FACTS: A judgment in favor of Blue Goose Motor Coach Co. (D) was rendered against Little (P) in a justice court for negligently operating his vehicle. Because of a lack of prosecution, Little's (P) appeal from the judgment was dismissed, but, during the pendency of that suit, he commenced an action for personal injury against Blue Goose (D). Little (P) died, and his executrix (P) initiated a wrongful death action against Blue Goose (D) for negligence and willful and wanton negligence. A judgment for executrix (P) was reversed on appeal. The executrix (P) appealed.

ISSUE: Does a previous justice court judgment constitute an estoppel by verdict to a subsequent action involving the same parties, issues, and transaction?

HOLDING AND DECISION: (Per curiam) Yes. Where a former adjudication is a bar to a subsequent action, there must have been an identity of the parties and subject matter. Here, the issue of fact upon which both Little's (P) and his executrix's (P) case was based was the negligence of Little (P) as determined by the justice court. When the justice court judgment became final, it bound both parties. The fact that the executrix (P) charged Blue Goose (D) with willful and wanton negligence does not overcome the finding in the justice court that Little (P) was negligent. Affirmed.

▶ *ANALYSIS*

Estoppel by verdict may be interposed as a defense whenever there is an identity between parties, subject matter, and transaction in a previous lawsuit where judgment was allowed to become final. The policy behind this is to protect the finality of prior judgments and to put an end to litigation.

Quicknotes

FINAL JUDGMENT A decision by the court settling a dispute between the parties on its merits and which is appealable to a higher court.

NEGLIGENCE Conduct falling below the standard of care that a reasonable person would demonstrate under similar conditions.

WRONGFUL DEATH An action brought by the beneficiaries of a deceased person, claiming that the deceased's death was the result of wrongful conduct by the defendant.

Hardy v. Johns-Manville Sales Corporation

Exposed workers (P) v. Asbestos manufacturer (D)

681 F.2d 334 (5th Cir. 1982).

NATURE OF CASE: Appeal of collateral estoppel order in action for damages for personal injury.

FACT SUMMARY: A trial court entered a collateral estoppel order regarding a failure-to-warn basis for products liability, although the jury in the prior action could have based its finding on one of several theories.

> ## 🏛 RULE OF LAW
> Collateral estoppel may not be applied when the fact finder based its decision on one of several possible bases.

FACTS: A class of plaintiffs sued various defendants for personal injury related to asbestos exposure. One theory of recovery was products liability based on a failure to warn. The plaintiffs moved for a collateral estoppel order based on a jury finding in a prior case that the same defendants had failed to warn of the danger of asbestos. However, it was unclear from the record of the prior case as to when the jury believed the duty to warn came into being. In the present action, warnings were placed by Johns-Manville Sales Corporation (D) at various times from 1964 through 1969. The district court entered summary adjudication as to the failure-to-warn theory, and Johns-Manville (D) appealed.

ISSUE: May collateral estoppel, be applied when the fact finder based its decision on one of several possible bases?

HOLDING AND DECISION: (Gee, J.) No. Collateral estoppel may not be applied when the fact finder based its decision on one of several possible bases. Collateral estoppel may be applied only when there is an identity of issues. When the prior judgment is ambivalent, the doctrine is not to be utilized. Here, the jury in the prior action could have found that the duty to warn arose any time between 1963 and 1969. When it held the duty to have arisen is unclear from the record. Here, some defendants began issuing warnings as early as 1964. Therefore, it is possible that they fulfilled any duty to warn they may have had. This being so, collateral estoppel was incorrectly applied. Reversed.

▌ANALYSIS

Most actions involve general verdicts without specific findings by juries. It is difficult to find an identity of issues in such situations. Collateral estoppel is usually more readily available when the prior case contained special interrogatories.

Quicknotes

COLLATERAL ESTOPPEL A doctrine whereby issues litigated and determined in a prior proceeding are binding upon all subsequent litigation between the parties regarding that issue.

DUTY TO WARN An obligation owed by an owner or occupier of land to persons who come onto the premises, to inform them of defects or active operations which may cause injury.

INTERROGATORY A method of pretrial discovery in which written questions are provided by one party to another who must respond in writing under oath.

PRODUCT LIABILITY The legal liability of manufacturers and sellers for damages and injuries suffered by buyers, users, and even bystanders because of defects in goods purchased.

■=■

Commissioner of Internal Revenue v. Sunnen

Regulatory agency (P) v. Patentee (D)

333 U.S. 591 (1948).

NATURE OF CASE: Action in tax court challenging deficiency assessment made by the IRS.

FACT SUMMARY: Sunnen (D), having won a favorable determination in a prior year, sought to invoke the decision as res judicata to bar later challenges for other years where there was a complete identity of facts, issues, and parties.

🏛 RULE OF LAW
Where two cases involve taxes in different taxable years, collateral estoppel will be confined to situations where the matter raised in the second suit is identical in all respects with that decided in the first proceeding and where the controlling facts and applicable legal rules remain unchanged.

FACTS: In 1928, Sunnen (D) had licensed his corporation to use his patents in exchange for a royalty. In various years following, Sunnen (D) assigned his interest in these agreements to his wife who reported this income on her income tax returns. In 1935, Sunnen (D) prevailed in a tax court proceeding brought by the Commissioner of Internal Revenue (P), who had contended that the income was taxable to Sunnen (D) himself. Later, the exact same action was brought by the Commissioner (P) against Sunnen (D) on the same issue, except this time for royalties paid in 1937.

ISSUE: Where two cases involve taxes in different taxable years, will collateral estoppel be confined to situations where the matter raised in the second suit is identical in all respects with that decided in the first proceeding and where the controlling facts and applicable legal rules remain unchanged?

HOLDING AND DECISION: (Murphy, J.) Yes. Collateral estoppel does apply in the income tax field but only insofar as it extends to any subsequent proceeding involving the same claim and the same tax year. Where a taxpayer secures a judicial determination of a particular tax matter which may recur without substantial variation for some years thereafter, a subsequent modification of the significant facts after a change or development in the controlling legal principles may make that determination obsolete, or erroneous, at least for future years. Permitting a taxpayer to invoke his decision in a single year for a number of years is unfair to other taxpayers causing inequalities in the administration of taxes, discriminatory distinctions in tax liability, and a fertile basis for litigious confusion. Tax inequality can result as readily from neglecting legal modulations by the Supreme Court as from disregarding factual changes wrought by state courts.

This reasoning is particularly apposite here since, if Sunnen (D) had not had the benefit of the earlier decision, his claim, in view of recent legal developments in the tax field, would have failed if brought now for the first time. Collateral estoppel should not have been used by the Tax Court in the instant proceeding to perpetuate the 1935 viewpoint of the assignment.

▶ ANALYSIS

The Court's opinion here may be difficult to reconcile with its earlier decision in *Tait v. Western Maryland Ry.*, 289 U.S. 620, 624 (1933), where it was said: "The scheme of the Revenue Acts is an imposition of tax for annual periods, and the exaction for one year is distinct from that for any other. But it does not follow that Congress, in adopting this system, meant to deprive the government and the taxpayer of relief from redundant litigation of the identical question of the statute's application to the taxpayer's status . . . Alteration of the law in this respect is a matter for the lawmaking body rather than the courts . . . It cannot be supposed that Congress was oblivious of the scope of the doctrine (of res judicata), and in the absence of a clear declaration of such purpose, we will not infer from the annual nature of the exaction an intention to abolish the rule in this class of cases."

■━■

Quicknotes

COLLATERAL ESTOPPEL A doctrine whereby issues litigated and determined in a prior proceeding are binding upon all subsequent litigation between the parties regarding that issue.

FINAL JUDGMENT A decision by the court settling a dispute between the parties on its merits and which is appealable to a higher court.

ISSUE PRECLUSION When a particular issue has already been litigated, further litigation of the same issue is barred.

RES JUDICATA The rule of law that a final judgment by a court precludes subsequent litigation between the parties regarding the same cause of action.

■━■

Halpern v. Schwartz

Borrower (P) v. Bankruptcy trustee (D)

426 F.2d 102 (2d Cir. 1970).

NATURE OF CASE: Appeal of order denying bankruptcy discharge.

FACT SUMMARY: A bankruptcy referee denied Halpern (P) a discharge in bankruptcy based on intent to defraud having been found earlier in the bankruptcy, although such intent was involved in only one of three possible bases for the prior decision.

RULE OF LAW
When a prior judgment adjudicating one a bankrupt rests on two or more alternative grounds, it is not conclusive to discharge issues if less than all grounds in the bankruptcy adjudication involved such issues.

FACTS: Several creditors petitioned to put Halpern (P) into involuntary bankruptcy, alleging three different bases therefor. Only one of these involved an element of intent. The bankruptcy referee held all three bases fulfilled and held Halpern (P) bankrupt. Subsequently, Halpern (P) petitioned for discharge. Schwartz (D), the bankruptcy trustee, opposed this, contending that Halpern (P) had effected certain property transfers with the intent of defrauding creditors, a ground for denying discharge under 11 U.S.C. § 32(c)(4). The bankruptcy court held that the earlier finding of bankruptcy precluded litigation of the intent issue and denied the petition. Halpern (P) appealed.

ISSUE: When a prior judgment adjudicating one a bankrupt rests on two or more alternative grounds, is it conclusive to discharge issues if less than all grounds in the bankruptcy adjudication involved such issues?

HOLDING AND DECISION: (Smith, J.) No. When a prior judgment adjudicating one a bankrupt rests on two or more alternative grounds, it is not conclusive to discharge issues if less than all grounds in the bankruptcy adjudication involved such issues. It is established that, even if an issue was fully litigated in a prior proceeding, preclusive effect will not be given if the resolution of that issue was not necessary for the judgment below. This is based on the notion that if an issue is not necessary for the result in the first action, a party may not be motivated to fully litigate it. To subsequently consider it precluded would therefore work to the litigant's prejudice if it is determinative in the subsequent action. Here, the bankruptcy referee could have held Halpern (P) bankrupt with or without a finding of intent. In the present controversy, such a finding is necessary for Halpern (P) to lose. This

being so, collateral estoppel on the issue of intent would be improper. Reversed.

ANALYSIS

At first glance, it might appear that the rule established in this decision would effectively preclude the application of collateral estoppel whenever a prior decision is based on alternative grounds. This, at least theoretically, is not so. If an issue is a necessary element of each ground, then preclusion would be appropriate.

■=■

Quicknotes

COLLATERAL ESTOPPEL A doctrine whereby issues litigated and determined in a prior proceeding are binding upon all subsequent litigation between the parties regarding that issue.

ISSUE PRECLUSION When a particular issue has already been litigated, further litigation of the same issue is barred.

■=■

Taylor v. Sturgell

FOIA requester (P) v. Federal official (D)

553 U.S. __, 128 S. Ct. 2161 (2008).

NATURE OF CASE: Appeal from affirmance of summary judgment for defendant in action under the Freedom of Information Act (FOIA).

FACT SUMMARY: Taylor (P) contended that his Freedom of Information Act (FOIA) suit seeking records from the Federal Aviation Administration (FAA) (D) should not have been dismissed on grounds of claim preclusion—on the theory of "virtual representation"—merely because his friend and close associate, Herrick, had filed a similar suit seeking the same records.

RULE OF LAW

A claim may not be precluded under a doctrine of "virtual representation" where a second claimant brings a suit identical to a first claimant and, although the claimants know each other, there is no legal relationship between them and there is no evidence that the second claimant controlled, financed, participated in, or even had notice of the earlier suit.

FACTS: Herrick, an antique aircraft enthusiast sought to restore a vintage airplane manufactured by the Fairchild Engine and Airplane Corporation (FEAC). He filed a Freedom of Information Act (FOIA) request asking the Federal Aviation Administration (FAA) (D) for copies of technical documents related to the airplane. The FAA (D) denied his request based on FOIA's exemption for trade secrets. Herrick took an administrative appeal, but when Fairchild Corporation (Fairchild) (D), FEAC's successor, objected to the documents' release, the FAA (D) adhered to its original decision. Herrick then filed a FOIA lawsuit to secure the documents, which was dismissed on summary judgment by the district court and later affirmed by the court of appeals. Less than a month after that suit was resolved, Taylor (P), Herrick's friend and an antique aircraft enthusiast himself, made a FOIA request for the same documents Herrick had unsuccessfully sued to obtain. When the FAA (D) failed to respond, Taylor (P) filed suit in federal district court. Holding the suit barred by claim preclusion, the district court granted summary judgment to the FAA (D) and to Fairchild (D), as intervener in Taylor's (P) action. The court acknowledged that Taylor (P) was not a party to Herrick's suit, but held that a nonparty may be bound by a judgment if she was "virtually represented" by a party. The court of appeals affirmed, announcing a five-factor test for "virtual representation." The first two factors of that test—"identity of interests" and "adequate representation"—are necessary but not sufficient for virtual representation. In addition, at least one of three other factors must be established: "a close relationship between

the present party and his putative representative," "substantial participation by the present party in the first case," or "tactical maneuvering on the part of the present party to avoid preclusion by the prior judgment." The court of appeals acknowledged the absence of any indication that Taylor (P) participated in, or even had notice of, Herrick's suit. It nonetheless found the "identity of interests," "adequate representation," and "close relationship" factors satisfied because the two men sought release of the same documents, were "close associates," had discussed working together to restore Herrick's plane, had used the same lawyer to pursue their suits, and Herrick had given Taylor (P) documents Herrick had obtained from the FAA (D) during discovery in his suit. Because these conditions sufficed to establish virtual representation, the court left open the question whether Taylor (P) had engaged in tactical maneuvering to avoid preclusion. The United States Supreme Court granted certiorari.

ISSUE: May a claim be precluded under a doctrine of "virtual representation" where a second claimant brings a suit identical to a first claimant and, although the claimants know each other, there is no legal relationship between them and there is no evidence that the second claimant controlled, financed, participated in, or even had notice of the earlier suit.

HOLDING AND DECISION: (Ginsburg, J.) No. A claim may not be precluded under a doctrine of "virtual representation" where a second claimant brings a suit identical to a first claimant and, although the claimants know each other, there is no legal relationship between them and there is no evidence that the second claimant controlled, financed, participated in, or even had notice of the earlier suit. The preclusive effect of a federal-court judgment is determined by federal common law, subject to due process limitations. Extending the preclusive effect of a judgment to a nonparty runs up against the "deep-rooted historic tradition that everyone should have his own day in court." Indicating the strength of that tradition, this Court has often repeated the general rule that "one is not bound by a judgment in personam in a litigation in which he is not designated a party or to which he has not been made a party by service of process." The rule against nonparty preclusion is subject to exceptions, currently grouped into six categories. First, "[a] person who agrees to be bound by the determination of issues in an action between others is bound in accordance with the [agreement's] terms," Restatement (Second) of Judgments § 40.

Continued on next page.

[handwritten note: 6 categories of exception to the rule against nonparty preclusion]

Second, nonparty preclusion may be based on a pre-existing substantive legal relationship between the person to be bound and a party to the judgment, e.g., assignee and assignor. Third, "in certain limited circumstances," a nonparty may be bound by a judgment because she was "adequately represented by someone with the same interests who [wa]s a party" to the suit. Fourth, a nonparty is bound by a judgment if he "assume[d] control" over the litigation in which that judgment was rendered. Fifth, a party bound by a judgment may not avoid its preclusive force by relitigating through a proxy. Preclusion is thus in order when a person who did not participate in litigation later brings suit as the designated representative or agent of a person who was a party to the prior adjudication. Sixth, a special statutory scheme otherwise consistent with due process, e.g., bankruptcy proceedings, may "expressly foreclos[e] successive litigation by nonlitigants." Reaching beyond these six categories, the court of appeals recognized a broad "virtual representation" exception to the rule against nonparty preclusion. None of the arguments advanced by that court, the FAA (D), or Fairchild (D) justify such an expansive doctrine. The court of appeals purported to ground its doctrine in this Court's statements that, in some circumstances, a person may be bound by a judgment if she was adequately represented by a party to the proceeding yielding that judgment. But the court of appeals' definition of "adequate representation" strayed from the meaning this Court has attributed to that term. In one case, *Richards v. Jefferson County*, 517 U.S. 793 (1996), the Alabama Supreme Court had held a tax challenge barred by a judgment upholding the same tax in a suit by different taxpayers. This Court reversed, holding that nonparty preclusion was inconsistent with due process where there was no showing (1) that the court in the first suit "took care to protect the interests" of absent parties, or (2) that the parties to the first litigation "understood their suit to be on behalf of absent [parties]." In holding that representation can be "adequate" for purposes of nonparty preclusion even where these two factors are absent, the court of appeals misapplied *Richards*. Fairchild (D) and the FAA (D) ask the Court to abandon altogether the attempt to delineate discrete grounds and clear rules for nonparty preclusion. Instead, they contend, only an equitable and heavily fact-driven inquiry can account for all of the situations in which nonparty preclusion is appropriate. This argument is rejected. First, the balancing test they propose is at odds with the constrained approach advanced by this Court's decisions, which have endeavored to delineate discrete, limited exceptions to the fundamental rule that a litigant is not bound by a judgment to which she was not a party. Second, a party's representation of a nonparty is "adequate" for preclusion purposes only if, at a minimum: (1) the interests of the nonparty and her representative are aligned, and (2) either the party understood herself to be acting in a representative capacity or the original court took care to protect the nonparty's interests. Adequate representation may also require (3) notice of the original

suit to the persons alleged to have been represented. In the class-action context, these limitations are implemented by Fed. R. Civ. P. 23's procedural safeguards. But an expansive virtual representation doctrine would recognize a common-law kind of class action that would lack these protections. Third, a diffuse balancing approach to nonparty preclusion would likely complicate the task of district courts faced in the first instance with preclusion questions. Finally, the FAA (D) maintains that nonparty preclusion should apply more broadly in "public-law" litigation than in "private-law" controversies. First, the FAA (D) points to *Richards*'s acknowledgment that when a taxpayer challenges "an alleged misuse of public funds" or "other public action," the suit "has only an indirect impact on [the plaintiff's] interests," and "the States have wide latitude to establish procedures [limiting] the number of judicial proceedings that may be entertained." In contrast to the public-law litigation contemplated in *Richards*, however, a successful FOIA action results in a grant of relief to the individual plaintiff, not a decree benefiting the public at large. Furthermore, *Richards* said only that, for the type of public-law claims there envisioned, states were free to adopt procedures limiting repetitive litigation. While it appears equally evident that Congress can adopt such procedures, it hardly follows that this Court should proscribe or confine successive FOIA suits by different requesters. Second, the FAA (D) argues that, because the number of plaintiffs in public-law cases is potentially limitless, it is theoretically possible for several persons to coordinate a series of vexatious repetitive lawsuits. But this risk does not justify departing from the usual nonparty preclusion rules. Stare decisis will allow courts to dispose of repetitive suits in the same circuit, and even when stare decisis is not dispositive, the human inclination not to waste money should discourage suits based on claims or issues already decided. The remaining question is whether the result reached by the courts below can be justified based on one of the six established grounds for nonparty preclusion. With one exception, those grounds plainly have no application here. The FAA (D) and Fairchild (D) argue that Taylor's (P) suit is a collusive attempt to relitigate Herrick's claim. That argument justifies a remand to allow the courts below the opportunity to determine whether the fifth ground for nonparty preclusion—preclusion because a nonparty to earlier litigation has brought suit as an agent of a party bound by the prior adjudication—applies to Taylor's (P) suit. However, courts should be cautious about finding preclusion on the basis of agency. A mere whiff of "tactical maneuvering" will not suffice; instead, principles of agency law indicate that preclusion is appropriate only if the putative agent's conduct of the suit is subject to the control of the party who is bound by the prior adjudication. Finally, the Court rejects Fairchild's (D) suggestion that Taylor (P) must bear the burden of proving

Continued on next page.

he is not acting as Herrick's agent. Claim preclusion is an affirmative defense for the defendant to plead and prove. Vacated and remanded.

ANALYSIS

This case presented an issue of first impression in the sense that the Supreme Court had never before addressed the doctrine of "virtual representation" adopted (in varying forms) by several circuits and relied upon by the district court and court of appeals below. For example, the Eighth Circuit had developed a seven-factor test for virtual representation, which was adopted by the district court in this case. The Eighth Circuit test requires an "identity of interests" between the person to be bound and a party to the judgment. Six additional factors counsel in favor of virtual representation under the Eighth Circuit's test, but are not prerequisites: (1) a "close relationship" between the present party and a party to the judgment alleged to be preclusive; (2) "participation in the prior litigation" by the present party; (3) the present party's "apparent acquiescence" to the preclusive effect of the judgment; (4) "deliberat[e] maneuver[ing]" to avoid the effect of the judgment; (5) adequate representation of the present party by a party to the prior adjudication; and (6) a suit raising a "public law" rather than a "private law" issue. These factors, the court of appeals (D.C. Circuit) in this case observed, "constitute a fluid test with imprecise boundaries" and call for "a broad, case-by-case inquiry." The D.C. Circuit adopted a five-factor test. The Supreme Court resolved these different approaches by rejecting the doctrine of virtual representation altogether, instead relying on well-established principles of due process and claim preclusion.

■■■

Quicknotes

CLAIM PRECLUSION A procedural rule or order prohibiting the support or opposition to certain claims or defenses.

DUE PROCESS The constitutional mandate requiring the courts to protect and enforce individuals' rights and liberties consistent with prevailing principles of fairness and justice and prohibiting the federal and state governments from such activities that deprive its citizens of life, liberty, or property interest.

INTERVENOR A party, not an initial party to the action, who is admitted to the action in order to assert an interest in the subject matter of a lawsuit.

PARTY Person designated as either the defendant or plaintiff in a lawsuit.

■■■

Parklane Hosiery Co. v. Shore

Stocking manufacturer (D) v. Shareholders (P)

439 U.S. 322 (1979).

NATURE OF CASE: Review of order reversing denial of summary adjudication of issues in an action based on violation of securities laws.

FACT SUMMARY: Shore (P), representing a shareholder class in a derivative action, sought to use the result of a prior Securities Exchange Commission (SEC) enforcement action to preclude issue litigation regarding liability against Parklane Hosiery Co. (D).

🏛 RULE OF LAW
A nonparty to a prior equitable action may assert collateral estoppel in a subsequent action at law.

FACTS: Shore (P) filed a derivative action against Parklane Hosiery Co. (Parklane) (D), alleging fraud in a proxy statement. Concurrently, the SEC filed an enforcement action, seeking an injunction. The district court held the proxy statement to have been fraudulent and enjoined further such action. Shore (P) moved for summary adjudication, contending that liability had been determined in the SEC action. The district court denied the motion, but the court of appeals reversed. The Supreme Court granted review.

ISSUE: May a nonparty to a prior equitable action assert collateral estoppel in a subsequent action at law?

HOLDING AND DECISION: (Stewart, J.) Yes. A nonparty to a prior equitable action may assert collateral estoppel in a subsequent action at law. The old rule of mutuality for the application of collateral estoppel has been jettisoned. Now, collateral estoppel may be used defensively in most circumstances. Its use in an offensive capacity is suspect, however. The issue may have been minor in the previous action, and it would be unfair to allow the issue to be precluded in another action where the issue is vital. Also, the whole purpose of the preclusion doctrine is to avoid multiple litigations. The offensive use of preclusion may work against this, however, as it would permit a party to wait for the issue to be resolved, and then file its own suit. However, the best solution to this problem is to look at these factors in the context of each case. Whether the prior case was legal or equitable really is of no import. Here, Parklane (D) certainly had ample motivation to fully litigate the issue of fraud in the prior action. Further, it is unlikely that Shore (P) could have been a party to the SEC action. Since no policy reason for not permitting the offensive use of collateral estoppel exists, its use would be appropriate. Affirmed.

DISSENT: (Rehnquist, J.) The application of collateral estoppel in this action violates Parklane's (D) Seventh Amendment right to trial by jury.

▶ ANALYSIS

Mutuality was a requirement for any use of collateral estoppel for many years. The Supreme Court abandoned mutuality as a per se requirement in *Blonder-Tongue Laboratories v. University of Illinois Foundation*, 402 U.S. 313 (1971), which dealt with "defensive" collateral estoppel. As the present case illustrates, "offensive" use is still in a state of flux.

Quicknotes

COLLATERAL ESTOPPEL A doctrine whereby issues litigated and determined in a prior proceeding are binding upon all subsequent litigation between the parties regarding that issue.

Stephenson v. Dow Chemical Co.

Agent Orange victim (P) v. Agent Orange manufacturer (D)

273 F.3d 249 (2d Cir. 2001), *aff'd*, 539 U.S. 111 (2003).

NATURE OF CASE: Appeal from dismissal.

FACT SUMMARY: Isaacson and Stephenson (P) sued chemical manufacturers for damages related to their exposure to Agent Orange in Vietnam. The suits were dismissed because of an earlier class action settlement and judgment concerning the same issue. Plaintiffs appeal, claiming the settlement should not be immune from collateral attack because of inadequate representation.

> ### 🏛 RULE OF LAW
> Collateral attack on class action judgments is allowed if the class did not adequately represent the plaintiffs, thus rendering them improper parties to the previous litigation who cannot be bound to the settlement.

FACTS: Many of the U.S. military were exposed to Agent Orange chemicals during the Vietnam War, resulting in a host of illnesses and cancers. A class was certified to sue, among others, the manufacturer of Agent Orange. The certified class included all injured plaintiffs who did not opt out after notice up to May 1, 1984. The certified class also included "at-risk" persons whose injuries had not yet manifested. A settlement was reached on May 6, 1984, wherein veterans or their families would receive payments or agency benefits for ten years. Potential plaintiffs whose injuries manifested during those ten years were provided for in the settlement. After the fund was depleted, Stephenson's (P) and Isaacson's injuries were diagnosed. The district court dismissed the plaintiffs' (P) complaints as barred by the 1984 settlement, and Stephenson (P) appealed.

ISSUE: Is collateral attack on class action judgments allowed if the class did not adequately represent the plaintiffs, thus rendering them improper parties to the previous litigation?

HOLDING AND DECISION: (Parker, J.) Yes. Collateral attack on class action judgments is allowed if the class did not adequately represent the plaintiffs, thus rendering them improper parties to the previous litigation who cannot be bound to the settlement. Prior consideration of similar plaintiffs' claims resulted in dismissal, but no court has addressed the claims of plaintiffs who manifested injury after the fund was depleted. These plaintiffs must have been vigorously represented by the certified class for the claims to be barred. Isaacson and Stephenson (P) claim they were not a proper party, rather than attacking the settlement or judgment as inadequate. Because they were not a proper party, the collateral attack is allowed. The 1984 class represented plaintiffs with present injuries and those whose injuries had not yet manifested. The Supreme Court has previously held that this creates a conflict because the presently injured seek immediate, substantial payments while the future injured seek substantial sums be set aside and protected. Adequate representation for the presently injured necessarily means subordinating the future needs of those whose injuries have not yet manifested. Because Isaacson and Stephenson (P) fall into this latter group, the 1984 class did not adequately represent them and the collateral attack is allowed. The dismissal is vacated and the case remanded.

▶ ANALYSIS

This case rests on the "bright line" holding of *Amchem Products, Inc. v. Windsor*, 521 U.S. 591 (1997), where the Supreme Court required a split of present and future class claimants. Few cases will fall into such a fact-specific pattern, so the finality of class action judgments is not threatened. Defendant companies could otherwise face decades of continuing litigation over the same issues as settlement funds were depleted.

■=■

Quicknotes

CLASS ACTION A suit commenced by a representative on behalf of an ascertainable group that is too large to appear in court, who share a commonality of interests and who will benefit from a successful result.

COLLATERAL ATTACK A proceeding initiated in order to challenge the integrity of a previous judgment.

■=■

United States v. Mendoza

Federal government (D) v. Philippine national (P)

464 U.S. 154 (1984).

NATURE OF CASE: Review of order precluding issue litigation in action seeking naturalization.

FACT SUMMARY: Mendoza (P), seeking naturalization, relied on an earlier action in which applicants similar to him had obtained naturalization.

RULE OF LAW
Nonmutual offensive use of collateral estoppel may not be applied against the federal government.

FACTS: Mendoza (P), a Philippine national, sought naturalization as a U.S. citizen based on his reading of a certain statute. This was denied, the Government (D) contending that the statute did not apply to him. Mendoza (P) appealed, contending that a prior, successful action by individuals similarly situated to him precluded relitigation of his claim. The court of appeals agreed and ordered Mendoza (P) naturalized. The Government (D) petitioned for certiorari.

ISSUE: May nonmutual offensive use of collateral estoppel be applied against the federal government?

HOLDING AND DECISION: (Rehnquist, J.) No. Nonmutual offensive use of collateral estoppel may not be applied against the federal government. The federal government is situated sufficiently differently from private litigants to warrant disparate treatment. The federal government is by far the most frequent litigant in federal actions. To hold an issue decided in one action to be forever precluded from relitigation would thwart the development of important issues of law, as conflicts in the circuits, a common reason for grants of certiorari, would no longer occur. Further, it is natural and proper for successive executive administrations to take differing positions on issues, and the use of collateral estoppel against the federal government would hinder this. For these reasons, use of collateral estoppel in an offensive manner against the government cannot be allowed. Reversed.

ANALYSIS

Critics argue that the government's sheer size and ability to participate in protracted litigation should result in the government being required to abide by judicial decisions concerning it. Allowing the government multiple chances at the same issue does not seem quite fair to some, but the Court argues that it is an appropriate allocation of the government's limited resources. The government can choose when to appeal or wait to see if a conflict develops. This method does, however, allow the government the ability to pick and choose—to a certain extent—which judicial decisions to follow and which to ignore.

Quicknotes

COLLATERAL ESTOPPEL A doctrine whereby issues litigated and determined in a prior proceeding are binding upon all subsequent litigation between the parties regarding that issue.

OFFENSIVE COLLATERAL ESTOPPEL A doctrine that may be invoked by a plaintiff whereby a defendant is prohibited from relitigating issues litigated and determined in a prior proceeding against another plaintiff.

Glossary

Common Latin Words and Phrases Encountered in the Law

A FORTIORI: Because one fact exists or has been proven, therefore a second fact that is related to the first fact must also exist.

A PRIORI: From the cause to the effect. A term of logic used to denote that when one generally accepted truth is shown to be a cause, another particular effect must necessarily follow.

AB INITIO: From the beginning; a condition which has existed throughout, as in a marriage which was void ab initio.

ACTUS REUS: The wrongful act; in criminal law, such action sufficient to trigger criminal liability.

AD VALOREM: According to value; an ad valorem tax is imposed upon an item located within the taxing jurisdiction calculated by the value of such item.

AMICUS CURIAE: Friend of the court. Its most common usage takes the form of an amicus curiae brief, filed by a person who is not a party to an action but is nonetheless allowed to offer an argument supporting his legal interests.

ARGUENDO: In arguing. A statement, possibly hypothetical, made for the purpose of argument, is one made arguendo.

BILL QUIA TIMET: A bill to quiet title (establish ownership) to real property.

BONA FIDE: True, honest, or genuine. May refer to a person's legal position based on good faith or lacking notice of fraud (such as a bona fide purchaser for value) or to the authenticity of a particular document (such as a bona fide last will and testament).

CAUSA MORTIS: With approaching death in mind. A gift causa mortis is a gift given by a party who feels certain that death is imminent.

CAVEAT EMPTOR: Let the buyer beware. This maxim is reflected in the rule of law that a buyer purchases at his own risk because it is his responsibility to examine, judge, test, and otherwise inspect what he is buying.

CERTIORARI: A writ of review. Petitions for review of a case by the United States Supreme Court are most often done by means of a writ of certiorari.

CONTRA: On the other hand. Opposite. Contrary to.

CORAM NOBIS: Before us; writs of error directed to the court that originally rendered the judgment.

CORAM VOBIS: Before you; writs of error directed by an appellate court to a lower court to correct a factual error.

CORPUS DELICTI: The body of the crime; the requisite elements of a crime amounting to objective proof that a crime has been committed.

CUM TESTAMENTO ANNEXO, ADMINISTRATOR (ADMINISTRATOR C.T.A.): With will annexed; an administrator c.t.a. settles an estate pursuant to a will in which he is not appointed.

DE BONIS NON, ADMINISTRATOR (ADMINISTRATOR D.B.N.): Of goods not administered; an administrator d.b.n. settles a partially settled estate.

DE FACTO: In fact; in reality; actually. Existing in fact but not officially approved or engendered.

DE JURE: By right; lawful. Describes a condition that is legitimate "as a matter of law," in contrast to the term "de facto," which connotes something existing in fact but not legally sanctioned or authorized. For example, de facto segregation refers to segregation brought about by housing patterns, etc., whereas de jure segregation refers to segregation created by law.

DE MINIMIS: Of minimal importance; insignificant; a trifle; not worth bothering about.

DE NOVO: Anew; a second time; afresh. A trial de novo is a new trial held at the appellate level as if the case originated there and the trial at a lower level had not taken place.

DICTA: Generally used as an abbreviated form of obiter dicta, a term describing those portions of a judicial opinion incidental or not necessary to resolution of the specific question before the court. Such nonessential statements and remarks are not considered to be binding precedent.

DUCES TECUM: Refers to a particular type of writ or subpoena requesting a party or organization to produce certain documents in their possession.

EN BANC: Full bench. Where a court sits with all justices present rather than the usual quorum.

EX PARTE: For one side or one party only. An ex parte proceeding is one undertaken for the benefit of only one party, without notice to, or an appearance by, an adverse party.

EX POST FACTO: After the fact. An ex post facto law is a law that retroactively changes the consequences of a prior act.

EX REL.: Abbreviated form of the term ex relatione, meaning upon relation or information. When the state brings an action in which it has no interest against an individual at the instigation of one who has a private interest in the matter.

FORUM NON CONVENIENS: Inconvenient forum. Although a court may have jurisdiction over the case, the action should be tried in a more conveniently located court, one to which parties and witnesses may more easily travel, for example.

GUARDIAN AD LITEM: A guardian of an infant as to litigation, appointed to represent the infant and pursue his/her rights.

HABEAS CORPUS: You have the body. The modern writ of habeas corpus is a writ directing that a person (body) being detained (such as a prisoner) be brought before the court so that the legality of his detention can be judicially ascertained.

IN CAMERA: In private, in chambers. When a hearing is held before a judge in his chambers or when all spectators are excluded from the courtroom.

IN FORMA PAUPERIS: In the manner of a pauper. A party who proceeds in forma pauperis because of his poverty is one who is allowed to bring suit without liability for costs.

INFRA: Below, under. A word referring the reader to a later part of a book. (The opposite of supra.)

IN LOCO PARENTIS: In the place of a parent.

IN PARI DELICTO: Equally wrong; a court of equity will not grant requested relief to an applicant who is in pari delicto, or as much at fault in the transactions giving rise to the controversy as is the opponent of the applicant.

IN PARI MATERIA: On like subject matter or upon the same matter. Statutes relating to the same person or things are said to be in pari materia. It is a general rule of statutory construction that such statutes should be construed together, i.e., looked at as if they together constituted one law.

IN PERSONAM: Against the person. Jurisdiction over the person of an individual.

IN RE: In the matter of. Used to designate a proceeding involving an estate or other property.

IN REM: A term that signifies an action against the res, or thing. An action in rem is basically one that is taken directly against property, as distinguished from an action in personam, i.e., against the person.

INTER ALIA: Among other things. Used to show that the whole of a statement, pleading, list, statute, etc., has not been set forth in its entirety.

INTER PARTES: Between the parties. May refer to contracts, conveyances or other transactions having legal significance.

INTER VIVOS: Between the living. An inter vivos gift is a gift made by a living grantor, as distinguished from bequests contained in a will, which pass upon the death of the testator.

IPSO FACTO: By the mere fact itself.

JUS: Law or the entire body of law.

LEX LOCI: The law of the place; the notion that the rights of parties to a legal proceeding are governed by the law of the place where those rights arose.

MALUM IN SE: Evil or wrong in and of itself; inherently wrong. This term describes an act that is wrong by its very nature, as opposed to one which would not be wrong but for the fact that there is a specific legal prohibition against it (malum prohibitum).

MALUM PROHIBITUM: Wrong because prohibited, but not inherently evil. Used to describe something that is wrong because it is expressly forbidden by law but that is not in and of itself evil, e.g., speeding.

MANDAMUS: We command. A writ directing an official to take a certain action.

MENS REA: A guilty mind; a criminal intent. A term used to signify the mental state that accompanies a crime or other prohibited act. Some crimes require only a general mens rea (general intent to do the prohibited act), but others, like assault with intent to murder, require the existence of a specific mens rea.

MODUS OPERANDI: Method of operating; generally refers to the manner or style of a criminal in committing crimes, admissible in appropriate cases as evidence of the identity of a defendant.

NEXUS: A connection to.

NISI PRIUS: A court of first impression. A nisi prius court is one where issues of fact are tried before a judge or jury.

N.O.V. (NON OBSTANTE VEREDICTO): Notwithstanding the verdict. A judgment n.o.v. is a judgment given in favor of one party despite the fact that a verdict was returned in favor of the other party, the justification being that the verdict either had no reasonable support in fact or was contrary to law.

NUNC PRO TUNC: Now for then. This phrase refers to actions that may be taken and will then have full retroactive effect.

PENDENTE LITE: Pending the suit; pending litigation underway.

PER CAPITA: By head; beneficiaries of an estate, if they take in equal shares, take per capita.

PER CURIAM: By the court; signifies an opinion ostensibly written "by the whole court" and with no identified author.

PER SE: By itself, in itself; inherently.

PER STIRPES: By representation. Used primarily in the law of wills to describe the method of distribution where a person, generally because of death, is unable to take that which is left to him by the will of another, and therefore his heirs divide such property between them rather than take under the will individually.

PRIMA FACIE: On its face, at first sight. A prima facie case is one that is sufficient on its face, meaning that the evidence supporting it is adequate to establish the case until contradicted or overcome by other evidence.

PRO TANTO: For so much; as far as it goes. Often used in eminent domain cases when a property owner receives partial payment for his land without prejudice to his right to bring suit for the full amount he claims his land to be worth.

QUANTUM MERUIT: As much as he deserves. Refers to recovery based on the doctrine of unjust enrichment in those cases in which a party has rendered valuable services or furnished materials that were accepted and enjoyed by another under circumstances that would reasonably notify the recipient that the rendering party expected to be paid. In essence, the law implies a contract to pay the reasonable value of the services or materials furnished.

QUASI: Almost like; as if; nearly. This term is essentially used to signify that one subject or thing is almost analogous to another but that material differences between them do exist. For example, a quasi-criminal proceeding is one that is not strictly criminal but shares enough of the same characteristics to require some of the same safeguards (e.g., procedural due process must be followed in a parole hearing).

QUID PRO QUO: Something for something. In contract law, the consideration, something of value, passed between the parties to render the contract binding.

RES GESTAE: Things done; in evidence law, this principle justifies the admission of a statement that would otherwise be hearsay when it is made so closely to the event in question as to be said to be a part of it, or with such spontaneity as not to have the possibility of falsehood.

RES IPSA LOQUITUR: The thing speaks for itself. This doctrine gives rise to a rebuttable presumption of negligence when the instrumentality causing the injury was within the exclusive control of the defendant, and the injury was one that does not normally occur unless a person has been negligent.

RES JUDICATA: A matter adjudged. Doctrine which provides that once a court of competent jurisdiction has rendered a final judgment or decree on the merits, that judgment or decree is conclusive upon the parties to the case and prevents them from engaging in any other litigation on the points and issues determined therein.

RESPONDEAT SUPERIOR: Let the master reply. This doctrine holds the master liable for the wrongful acts of his servant (or the principal for his agent) in those cases in which the servant (or agent) was acting within the scope of his authority at the time of the injury.

STARE DECISIS: To stand by or adhere to that which has been decided. The common law doctrine of stare decisis attempts to give security and certainty to the law by following the policy that once a principle of law as applicable to a certain set of facts has been set forth in a decision, it forms a precedent which will subsequently be followed, even though a different decision might be made were it the first time the question had arisen. Of course, stare decisis is not an inviolable principle and is departed from in instances where there is good cause (e.g., considerations of public policy led the Supreme Court to disregard prior decisions sanctioning segregation).

SUPRA: Above. A word referring a reader to an earlier part of a book.

ULTRA VIRES: Beyond the power. This phrase is most commonly used to refer to actions taken by a corporation that are beyond the power or legal authority of the corporation.

Addendum of French Derivatives

IN PAIS: Not pursuant to legal proceedings.

CHATTEL: Tangible personal property.

CY PRES: Doctrine permitting courts to apply trust funds to purposes not expressed in the trust but necessary to carry out the settlor's intent.

PER AUTRE VIE: For another's life; during another's life. In property law, an estate may be granted that will terminate upon the death of someone other than the grantee.

PROFIT A PRENDRE: A license to remove minerals or other produce from land.

VOIR DIRE: Process of questioning jurors as to their predispositions about the case or parties to a proceeding in order to identify those jurors displaying bias or prejudice.

Casenote Legal Briefs

How Do They Grow?

From Lamb to Sheep

by Jillian Powell

RAINTREE
STECK-VAUGHN
PUBLISHERS

A Harcourt Company

Austin · New York
www.raintreesteckvaughn.com

Published by Raintree Steck-Vaughn Publishers, an imprint of Steck-Vaughn Company

Library of Congress Cataloging-in-Publication Data
Powell, Jillian.
From lamb to sheep / by Jillian Powell.
    p.   cm.—(How do they grow?)
    Includes bibliographical references (p.).
    ISBN 0-7398-4425-3
    1. Lambs—Juvenile literature. 2. Sheep—Development—
    Juvenile literature. [1. Sheep. 2. Animals—Infancy.]
    I. Title.

    SF375.2 .P68 2001
    636.3'07—dc21   2001018568

Printed in Italy. Bound in the United States.
1 2 3 4 5 6 7 8 9 0 05 04 03 02 01

Picture acknowledgments
Agripicture (Peter Dean) 25; Chris Fairclough Color Library 21; HWPL 9; Jane Upton title page, 4, 5, 6, 7, 8, 10, 11, 12, 13, 14, 15, 16, 17, 18, 19, 20, 22, 23, 24, 26, 27, 28, 29.

Contents

Words in **bold** in the text can be found in the glossary on page 30.

Lambing Time

These **ewes** are in a lambing shed, ready to give birth. Most lambs are born in the early spring.

A ewe often gives birth lying down. The lamb's
nose and front legs appear first.

5

The New Lamb

The lamb is born.
Its coat is wet.
The ewe licks it
to clean and dry it.
This keeps the lamb warm.

The lamb tries to stand up, but its legs are shaking. The lamb is hungry. It wants to drink its mother's milk.

Starting to Feed

This lamb is
drinking milk.
Milk helps it to grow
strong and fight off **germs**. Lambs feed
on their mother's milk for about 12 weeks.

This lamb is fed milk from a bottle.

Lambs are fed in this way if their mothers are

not able to feed them.

Lambs' Tails

Lambs are born with long tails. Their tails can pick up dirt and germs when they are out in the fields.

These lambs have had their tails cut.
This is called **docking**. A farmer often docks the
tails to help keep the **flock** healthy.

Feeding the Lambs

These lambs are three weeks old. They are being fed by bottles. In a few weeks these lambs will be **weaned** from their mothers' milk.

The lambs are now eating solid food.
These children are giving the lamb **pellets**.
Pellets are small pieces of food to eat.

Telling the Lambs Apart

The farm worker puts a **tag** in each lamb's ear. This tag has a number. This helps the farmer to tell one lamb from another lamb out in the fields.

14

She puts a mark on the lambs' coats. This way they can be matched up with their mothers or their brothers and sisters.

Special Food

These lambs are three months old and growing fast. The lambs eat their food from a **trough**. The mixture is a dry food made of **grains**.

The lambs eat hay from a hay rack.
Hay is grass that has been
dried by the sun.

Drinking and Grazing

The lambs need to drink water every day. This lamb is drinking clean water from a trough in the field.

The lambs **graze** in the fresh grass. They pull at the grass and chew it until it is soft enough to swallow.

Healthy Lambs

A vet checks all the lambs to make sure they are healthy. He checks that there are no problems with each lamb's teeth or its feet.

Lambs are given **medicine** to keep them from getting sick. The vet gives medicines to prevent **worms** or diseases.

Weighing the Lambs

These lambs have grown big and heavy.
Their wool coats are longer and thicker.

When they were born, the lambs weighed about 10 pounds (4.5 **kilograms**). This lamb is now four months old and weighs between 70 pounds (32 kg) and 88 pounds (40 kg).

Ready to Be Sold

These lambs are ready to be sold.
They are loaded onto a truck that will take
them to a **livestock market**.

Some lambs are sold for meat. Others stay on the sheep farm for breeding. This means more lambs will be born every year.

Ewes and Rams for Breeding

Lambs kept for breeding stay on the farm with the older sheep. When a ewe is in her second year she is ready to **mate**.

The farmer keeps a **ram** to mate with the ewes. After they have mated, some of the ewes will have baby lambs growing inside them.

Having Lambs

The ewes carry the tiny baby lambs inside their bodies for five months. A ewe may give birth to one, two, or three lambs.

When her lambs are born, the ewe feeds and looks after them. Like her, they will grow up to be strong and healthy sheep.

Glossary

Disease (duh-ZEEZ) Illness or sickness.

Docking (DOK ing) Making an animal's tail shorter.

Ewe (yoo) A female sheep.

Flock (flok) A large group of animals, such as sheep.

Germs (jurmz) Tiny living things around us that can carry disease.

Grains (graynz) The seeds of a cereal crop.

Graze (grayz) To feed on grass.

Kilograms A kilogram is 1,000 grams.

Livestock market (LIVE-stok MAR-kit) A place where farmers can meet to buy and sell animals.

Mate When a male and female come together to have babies. A male gives a female a seed which makes a female egg grow into a baby animal.

Medicine (MED-uh-suhn) Drugs that are taken to avoid illness or disease.

Pellet (PEL-it) Small, round piece of food.

Ram A male sheep.

Tag A label that gives something a name, number, or identity.

Trough (Trawf) A long holder for food or water for farm animals.

Weaned (weend) When an animal no longer drinks its mother's milk.

Worms (wurmz) Small thin animals that can live inside other animals and feed from them.

Further Information

Books

Helweg, Hans. *Farm Animals.* (Pictureback series). Random, 1980.

Kalman, Bobbie. *In the Barn.* Crabtree Publishing Company, 1997.

Kratky, Lada J. *The Shaggy Sheep: Big Book.* (Wonders! series). Hampton-Brown, 1992.

Losito, Linda. *Pets and Farm Animals.* (Encyclopedia of the Animal World Series). Facts On File, 1990.

Perols, Sylvaine and Gallimard Jeunesse. *Farm Animals.* (First Discovery Books). Scholastic Inc., 1998.

Spinelli, Eileen. *Farm Animals.* (Childrens' Nature Library). Forest House, 1992.

Stone, Lynn M. *Sheep.* (Farm Animal Discovery Library). Rourke Corporation, 1990.

Video

Farm Animals narrated by Johnny Morris (Dorling Kindersley)

On the Farm: Baby Animals (Dorling Kindersley)

Let's Go to the Farm/Baby Animals (Countryside Products). Visit their website at:
www.countrysidevideos.com

Websites

www.4-H.org

www.areyouintoit.com

A site with links to 4-H clubs in your state.

www.kidsfarm.com

A fun site about the people and animals on ranches in Colorado, USA.

www.sheepusa.org

Lots of information about sheep, lambs, and their wool.

Useful Addresses

National 4-H Council
7100 CT Avenue
Chevy Chase, MD 20815
(Phone: (301) 961-2800)

4-H Center
25236 Hillman Highway
Abington, VA 24210
(Phone: (540) 676-6180)
E-mail: ex269@vt.edu

Index

B

birth 4, 5, 28, 29

bottle feeding 9, 12

breeding 25, 26

C

chewing 19

coat 6, 15, 22

D

diseases 21

docking 11

drinking 7, 8, 18

F

feet 20

fields 10, 14, 18

flock 11

food 13, 16, 17

G

germs 8, 10

grass 17, 19

grazing 19

H

hay 17

L

lambing shed 4

livestock market 24, 25

M

marking 15

mating 26, 27

meat 25

medicine 21

milk 7, 8, 9

R

rams 27

T

tagging 14

tails 10, 11

teeth 20

trough 16, 18

V

vet 20, 21

W

water 18

weaning 12

weighing 23

wool 22

worms 21